MORALITY AND SOCIAL CLASS IN EIGHTEENTH-CENTURY FRENCH LITERATURE AND PAINTING

WARREN ROBERTS

Morality and Social Class in Eighteenth-Century French Literature and Painting

UNIVERSITY OF TORONTO PRESS

© University of Toronto Press 1974
Toronto and Buffalo
Printed in Canada
ISBN 0–8020–5250–9
LC 79–185732

University of Toronto Romance Series 25

Contents

Illustrations

Acknowledgments

The idea for this study first came to me in one of Richard Herr's provocative and stimulating lectures. As it turned out, he, more than any other person, came to be associated with the project as it progressed. To him I feel a keen sense of indebtedness not only for his lucid and penetrating comments but also for the example of his uncompromising integrity. To work with Richard Herr is to respect the historian's craft. Although Robert Brentano had nothing to do with this study I think I can safely say that without him it would never have been undertaken. Invaluable assistance from the SUNY Research Foundation and the National Humanities Foundation freed my summers for the necessary work. Paul Wheeler, a fine and resourceful dean, gave quick and effective help when it was needed. I received very different support and encouragement from my parents, my wife, and four children. Their help was gratefully received, and it is warmly and gladly acknowledged.

I wish to express my appreciation to the Musée du Louvre, The Frick collection in New York, the Prado in Madrid, the Nationalmuseum in Stockholm, the Alte Pinakothek in Munich, and the Musée des Beaux-Arts in Lille for permission to reproduce pictures, and to express my regrets if, in spite of my continued efforts to obtain precise information on the ownership of paintings, any incorrect acknowledgment has resulted or any has been omitted. This work has been published with the help of grants from the State University of New York at Albany, from the Humanities Research Council of Canada, using funds provided by the Canada Council, and from the Publications Fund of the University of Toronto Press.

WARREN ROBERTS
State University of New York at Albany

Introduction

As France awaited the meeting of the Estates General a pamphleteer defined patriotism as 'l'attachement que l'on a pour ses parens, pour sa famille, pour son pays ...'[1] Four years later, in the *Catéchisme du citoyen français* (1793) Constantin-François Volney considered conjugal love a virtue 'Parce que la concorde et l'union qui résultent de l'amour des époux éstablissent au sein de la famille une foule d'habitudes utiles à sa prospérité et à sa conservation.'[2] In the following year, when Volney, a Girondin, was languishing in prison because of his political views, Robespierre announced that national festivals would be celebrated every tenth day. Among the virtues that were to be honoured on these *décadis* were conjugal fidelity, fatherly affection, mother love, filial piety, childhood, youth, and old age. In 1795, after the fall of Robespierre, a Declaration of the Rights and Duties of Man and Citizen proclaimed that 'no one is a good citizen if he is not a good son, good father, good brother, good friend, and good husband.'[3]

Why, the historian might ask, did the Revolution throw its support so firmly behind conjugal fidelity and the family? Perhaps the answer is in Volney's *Catéchisme*. In the section on domestic virtue he not only idealized the family, but also attacked 'dissipation,' 'prodigalité,' and 'adultère.' The latter vice, he claimed, 'traîne avec lui une foule d'habitudes nuisibles aux époux et à la famille. La femme ou le mari, épris d'affections étrangères, négligent leur maison ... [the result will be] les querelles, les scandales, les procès, le mépris des enfants et des domestiques, le pillage et la ruine finale de toute la maison.'[4] Obviously Volney was condemning adultery because he considered it a social and moral abuse.

To the student of eighteenth-century French literature, it is clear that the above attitudes toward love and marriage did not originate in 1789. In fact, the moralistic tendencies that culminated in the Republic of Virtue had long been at work, and can be traced in literature back to the late seventeenth century. And consistent with the moralistic current that passed through eighteenth-century literature was another, rival current. In the 1690's two separate and antithetical moralities began to take shape, both of which grew, developed, and found literary and also artistic expression time and again, until the very end of the Ancien Regime. One was erotic and libertine, the other sentimental and romantic; the former rejected, while the latter defended, the Christian idea of love and marriage.

This study is intended to be a history of the impact on contemporary French society of these two currents, one literary, the other artistic. Similar work has been undertaken by others, including a number of Marxist critics. In fact, it has been said that Marxist literary criticism began with the celebrated essay by G.V. Plekhanov, 'French Dramatic Literature and French Eighteenth Century Painting from the Sociological Standpoint.' Perhaps it was because Plekhanov was a Marxist first, and then turned to literary analysis in order to prove his philosophy and political theories, that he emphasized the rise of the bourgeoisie in his essay. While Plekhanov assumed that the erotic paintings of Boucher appealed to the 'dissolute and degenerate aristocracy,' he did not examine the libertine tradition in either literature or art. Concerned as he seems to have been with the progressive element in history, he concentrated on the moralistic tradition which, in his opinion, was bourgeois and therefore reflected the forces of social change.

Another and more recent Marxian interpretation of eighteenth-century literature and art has taken the erotic-libertine tradition into account. In his *Social History of Art* Arnold Hauser has shown how logically and, it seems, necessarily, that tradition fits into the Marxian interpretation of history. When he discussed 'erotic motifs' in a chapter titled 'The Dissolution of Courtly Art,' Hauser revealed the connection that he saw between the erotic-libertine tradition, the aristocracy, and the process of cultural change. Eighteenth-century courtly art was erotic, it was by definition aristocratic, and it was breaking down. At the same time that Hauser saw one culture passing out of sight, he saw another rising and taking its place. Already, in his chapter on courtly art, the bourgeois art of

Chardin and Greuze has made an appearance. As a dialectician, Hauser saw a new culture emerging from the decrepitude and decadence of another. Thus did the culture of one class, the aristocracy, fall before that of another, the rising bourgeoisie. As Hauser puts it, 'the break with the rococo takes place in the second half of the century; the cleft between the art of the upper classes and that of the middle classes is obvious.'[5] According to his aggument, there was an aristocratic culture, in which 'erotic motifs' figured importantly, and there was a bourgeois culture, which was sentimental and moralistic. There was between the two a dialectical connection; each was a conscious rejection of the other. Also, Hauser assumed in good Marxian fashion that bourgeois culture rested upon material change. His chapter on the 'Dissolution of Courtly Art' is followed by one on the 'New Reading Public,' and another on the 'Origins of Domestic Drama,' both of which attempt to establish a connection between literary and artistic change on the one hand and the economic rise of the bourgeoisie on the other.

While Marxian analysis naturally lends itself to a sociological approach to literature and art, Marxists have by no means been alone in following this approach. Not only did such a traditionalist scholar as Brunetière interpret eighteenth-century literature sociologically; he did so in a way that won the approval of Plekhanov. In fact, Plekhanov borrowed heavily from Brunetière, and for reasons which are made clear in the following passage from the latter's *Les Époques du théâtre français*.

From the failure of Law's bank onwards – to go no further back – the aristocracy loses ground every day. Everything a class can do to discredit itself, it hastens to do ... But above all, it ruins itself while the bourgeoisie, the third estate, enriches itself in proportion, grows in importance and acquires a new consciousness of its rights. Existing inequalities appear ever more abominable, abuses more insupportable. Hearts are 'great with hatred,' as a poet has since expressed it, and 'a thirst for justice' ... Is it possible that, with such a means of propaganda and action as the theatre at its disposal, the bourgeoisie should not use it? That it should not take as matter for serious treatment, almost for tragedy, those inequalities which only amused the author of *Le Bourgeois gentilhomme* and *Georges Dandin*? And above all, could this already triumphant bourgeoisie reconcile itself to the constant portrayal on the stage of emperors and kings, or refrain from spending some of its savings, if one may so express oneself, on having its own portrait painted?[6]

Plekhanov quoted this passage because it supported his own interpretation, in which the aristocracy declined as the ambitious, energetic bourgeoisie was laying the foundations for a new and more productive economic system, from which a new political edifice would ultimately rise. In other words, capitalism undercut the feudal base of the Ancien Regime and rendered inevitable a new system of government, one that would represent the dissolution of one social order and the emergence of another. According to this argument, it was during the Revolution that the bourgeoisie pushed aside the aristocracy and rebuilt the state in its own interest.

As a materialist, Plekhanov saw a direct connection between the economic base of a society and its thought and culture. In his opinion, there were 'causal ties between *being* and *consciousness*, between the technique and the economics of society on the one hand, and its art on the other.'[7] And it seems that Brunetière had a similar point of view: the bourgeoisie had been rising 'since the time of the failure of Law's bank,' and as it did so it acquired 'a new consciousness of its rights.' Here, Brunetière said, was a social class that developed a new awareness of itself and its importance, and from this awareness came a new genre of literature, the *comédie larmoyante*, or sentimental comedy. Thus did both Brunetière and Plekhanov consider the appearance of a new type of play to be an index of economic change. Further, both thought that this literary development heralded the rise of the bourgeoisie and for that reason anticipated the political breakthrough of the middle class in 1789.

The non-Marxist literary criticism of Brunetière agrees with the Marxist criticism of Plekhanov because both rest upon a similar interpretation of eighteenth-century French history. At the beginning of the Restoration, Guizot saw a direct connection between the rise of the bourgeoisie and the political upheaval that had begun in 1789 and only recently subsided. And other French historians of both the Restoration and July Monarchy worked out a social interpretation of the Revolution that looked toward and even contributed to the later Marxian interpretation. Undoubtedly this helps to explain the literary criticism of Brunetière, whose historical outlook was influenced not by Marx and his followers, but rather by Guizot and his. It was not subversive for Brunetière to see the bourgeoisie rising in eighteenth-century France, it was not unusual for him to see the Revolution as a product of that social change, nor was it exceptional that he saw a reflection of one and an anticipation of the other in the literature of the time. It seems that historians, literary critics, and art historians of both a Marxian and non-Marxian persuasion can trace the decline of the aristocracy and the rise of the bourgeoisie in eighteenth-century French literature and painting. Certainly until now they have often done so.

In my opinion, it is time to challenge the point of view explained above, whether it be set forth by Brunetière, by Plekhanov, or by Hauser. If we are to challenge this theory of literature and art, it is necessary to question the interpretation of French history in which it is rooted. And recently historians have questioned that interpretation. We now know that the aristocracy became more powerful in the eighteenth century, and that it did so both politically and economically. All historians, Marxist and non-Marxist, understand this to be the case, just as they agree that the bourgeoisie was rising in the economic sense. Assuming that the bourgeoisie became more powerful as a result of commercial expansion, historians have tended to see the Revolution as a collision between two moving forces, one aristocratic and the other bourgeois, both of which were becoming stronger, but between which there were critical differences in social outlook and political thought. One was élitist and feudal, the other egalitarian and capitalistic. This interpretation of the Revolution, which we can call 'orthodox,' has recently come under attack by a group of historians who think of themselves as 'revisionists.'[8]

The 'revisionists' question what is probably the most basic assumption of the 'orthodox' school, the assumption that class antagonism took place within the framework of the estates. According to the 'orthodox' argument, society was split into juridically separate parts, and as a result of that cleavage the individual Frenchman not only was identifiable by his position in the social hierarchy, but also thought and acted accordingly. A peasant derived his orientation from his position in the peasantry, a bourgeois from his position in the bourgeoisie, and so on. The 'revisionist' argues that Frenchmen did not think and act only, or even primarily, as members of a legal class. Rather, they had many interests, and lined up on particular issues in various ways. In order to bring out the complexity of French society and to reinterpret the Revolution, 'revisionist' historians have worked out a new social terminology. They divide society into town and country, rich and poor, capitalists and non-capitalists, and in doing so they have drawn lines that cut through the horizontal, juridical lines dear to the 'orthodox' interpretation. Thus, a noble can be rich or poor, rural or urban, capitalistic or non-capitalistic, and his alignment on concrete issues will reflect his position in any of these categories. On one issue his interests might coincide with men who, in the traditional terminology, were bourgeois, while on another issue they might have conflicting interests.

For the purpose of this study the debate between 'orthodox' and 'revisionist' historians is important if only because it forces us to question a certain view of eighteenth-century French history, one that with modification has held sway from the time of Guizot right down to the present. We will not assume that the bourgeoisie was rising, we will not assume that there was conflict between that class and the aristocracy, and we will not assume that the bourgeoisie, riding the crest of historical change, came to power during the Revolution. All this might in fact have been the case, but we shall say that we do not know that it was so. Having discarded the framework on which most sociological interpretations of eighteenth-century French literature and art have been constructed, we are free to approach our materials without the preconceptions that have preceded most other studies.

And yet, when this study was first undertaken, it did assume the 'orthodox' interpretation of eighteenth-century French history. It began with that interpretation, and it sought more or less consciously to use literature and art in order to prove it. In an earlier version I thought that this had been achieved. I concluded that erotic literature and art reflected aristocratic decadence, and that the appearance of bourgeois literature announced the rise of the middle class and hence anticipated the Revolution. In other words, I agreed with Brunetière, Plekhanov, and Hauser. Up to a point, the form of the present study still bears the stamp of the earlier version. It asks the same questions as before: was this group of novels or that collection of paintings aristocratic or bourgeois? However, it had become clear to me that the previous answers to these questions were unsatisfactory, and it was necessary to reach new conclusions concerning the social context of French literature and art. The original aristocratic and bourgeois categories were not eliminated, but they were seen in a different light. Since one no longer assumed that the aristocracy had to fall before the rising bourgeoisie, it was possible to raise questions about the social context of literature and art, rather than to prove one's own preconceptions. Also, as the work progressed, it became necessary to introduce new categories, in order to define the social framework with greater precision. As a result, this study utilizes such terms as 'la cour et la ville,' rural society, urban society, capitalism, the commercial nobility, and the office-holding class, all of which cut through the two earlier categories. I hope that others who traverse this ground will move further in the same direction.

MORALITY AND SOCIAL CLASS IN EIGHTEENTH-CENTURY FRENCH LITERATURE AND PAINTING

1

The Christian idea
of love and marriage

The scene is the bedroom of the heroine, Cidalise. Talking to her about philosophy and morals is the hero, Clitandre, who says that, before the age of modern philosophy, moral conduct was really little different than at present. An absurd desire to appear respectable had interfered with pleasure until, guided by reason, society finally gave up its pointless pretensions. And what, he asked, were the results?

Jamais les femmes n'ont mis moins de grimaces dans la société; jamais l'on n'a moins affecté la vertu. On se plaît, on se prend. S'ennuie-t-on l'un avec l'autre? on se quitte avec tout aussi peu de cérémonie que l'on s'est pris. Revient-on à se plaire? On se reprend avec autant de vivacité que si c'était la première fois qu'on s'engageât ensemble. On se quitte encore, et jamais on ne se brouille. Il est vrai que l'amour n'est entré pour rien dans tout cela; mais l'amour, qu'était-il, qu'un désir que l'on se plaisait à s'exagérer, un mouvement des sens, dont il avait plu à la vanité des hommes de faire une vertu? On sait aujourd'hui que le goût seul existe; et si l'on se dit encore qu'on s'aime, c'est bien moins parce qu'on le croit, que parce que c'est une façon plus polie de se demander réciproquement ce dont on sent qu'on a besoin ... et je crois, à tout prendre, qu'il y a bien de la sagesse à sacrifier à tant de plaisirs quelques vieux préjugés qui rapportent assez peu d'estime, et beaucoup d'ennui à ceux qui en font encore la règle de leur conduite.[1]

While Clitandre assumed that 'before' his own enlightened age (the novel was written in 1736), 'nous faisions sûrement tout ce que nous faisons aujourd'hui,' he contended that moral attitudes had been different.

'Vieux préjugés' persisted until 'raison' dispersed them. Clitandre's conduct in the novel would indicate that he was a man of action rather than a student of western morals; yet, in this passage he advanced a valid historical argument. His age, the age of the Enlightenment, did reorient its moral outlook; part of this reorientation – the part that Clitandre emphasized – pertained to sexual mores. When Clitandre rejected 'vieux préjugés' he meant the Christian attitudes that had long dominated sexual standards, and from which, in his opinion, his age was happily being disengaged.

Asceticism was a marked characteristic of Christianity as early as the first century. But Christianity was not the first religion to shrink from the world. Rather, it was an important channel that would receive many ascetic currents already well formed by the time of Jesus. Long before the first century AD the Mediterranean world, especially its eastern part, was in the throes of a profound moral crisis. By the fourth century BC the Greek city state had lost its vitality and, simultaneously, the Olympian gods had lost much of their appeal. There emerged from this milieu new schools of philosophy whose doctrines were grounded in despair: a mood of apprehension gave rise to Cynicism, Scepticism, Stoicism, and Epicureanism.

Another clue to the moral trauma of the Hellenistic world is the emergence of a more subjective ethical outlook. It became necessary for an individual to choose between right and wrong. In Aristotle, conflict had been absent from ethical conduct. The virtuous person, in this philosopher's opinion, was not tempted: in the *Ethics* an absence of moral effort was the symptom of virtue. Antithetical to the Aristotelian concept of virtue was that of the Stoics. 'The life of every man is a soldier's service,' wrote Epictetus. Seneca argued that 'we must all be soldiers, and in a campaign where there is no intermission and rest.' In a similar vein he said, 'let us also conquer all things. For our prize is not a crown nor a palm nor a herald calling silence to cry our name, but virtue, and strength of mind, and peace.'[2] How familiar the utterances of Epictetus and Seneca sound to the Christian moralist, and how strange are those of Aristotle. To Aristotle moral effort was a vice; to the Stoic it was the pivot of the virtuous life. Obviously Stoicism was part of a moral outlook that anticipated Christianity. As C.S. Lewis says, a similar state of mind is observable in Seneca, Paul, Epictetus, Marcus Aurelius, and Tertullian.[3]

Implicit in Stoic ethics was a firm notion of right and wrong, good and evil. The Hellenized form of Persian dualism, Gnosticism, achieved in the area of religion a similar polarization. There was in Gnosticism an absolute opposition between light and darkness, good and evil, and spirit and matter. Man, being tied to matter, strove to ascend to the higher world of the spirit. While there were obvious affinities between Gnosticism and Christianity, it is difficult to assess the impact of the former on the latter. Gnosticism did penetrate Christianity, and when it did it was declared heretical. Clearly a religion whose main thrust was to deny the world could not maintain the delicate balance between this world and the next that was essential to Christianity. If matter were completely denigrated, the human side of Jesus' teachings would be meaningless, and the doctrine of reincarnation would be pointless. How could God assume material form if matter were imperfect? The Church had to fight, and did fight, a heresy extravagant in its asceticism.

And yet, Gnosticism did influence Christianity. The very teachings of Jesus could encourage other-worldliness and in the moral climate of the first century they did. Certainly Jesus accepted the world, and he fashioned an ethic that would make life here and now decent and humane. Man could enjoy a simple, honest happiness during his worldly stay. But the predominance given to the spiritual life and the eagerness with which man should prepare himself for heaven meant inevitably that life in this world was of only secondary importance. Further, God would soon gather up all his flock. The world was not long to be. The other-worldly side of Jesus' teachings could weaken the humanistic teachings.

In Paul the shift towards asceticism is already evident. His doctrine of the flesh and spirit denigrated the material order, and his doctrine of redemption encouraged man to overcome the flesh and rise to a higher, spiritual world. Paul feared the flesh, in which he believed all sin was rooted. While he considered sexual activity legitimate in marriage, he thought that even then it separated man from God. His ideal was chastity.[4] While Paul's suspicion of the flesh can be explained partly by Judaic tradition, in which the First Fall resulted from physical desire, his asceticism has another source. In his opposition between sense and spirit Paul reveals the influence of Gnosticism on Christianity.[5]

The world-denying forces implicit in Jesus' teachings and explicit in Paul's writings flourished in a world that had already found room for Gnosticism. These forces were given further encouragement by the languid, hedonistic society of first-century Rome. The world into which Christianity moved was being morally polarized. At one extreme was satiety, at the other its dialectical opposite, asceticism. Christianity naturally merged with the ascetic movement, but at the same time had to harness the most extravagant flights of asceticism. While Paul accepted marriage, some Christians were soon practising 'spiritual marriages.' The impetus for chaste marriages was spontaneous, not official; in fact, the Church strove to limit the practice.[6]

Try as the Church did to check inordinate asceticism, an ascetic outlook could not avoid becoming an important Christian characteristic. All the Fathers suspected the flesh, and all had grave reservations about sexual life. Origen so abominated his own person that he castrated himself. In a letter to Eustochium, Jerome described the lust that flared up in him in the desert, and how he struggled with his rebellious flesh by seven days' fasting. While Ambrose accepted the legitimacy of sexual activity in marriage, the purpose of this activity was to have children. The married couple should not only regulate their sexual life carefully, but also look to chastity as an ideal.[7] In his *Exhortatio virginitatis* Ambrose considered the state of virginity higher than marriage. 'There is nothing fairer than that which I commend to you, that you should be angels among men, bound by no marriage tie. Those who do not take wives for themselves in marriage are like angels upon the earth. They do not feel the tribulation of the flesh; they know no servitude; they are preserved from the contagion of worldly thoughts; and they attend wholly to divine things.'[8] In book ten of the *Confessions* Augustine described a dream in which he saw in himself the sin of concupiscence. His superb rhetoric reveals the intensity of his revulsion and fear, and also the depth of his relief when he awakened to discover that he had only been dreaming. Augustine's fear of the flesh is nowhere more transparent than in a vision – perhaps fantasy is more accurate – that appears in *The City of God* (xiv, xxvi). In the innocence and perfection of life before the Fall man begot children without lust, and without breaking woman's protective tissue. Both man and woman retained their virginity.

Conditioned by powerful historical forces, Christianity could not accept sexual activity as healthy. Celibacy became the highest Christian ideal, and even within the acceptable confines of marriage, desire was suspect. As these attitudes were transmitted to the Middle Ages, the Church strove to regulate sexual life by passing legislation that limited the number of days in which married couples could legitimately perform the sexual act. First, it was prohibited on Sundays, Wednesdays, and Fridays, and then for forty days prior to Easter, and forty days after Christmas. It was also forbidden three days before communion, from the time of conception to forty days after parturition, and during penance.

Penitentials from the eighth century through the Middle Ages devoted considerable attention to sexual conduct. Wives were urged to withhold their persons from their husbands, and penalties were listed for any non-marital intercourse. In one penitential, fornication carried a penalty of one year's penance. More extreme forms of misconduct, such as adultery or intercourse by members of the clergy, resulted in stiffer penalties, the latter in ten years' fast and perpetual lamentation and abstention from meat. Lesser offences, such as kissing and thinking of fornication, also resulted in penalties, the latter in forty days' penance.[9]

It is not surprising that the Church, through institutional channels, made society aware of the reservations with which it regarded sex. As Ansolde of Maule said to his wife, 'Lady, set me free, then, I pray thee, from my conjugal obligations and by thy good will let me give myself to God.' There was a certain type of dress, the *chemise cagoule*, made of heavy cloth, which permitted penetration without any other bodily contact. 'One should engender chastely,' wrote Abelard. Peter Lombard contended that it was a sin worse than adultery for a husband to love his wife too ardently. The Seigneur de Berze wrote in his Bible that it was sinful not only to commit the carnal act, but to recall it with pleasure.[10]

That Christians did not always live up to the ethical standards of their religion is both obvious and undeniable. No religion ever has or is likely to impose uniformly a moral outlook as austere as that of the early Church. The emergence of the indelicate, bawdy *fabliau* in the twelfth century indicates an undercurrent of sexuality in medieval life. One of the sources of this literature, the eastern tale, suggests the possibility of a continuous tradition of salacious stories circulating orally through all the Christian centuries until the twelfth, at which time they were written down. In any event, the first of the *fabliaux, Richeut* (c. 1159), is scurrilous throughout, and adultery, wantonness, and corruption of the clergy were to be commonplace in the one-hundred-and-fifty-two *fabliaux* that have been preserved.[11]

Love was one of the main themes in another genre of medieval literature, the courtly romance. But the romance had a different social context than the *fabliau*: while the *fabliau* was popular, the romance was aristocratic. From the former came the ribald, licentious tradition of *gauloiserie*, and from the latter a literature of love from which coarseness was purged, and in which sensuality was often sublimated. This is not to say that the courtly romance was brought into line with Christian teachings on sex. On the contrary. The doctrines of courtly love, which found literary expression in the romance, were sometimes a direct parody of Christian tradition. An example is the passage in Chrétien de Troyes' *Lancelot* (c, 1170) in which the hero proved his worth through sacrifice, suffering, and heroism. Finally, entering Guinevere's chamber, he genuflected before her, and then made love to her in an adulterous union, carrying sacrilege of the religion of love to its furthest limit.

The idealization of adultery in the medieval romance was rooted, at least partly, in the contemporary practice of arranged marriages. Marriage in the feudal class had little to do with love. Matches were generally based on material interest, and if that interest disappeared, it was not uncommon for the marriage to be dissolved. It is not surprising that such an approach to marriage led to widespread adultery among the nobility, nor is it unreasonable to say that the idealization of adultery in the romance may be seen in this social context. As C.S. Lewis argues, marital life was the drab background for the fanciful, refined, adulterous, courtly theory of love. Courtly society reacted against Christian teaching, and it fashioned a theory of love that was not only a mockery of Christian teachings on marriage, but also an attempt to establish an autonomous secular morality.[12]

It would seem, though, that the courtly romance did not fully liberate itself from Christian influence. Chrétien described Lancelot as a pious man, and he had him dismount when he passed a church and then enter and pray. A religious and ethical tension is even more apparent in *Tristan et Iseult*. Tristan was the physical superior of all his foes, even the king, and the manners of the time sanctioned the rights of the stronger.[13] And yet, even after Tristan conquered Iseult, he vowed to give her to his king, an act that secured Iseult's unremitting hatred. It required a potion to make the hero and heroine love one another, and even then it is doubtful that they achieved physical satisfaction. When the king discovered Tristan and Iseult sleeping together in the forest their bodies were separated by a sword, the symbol and guardian of chastity. The hero and heroine of this romance loved only under the effects of a potion; their love appears not to have been physical; and it led to their death. Also ambivalent toward love was the leading treatise on courtly love, the *De arte honeste amandi*, written by Andreas Capellanus in the early thirteenth century. At the very beginning the author contended that love must be consummated (i, i). He argued, further, that it must be adulterous, and, in parody of Christian grace, he held that love had the divine power of reward and punishment after death. Andreas Capellanus, too, tried to disengage love from the mandates of Christianity. But his effort failed; in the last book of the *De arte* he retracted. After trying to create a natural morality of love, to carve out a zone for an autonomous human morality, Andreas weakened.

Behind the precarious zone that he tried to delimit there loomed a vast ethical system secure in its higher, divine command.

By the time the Renaissance came to France, Marsiglio Ficino (1433–99) had fully elaborated his Neo-Platonic philosophy. Ficino drew not only from Plato, but also from the other-worldly pseudo-Dionysius and Plotinus. One result was what Ficino called 'Platonic love,' in which love was regarded as an ascent from the terrestial to the celestial. Human beauty was a spark of divine beauty, and inspired the soul to aspire to a realm of infinite beauty. The ideal, then, was spiritual love. Ficino's theories were transmitted to France through four French translations of his own works and through French translations of other Neo-Platonist Italian writings: Pico della Mirandola's *Comento sopra una canzona de amore da Hieronimo Benivieni* (one French edition), Pietro Bembo's *Asolani* (three French editions), Maria Equicola's *Libro di natura d'amore* (three French editions), Leone Ebreo's *Dialoghi d'amore* (five French editions), Caviceo's *Libro del Peregrino* (ten French editions), and, most of all, Castiglione's *Il Cortegiano* (seven French editions before 1600).[14]

The impact of Neo-Platonism on French literature was considerable. In Chrétien love was physical, just as in Andreas' formal theory of courtly love. But in the sixteenth century, under the influence of Ficino's Florentine school, spiritual love became imbedded in the writings of Maurice Scève, Marot, Bonaventure des Périers, Dolet, Héroët, the Ecole Lyonnaise, and the Pléiade poets. Seventeenth-century literature also idealized spiritual love, as seen in the following quote from the novelist Gerzan: 'Il faut prendre garde que les Amours que l'on traitera soient si chastes & si honnestes, qu'elles ne puissent desplaire aux oreilles les plus delicates, n'y aux pensées les plus scrupuleuses.'[15] In Honoré d'Urfé's *L'Astrée* (1610–27), Silvandre said that possession caused love to die. Here is a passage that indicates the Platonism of this enormously popular novel:

L'Ame raisonnable est celle par qui les hommes sont différents des brutes, et c'est elle-mesme, qui par le discours nous fait parvenir à la connoissance des choses, et qui à cette occasion s'appelle raisonnable. La matière est ce qui tombe sous les sens, qui s'embellit par les diverses formes que l'on luy donne, et par là vous pouvez juger, que celle que vous aimez peut bien avoir en perfection les deux dernières beautés que nous nommons corporelle et raisonnable, et que toutes fois nous pouvons dire sans l'offenser, qu'il y en a d'autres plus grandes que la sienne.[16]

The spiritualization of love in seventeenth-century literature was also encouraged by the widely-held theory that the love-passion was destructive. The love-passion was so represented in much of Racine, *Phèdre* being the best-known example. Novels, too, frequently decried lust. 'Qui ne me confessera que l'amour est un rage qui fait tourner les cervelles les mieux assises,' said one character. Another lamented that 'amour est un dangereux dereiglement de la raison, et qui tient beaucoup de la nature de ces fièvres aigues dont nos corps sont perileusement combattus.'[17] Not surprisingly, Platonic sentiments were sometimes mingled with condemnations of sexual passion.[18]

According to Magendie, the serious novel after *l'Astrée* further etherialized and spiritualized love.[19] Important, too, in the novel's depiction of love were the stylistic and structural changes that took place as the heroic and pastoral *roman* gave way to the *nouvelle*. The emergence of the latter in the second half of the seventeenth century gave the novelist a far more effective instrument for his didactic purpose. Moral point was easily lost in wandering, discursive dialogues that ran through the *roman*. The *nouvelle*, however, focused more sharply, developed its theme with fewer digressions, and reached its moralistic conclusion with a new impact.

The heroine of the *nouvelle*, the *honnête femme*, was conspicuous for her high moral conduct, which, it turned out, she was obliged to demonstrate. Forced into marriage, she did not love her husband and, to make matters worse, fell in love with another man. But, because she was virtuous, she refused to yield to her natural desires; she had to struggle with herself in order to overcome her passion and preserve her honour and fidelity. The *nouvelles* analysed by Dorothy Dallas obviously point in the direction of the most famous novelist of the genre, Marie Madeleine, comtesse de La Fayette (1634–92).[20]

Already in *La Princesse de Montpensier* (1662), Madame de La Fayette had described the destructiveness of passion. An aristocratic girl fell in love with a dashing young noble, but was forced to marry another man. While she never committed adultery, her passion for her original suitor revived in spite of her efforts to resist it. This led her into ruinous intrigues in which she was assisted by her husband's best friend, Chabannes. Chabannes was massacred on Saint Bartholomew's Eve; the Duc de Guise, the cause of her passion, betrayed her by falling in love with another lady; her husband, Montpensier, was overwhelmed by grief, and she, completely undone by this tragic turn of events, died of remorse, still in the prime of life, and 'une des plus belles princesses du monde.' The author concluded that '[elle] aurait été sans doute la plus heureuse, si la vertu et la prudence eussent conduit toutes ses actions.'[21]

Similar in situation and conclusion was Madame de La Fayette's masterpiece, *La Princesse de Clèves* (1678). Again, the heroine had to marry a man she did not love, and again, she developed a passion for another. While she did not deceive her husband, her actions allowed him to believe that she had done so and caused his death. The princess, realizing the terrible consequences of her passion, retired to the country, living part of the year in a convent. Stricken with grief and anxious to expiate her wrongs, she concerned herself with 'occupations plus saintes que celles des couvents les plus austères; et sa vie, qui fut assez courte, laissa des exemples de vertu inimitables!'[22]

It seems that the Christian view of love gradually, over a period of many centuries, permeated French literature. What is perhaps most interesting in Chrétien de Troyes' twelfth-century work, *Lancelot*, is its mockery of Christian love. Unsuccessful as the effort was, the medieval romance struggled against a view of love that was considered inhibiting and constraining. But the literature of the sixteenth and seventeenth centuries, subject to the influence of Neo-Platonism and a theory which regarded the love-passion as destructive, developed a view of love consistent with Christianity. Perhaps this development should be seen, in its most basic sense, as a product of the various cultural, intellectual, and religious currents that flowed into the Reformation. Particularly in the seventeenth century, France underwent a religious revival that pervaded all levels of society, and had a direct influence on literature. Corneille's *Le Cid*, written in 1636, showed certain passions as destructive, but not that of love. Don Rodrigue could marry the heroine and live happily ever after. Two years after Corneille wrote *Le Cid*, Cornelius Jansen died, and two years later his work, the *Augustinus* (1640), was published. The rapidity with which Jansenism took root in France scarcely needs comment. Obviously, the time was ripe for a deterministic theology. And as Jansenism articulated and intensified a view of life at once deterministic and pessimistic, it contributed to the representation in literature of an all-destructive love. That Racine was Jansenist-educated is well known and that his plays were conditioned by a Jansenist outlook stands to reason.[23] Phèdre struggled against a passion that could only degrade and eventually consume her. But she could not prevent the love-passion from dominating her and bringing about her ruin. This pessimistic attitude towards love frequently found expression in serious seventeenth-century literature.

Now we must return to the passage from Crébillon *fils' La Nuit et le moment* quoted at the beginning of this chapter. The hero, Clitandre, proclaimed the merits of hedonism and libertinism, and poured scorn upon the absurd 'préjugés' that only his own enlightened age had overcome. *La Nuit et le moment* belonged to a highly popular genre of eighteenth-century French literature, the *roman érotique*, and as such it reflected a moral orientation without precedent in the history of the French novel. What social and intellectual movements brought this genre into existence? From what element in French society did the *roman érotique* originate? What forces brought about a moral reorientation of that social element? Why did a stratum of French society create a literature that rejected the Christian view of love? Why was it that, after achieving an unprecedented victory in seventeenth-century literature, the Christian view of love came under direct attack in the *roman érotique* of the following century?

2

The inner connection
between the seventeenth-century *nouvelle* and
the eighteenth-century *roman érotique*

It was not accidental that the treatment of love in the eighteenth-century *roman érotique* was antithetical to that in the seventeenth-century *nouvelle*. Rather, it was a product of important social change. The eighteenth-century novelist belonged to a society that fell heir to the Christian view of love, that for the most part still accepted that view, but was increasingly questioning and reactionary towards it. The *roman érotique* was the chief product of that reaction in the field of literature. Precisely because the *roman érotique* was in the pattern of reaction, the novelist who worked in this genre could only approach love as the enemy dictated, for it was he who still held the field, and thereby determined the place and conditions of battle. Any society that reacts against the morals of a previous generation will necessarily come under its influence, and similarly the eighteenth-century *roman érotique* came unavoidably under the influence of the seventeenth-century *nouvelle*. Between the two there was a close inner connection.

Since they reflected the values of their audience, it is important to establish the social framework of both the *nouvelle* and the *roman érotique*. We find that the characters in both these genres are aristocratic and move in settings appropriate to the best society. They appear at the court, the masked ball, the theatre, the opera, and at country estates, where they hunt, stroll along shrub-lined lanes, and rest in pavilions; they gamble, converse, write letters, sometimes read, and seldom engage in demeaning commercial or entrepreneurial activities. Not only were characters and social setting aristocratic, but so too were authors. Amongst the writers treated in this study, we find a comtesse (Mme de La Fayette), a marquis (Joseph, Durey de Sauroy, marquis de Terrail, d. 1770), three barons (Pierre-Victor, baron de Besenval [1721–94], Dominique Vivant, baron de Denon [1747–1825], and Charles de Secondat, baron de Montesquieu [1689–1755]), a cadet of a noble family who entered the clergy (Claude-Henri Fusée de Voisenon [1708–1775]), two chevaliers (Pierre Choderlos, chevalier de Laclos [1741–1803], and Charles-Jacques Rochette, chevalier de La Morlière [1701–85]), and the son of a *procureur* (François-Augustin Paradis de Moncrif [1687–1770]). Only two authors were non-noble. One of these (Jean Galli da Bibiena [c. 1709–79]) came from a well-known Italian family of artists and architects, and the other (Crébillon *fils*) was educated at an élite Paris school, Louis le Grand. Several authors occupied socially influential positions. Mme de La Fayette was well connected at court, Moncrif was reader to Marie Leczinska, while Besenval was close to Marie-Antoinette.

The nexus between aristocratic society on the one hand and the *nouvelle* and *roman érotique* on the other is apparent in yet another way: literary form and structure. One important formal characteristic of the *nouvelle* is the elevated language in which it was written, indicating a connection with the aristocratic milieu of seventeenth-century salons. These salons attempted to purify the French language, by eliminating coarse colloquialisms. This objective reveals the élitist spirit dominating the salons and a concomitant disdain for the lower classes. The feeling of social superiority so highly developed in the salons carried over to the novel, influencing its development in a variety of ways. Just as aristocratic society wanted to see its sublime and lofty way of life reflected in literature, so it created the aristocratic novel. In projecting such a view of life the *nouvelle* belonged to the serious category of literature, in contrast to the comic literature appropriate to a less dignified social milieu. We shall see that the *roman érotique* fits into the formal and structural pattern of the *nouvelle*, so revealing its aristocratic orientation, but first we shall examine certain changes taking place within the aristocratic mentality in the seventeenth century, changes that would have a profound influence on the development of the novel.

Broad generalizations about the nature of aristocratic morality may be beyond the capacity of any historian. But we can treat as evidence the moral values recorded in formal, prescriptive writings which revealed certain class ideals. Of particular importance in this connection were two types of manual, the courtier's book and the treatise on *honnêteté*, both of which were vehicles through which the aristocracy articulated and developed its code. Since a third instrument by which the aristocracy conveyed its ideals was the serious novel, it is particularly appropriate that we compare moral attitudes in the novel and in manuals.

In both the courtier's book and the treatise on *honnêteté*, the *honnête homme* was a social type in whom the ideals of the seventeenth century aristocracy were embodied. As such, he was expected to live a Christian life, and to have a Christian view of love and marriage. Nicolas Faret, who wrote one of the most popular courtier's books of the seventeenth century (*L'Honneste homme*, 1630), argued that all the virtues of the *honnête homme* were rooted in religion. This being the case, it is not surprising that Faret condemned the courtier of 'badly composed soul' whose ignoble intentions and bragging could ruin the *honnête femme*.[1] In *Le Gentilhomme* (1611), Nicolas Pasquier contended that the gentleman who slipped into *volupté* stagnated and, his slothful soul seeking only gratification, ended up sunk in a life of evil.[2] Jacques de Caillières stated in *La Fortune des gens de qualité* (1658) that marriage was a sacrament and an indissoluble bond, and that in order to be supremely happy a man must love the woman he married.[3] Antoine de Courtin, to cite one more author, wrote in his *Suite de la civilité* (1675) that 'C'est par les semences d'honnesteté qu'elle [la Nature] a mises en nous, que nous jugeons que de perdre l'honneur de la pudicité, c'est une perte d'une irreparable que celle de la vie.'[4] He then contended that marriage was the first foundation of society, and essential to its preservation. Furthermore, the well-being of society required not only the preservation of chastity before marriage, but also no desire or attempt to seduce or corrupt the wife of another.[5]

With one exception, all of the manuals discussed above were written before 1660. After 1660, the Christian side of the *honnête homme* began to be eroded.[6] There had been elements in aristocratic society before 1660, such as the *libertins*, whose allegiance to Christianity was doubtful, but the code from 1600 to 1660 responded not to the *libertins* as much as to the dominant intellectual and religious forces of the age, Stoicism and the Counter-Reformation. While the Counter-Reformation was by no means over in 1660 the fashion of Stoicism did ebb sharply at that time, and as this occurred the most forbidden of pagan philosophers, Epicurus, was rehabilitated.[7]

The revival of Epicurus certainly helps to explain Antoine Gombaud, chevalier de Méré, whose writings indicate a shift in the theory of *honnêteté*, and he was not the only theorist whose work reflected this change. Méré did not disavow religion. 'La devotion et l'honnêteté,' he wrote, 'vont presque les mêmes voies, et qu'elles s'aident l'une à l'autre. La devotion rend l'honnêteté plus solide et plus digne de confiance; et l'honnêteté comble la devotion de bon-air et d'agrément.'[8] But in this statement religion became part of the refined baggage of the cultivated gentleman, who wished to move easily in society. Another desire legitimized by Méré was happiness. He argued that intelligent people realized that *honnêteté* made them happy, and that happiness (*félicité*) should be their objective. Méré was a hedonist, in the classical, philosophical, sense of the word. In a conversation with La Rochefoucauld he argued that 'dans la morale, Sénèque étoit un hypocrite et qu'Epicure étoit un saint.'[9]

As Méré reduced religion to a polite formality, he took the decisive step of rejecting the Christian view of love. Adultery to him was not only a fact of life within the society of *honnêtes gens*, but also a fact of which he approved.[10] By legitimizing love outside marriage while advancing an Epicurean argument for happiness, Méré arrived at a position that, if applied to literature, could support a non-Christian or, to be more accurate, anti-Christian view of love.

Having observed the penetration of philosophical hedonism into the social ideals of the French aristocracy, we must now examine the relationship between Epicureanism and the novel. If we use *La Princesse de Clèves* as a paradigm of the *nouvelle*, it would seem that there was no such relationship. Happiness could scarcely be the theme of a novel whose heroine denied the advances of a man she loved, and chose instead to retire from the world and end her days in a convent. Yet, it was in this very decision that the princess of Clèves acted consistently with Epicurean philosophy. When her lover, Nemours, proposed marriage to her, one of the grounds on which she declined was her own self interest. She pointed out to Nemours that he was an accomplished lover, that he had had many affairs, and that undoubtedly he would have many more. Since she had long known this she had ample opportunity to examine the consequences for herself, and having done so the results were clear. She was jealous, would always be so, and for that reason could not live tranquilly and happily with Nemours. Above all, she wanted *repos*, which, in her own way, was a solution to the happiness problem. In retiring from the world the princess sought to further her happiness, but the way in which she did so was consistent with Christian otherworldliness. Curious as it might seem, *La Princesse de Clèves* could either support a Jansenist view of life, or be reconciled with Epicureanism.

While it was possible to accommodate Epicureanism to a Jansenist outlook, it was difficult to do so. Saint-Évremond, one of the leading exponents of Epicureanism in the period 1660–1700, wavered endlessly between a commitment to traditional, Catholic Christianity and a philosophy that justified pleasure.[11] A similar ambivalence is seen in *La Princesse de Clèves*. While this novel ends with the heroine dying in a convent, she had wanted to achieve sexual happiness. The novel is, after all, about romance, intrigue, and love, love that was at once passionate and adulterous; had the heroine not fallen in love with a man the calibre of Nemours she would not have placed herself in a situation that forced her to retire from the world. That this did in fact happen reveals the precariousness of the moral world in which the heroine lived. Intrigue and adultery were commonplace at the court, and even the princess was guilty of meeting secretly with a man other than her husband and falling in love with him; she was tempted to participate in a way of life that surrounded her on all sides. Yet, strong as that temptation was, she resisted it, for only in her did absolute moral values remain firm. She can be seen, then, as the last protagonist of a morality whose force was ebbing from within.[12] So while Epicureanism did accommodate itself to a Jansenist view of life in *La Princesse de Clèves*, there were already signs of radical change. Any author who finds it necessary to tempt a heroine as Madame de La Fayette tempted the princess of Clèves is himself ambivalent about the high moral code which he maintains on the conscious level of his thought. And this was true of the *nouvelle* in general. It is not accidental that a type of novel appeared in 1660 that began with an unhappy marriage, went on to intrigue and adultery, and ended on a tragic note. The dénouements of such novels show that in the final analysis moral absolutes prevailed, but had the heroines not been attracted to illicit love they would never have been called upon to suffer tragically in order to maintain the traditional moral order.

This ambivalence was not new; on the contrary, it was as old as the medieval courtly romance. As we have seen, there was already uncertainty toward the Christian view of love in Chrétien de Troyes in the twelfth century; further, love was adulterous according to the dictates of courtly love. Aristocratic literature had always wanted to deny Christian love, but had never been able to do so completely. While it was not yet possible to realize this objective in the period 1660–1700, changes were occurring within aristocratic society that would soon end the ancient ambivalence. In the writings of the chevalier de Méré we can see a reorientation of aristocratic values. While Méré did not reflect the dominant attitudes of his class he did begin a trend which, as Philippe Ariès has argued, would gain force in the eighteenth century.[13] Aristocratic literature could not have rejected the Christian idea of love had not certain changes taken place within its society, changes which did in fact undermine the position of Christianity.[14]

While the serious novel of the period 1660–1700 did not advocate the new moral attitudes that found expression in aristocratic manuals, another genre at least suggested the breakthrough of those attitudes that was to occur in eighteenth-century literature. As Jacques Barchillon has shown, the fairy tale of the period 1685–1705 emerged from the aristocratic milieu of the *précieux*.[15] As in the *nouvelle*, love was a common theme in the fairy tale; further, the fairy tale required the same virtues in the hero and heroine as had the *nouvelle*. But, fissures were appearing in the moral structure of the *conte de fée*. In satirical and ironic fairy tales written at the end of the seventeenth century heroes were deflated and conventions of love were ridiculed. Further evidence of relaxed moral attitudes in the fairy tale is a veiled eroticism in some of La Fontaine's *contes*, and especially in his novelized fairy tale, *Psyché*. In the opinion of Barchillon, La Fontaine may have been the first to use the fairy tale as a medium for discreet, erotic insinuation.[16]

Not surprisingly, the serious novel of the eighteenth century reflected more relaxed moral attitudes than had its seventeenth-century predecessor. The *honnête homme* in Marivaux's novels was decent and kind, but at the same time he was inconstant in love, worldly, and sensual.[17] And, as Erich Auerbach has shown in his masterful analysis of Prévost's *Manon Lescaut* (1731), the novel after the Regency was intimately erotic in both descriptions and allusions.[18] *Désordre* in the feminine toilette, for instance, became a common motif. A 'charming disorder' was produced by a disturbed idyll, a gust of wind, or a fall or jump that revealed the normally covered parts of the body. During the classical epoch of the period of Louis xiv neither the novel nor the comedy had utilized even this type of eroticism.

But the complete breakthrough of eroticism did not take place in the eighteenth-century serious novel. Since it had maintained traditional values, and in particular stood behind the Christian view of love, the serious novel could hardly have served as a medium whose main function was to repudiate that view. There was a type of novel, the comic novel, that was in many ways better suited to realize this objective. Because it reflected the manners and morals of the people rather than the best society, the comic novel was realistic rather than idealistic, and not surprisingly, its coarse representation of life included indecency and immorality. This

novel, in the seventeenth century, perpetuated the ribald, licentious tradition of *gauloiserie*, and therefore one might think that it would have been
the perfect medium for the eighteenth-century novelist who rejected the
Christian view of love. But the eighteenth-century novelist did not turn to
the comic novel; rather, he created a new genre, the *roman érotique*, and for
reasons that deserve our attention.

In the first place, since the author of the *roman érotique* was a representative of the aristocracy rather than the people the comic novel was ruled
out. His heroes and heroines would belong to the same society as those of
the seventeenth-century serious novel, they would be every bit as refined
socially, and just as élitist in class attitude. However, this author wrote with
the conscious intention of repudiating the view of love that was predominant in the serious novel of the previous century. Since he aimed to
deny the sexual morality of the seventeenth-century novel, it is only
logical that he would attack it on its own ground, which he could not do
through the comic novel.

For these reasons, the *roman érotique* took over the technical apparatus
of the *nouvelle*, and thus, to return to an earlier proposition of this
chapter, it followed the form and structure of the *nouvelle*. It was written
in elevated language, observed the *bienséances*, defined love clearly,
created unity through few characters, made intrigue an integral part of
the plot, gave women the power to make key decisions, and stressed *gloire*
and *honneur*.[19] In addition to the formal continuity between the *nouvelle*
and the *roman érotique*, they had another link. In its effort to repudiate the
morality of the serious seventeenth-century novel the *roman érotique*
mocked and ridiculed the sublime and elevated ideals of the *nouvelle*. The
roman érotique, then, was a parody of the *nouvelle*.

A work that clearly illustrates the parodistic element in the *roman
érotique* is La Morlière's *Angola*. It begins at the court of a virtuous king and
queen, to whom prince Angola was born. Present at the hero's birth were
two fairies, one malicious and the other kind. The former prophesied that
when the prince grew up he would fall in love and become unhappy as a
result. On hearing this, the kind fairy offered to take Angola into her
protective custody when he reached the age of fifteen.

However, until his fifteenth year, Angola's education was a mockery of
the ideal set forth in the classical novel. The princess of Clèves' mother
devoted herself entirely to her daughter's education. Angola was turned
over to affected tutors who instructed him in social arts so absurd that they
can only be described as degenerate. Yet, the prince, being endowed with

a naturally virtuous character – like the classical hero – remained unsullied by the base environment to which he was exposed. Angola was chaste, sincere, and honest when he went to the court of the kind fairy.

The plan was to prevent the prince from falling in love. It was reasoned that if he did not, the prophecy of resulting misery could not come true. As in the classical novel, the love-passion was destructive, but now it had a different meaning. Both the princess of Clèves and Angola had to overcome passion; the former by denial and retreat from the world, the latter by learning to develop no feeling, affection, or love for the ladies who courted his favour. Eventually Angola was seduced. He was carried away by passion, and he was so intemperate as to want to continue the affair. His mentor, the experienced courtier, Almaïr, warned him of his folly. Women were only objects, Almaïr said, to be used discriminately. One should never start an affair without a plan to end it. That way the passions would never interfere with one's convenience.

Angola realized Almaïr's wisdom only after many affairs, when fatigued by love and bored to distraction. Suffering from a frightening degree of emptiness and anxious to find a remedy, he poured out his misery to his experienced friend. Now that his pupil was ready, Almaïr completed his education. Together they went to a country house (*petite-maison*), where no questions were asked and all liberties taken. Almaïr helped Angola overcome his *ennui* by arranging a brief liaison for which the prince was now prepared. It seemed that the destructive effects of passion could no longer threaten him. Now that he was fully educated, Angola realized that women were but objects to be used for momentary pleasure.

In *La Princesse de Clèves* the heroine dominated the action. She did so first by innocently drawing the hero into the net of love, and then, after she too was entrapped, she freed herself by retiring from the world in an attempt to overcome passion. As in the classical novel, the heroines in *Angola* shaped the action. They, too, drew the hero into the net of love. But while the princess of Clèves inspired love and passion through beauty, pride, and dignity, La Morlière's heroines employed a variety of devices in order to seduce the hero.

After attending the opera, Angola was offered a ride home by Zobéïde, a girl at Scintilla's court who took it upon herself to seduce him. The carriage, a *vis-à-vis*, placed the passengers in the most intimate positions. Although aroused, Angola was too innocent to take advantage of the situation. Upon arriving in her apartment, Zobéïde lay on a couch suggestively, making certain that her dress was partly open. After dinner, the heroine took the hero to a small specially furnished room at the end of the apartment. There were amorous paintings on every wall with mirrors between. A couch gave the appearance of an altar, consecrated to love. Reclining on the couch and dressed in a light negligée, Zobéïde led Angola along love's way until, at the strategic moment, she pretended to swoon. Frightened, Angola rang for help. This indiscretion exasperated Zobéïde, who told her still innocent lover never again to neglect a swooning woman. Parodying classical convention, the heroine inspired love, but love that was incomplete.

After this and several other unsuccessful attempts Scintilla herself decided to initiate Angola, and took him to an apartment that, like Zobéïde's, was furnished for love. The heroine made him a voyeur by undressing before a mirror whose reflections he could not avoid seeing. She then made him read from an erotic novel and helped him to imitate the descriptive passages. Eventually, Angola was able to proceed without the assistance of the novel, and so he was finally seduced. Again, in burlesque of the classical novel, the heroine's initiative dominated the action; she realized her objective no less than the princess of Clèves.

Many of the themes that appeared in *Angola* appeared also in other *romans érotiques*. As in *Angola*, love was commonly viewed as a strictly physical pleasure, from which the feelings or emotions should be withheld. Aristocratic parents often endangered their children's education by employing foppish tutors and by allowing decadent adults to corrupt youthful innocence. Heroines in the erotic novel typically took the lead in love, and they frequently seduced youths. The enterprising heroine often took her lover to her apartment or room, which contained furniture and paintings designed to stimulate and arouse. The obvious purpose of an amorously furnished room underlined the commonly-held view of love in the erotic novel: the view that love was strictly a physical sensation. Love in the classical novel was sometimes Platonic, sublime, and *spirituel*, sometimes destructive; in the erotic novel it was but a meeting of two skins. Consequently a variety of objects such as furniture, mirrors, and paintings, were used in order to maximize physical contact.

Both honour and glory demanded moral conduct of the highest order in the classical novel. Fearing that her married daughter had fallen in love with another man, the princess of Clèves' mother emphasized the importance of reputation. The heroine had to make whatever sacrifices were necessary in order to preserve honour, which forbade her to descend to the level of other women. In part, it was because she learnt these lessons that she attained such lofty virtue at the end; with her husband's death, and the removal of the last obstacle she could legitimately have married Nemours, but duty and honour obligated her to rise above love and extinguish passion.

The claims of honour were still present in the erotic novel, but in a completely different sense. In Crébillon *fils' Le Hasard du coin du feu* (1763), the heroine sat in a chair suggestively, thereby encouraging the hero, a complete stranger, to make advances, which he did. But the action was interrupted when the heroine resisted: the hero had not made a declaration of love, which his honour prevented him from doing, but which her honour required. The hero's refusal to make a declaration proved that he desired only her body, which was fair enough since she was interested only in his. Yet, she insisted on certain formalities, and because he refused to observe them her honour forced her to be equally frank. By making the hero agree to arrange an affair between herself and one of his friends the next morning she proved that for her, too, love was but the coming together of two skins. Thus did she satisfy her honour, and having done so she and the hero resumed the affair.

In another work by Crébillon *fils, Le Sopha*, honour was associated with sexual conquests, an obvious parody of the traditional, aristocratic, military concept of honour common in seventeenth-century literature. Laclos, of course, substituted sexual conquest for military conquest throughout *Les Liaisons dangereuses* (1781). As Harry Levin has shown, both the Marquise de Merteuil and Valmont employed elaborate strategies that suggested a military campaign, with primary and secondary objectives.[20] Pride of conquest rivalled that of the most dedicated general. Both hero and heroine strove for 'la gloire,' and both took immense pride in their achievements. After Valmont conquered Madame de Tourvel the marquise accused him of compromising his victory by falling in love. Always the man of honour, and unwilling to see another question his dignity, Valmont immediately severed his relationship with his mistress.

In one moral area the seventeenth-century novel (and this is true of both the *roman* and the *nouvelle*) agreed with the eighteenth-century erotic novel. Both condemned arranged marriages. Arranged marriages in the former were thought to bring disorder and unhappiness,[21] while in the latter they provided the background for infidelity and libertinism. The seventeenth-century novel argued for free marriage, whereas that of the eighteenth-century mocked the institution of marriage itself. A typical eighteenth-century heroine was the queen in Abbé Voisenon's *Tant mieux pour elle!* (1760): 'Cette reine méprisait son mari et ... faisait grand cas de l'amour et peu de ses amants: elle avait plus de sensations que de sentimens; elle était heureusement née.'[22] A count said to a countess in

Angola: 'Voilà des magots de la tournure la plus frappante, entre autres celui-ci: il ressemble comme *deux gouttes d'eau* a votre benêt de mari.'[23] The Marquise de Merteuil, in *Les Liaisons dangereuses*, wrote in one of her letters: 'je le lui ai si bien peint, que quand elle serait sa femme depuis dix ans, elle ne le hairait pas davantage.'[24] The heroine of Denon's *Point de lendemain!* (1777), long estranged from her husband, whom she knew slightly, was trying to bring about a reconciliation because of family pressure. Obliged to visit her husband at his estate, she nevertheless wanted to take her lover there. Fearing that her husband might resent her lover (mistakenly; he did not care), she tried to put him off his guard by taking another man the first night, having him leave the next day, and then receiving her lover. Her husband, she reasoned, would think the other man to be her lover, and would be so disarmed when he left that he would not suspect the truth. What began as marital infidelity of course became a double deception, for the heroine spent the first night making love with the other man.

The story which describes an aristocratic marriage in the greatest detail is Besenval's *La Spleen* (1777). An aristocratic father married his son to the daughter of a *fermier-général* whose large dowry helped improve the family's financial position. He did not consult his son in the matter, but simply presented the young lady that he was to marry. She was pretty, and they were attracted to each other in the early weeks of their marriage. But the initial excitement was soon replaced by indifference, and when the hero had to join his regiment he no longer loved his wife. While serving his regiment he fell in love with a married woman, Madame de Rennon. This caused him to rationalize his thoughts about marriage: '[Madame de Rennon] aimoit son mari, lorsque je la connus. Ce sentiment, source d'un bonheur bien vrai, ne se rapporte plus à nos moeurs; il gêne la liberté, qui fait le charme de la société de nos jours. La réserve et la décence que tout mari veut de sa femme, anéantit le plaisir: la gaieté même se ressent de l'éternelle présence dont un époux amoureux accable les maisons que fréquente une femme dont il est aimé. La société ... ridiculise, de son côté, cette sympathie conjugale.'[25]

When he returned home the hero learned that his wife had arrived at the same conclusion concerning marital fidelity. She was upset when he unexpectedly appeared, since she had previously arranged a party for that night, to which she had invited a number of her friends, including her current lover. This situation created a problem:

Je retombai dans un autre embarras, celui d'être *mari trompé*. Ce n'est pas assurément que j'en fusse affecté, quant a moi; mais l'étant il falloit en jouer le personnage, et ce rôle est plus difficile qu'on ne pense. Un mari prétend-il, interdire l'entrée de sa femme, il oblige l'un et l'autre à se chercher dans les lieux publics, à se donner des rendez-vous clandestins. Le premier moyen fait spectacle; le second se découvre, et tous les deux éternisent les propos. Si, plus fâcheux encore, il poursuit sa femme dans ces ressources, et les lui ravit, c'est le moyen d'amener des éclats, ou tout au moins de l'humeur et de la mésintelligence, qui lui font un enfer de sa maison; et bien souvent encore le fruit de ses peines n'est que de faire renvoyer l'amant en titre, pour en prendre un autre. Si, plus doux, et sûrement plus sage, il fait semblant de ne rien voir ...[26]

Under these circumstances, the hero worked out the best possible arrangement:

Je m'éloignai de la société de ma femme. Jamais je ne me trouvois chez moi, lorsqu'elle y donnoit a souper: et quand, par hasard, j'avois à lui parler, je me faisois annoncer comme une visite. Elle me recevoit toujours à merveille, parce que n'exigeant plus rien d'elle, elle ne me rendoit que ce qu'elle vouloit ... De mon côté, j'avois pris une petite maison où je donnois à souper à mes connoissances.[27]

To summarize, adultery did not appear for the first time in the eighteenth-century *roman érotique*. Rather, it was a theme in aristocratic French literature as far back as the twelfth century, and it continued to be so in every century up to the eighteenth. Indeed, in the *nouvelle* of the period 1660–1700 adultery was an integral part of the plot, resulting as it did from the unhappy marriage that took place at the beginning of the story. The *roman érotique* had only to take over the basic elements of the *nouvelle* and carry them to a different conclusion. That this did happen resulted from a reorientation of moral values that took place within the society of the French aristocracy. Finally, the aristocracy created a literary genre that reflected one of its most basic desires: rejection of the Christian view of love. This was the eighteenth-century *roman érotique*, which followed the formal and structural pattern of the seventeenth-century *nouvelle*, and it achieved its aim through parody. The relationship between the two types of novel was dialectical; in parodying the values of the *nouvelle* the *roman érotique* repudiated them. And as it rejected one view of love, it substituted another. The *roman érotique* projected an anti-Christian view of love by arguing that it was purely physical, and by separating it from marriage.

3

Aristocratic manners

Heroes and heroines of *romans érotiques* did not just enter into civilized relationships from which feelings were conveniently excluded. Aristocrats sought not only to win the game of love, but also to vanquish and destroy their opponents. Why were aristocrats so aggressive, why did they act out hostilities toward those with whom they might have shared pleasure? Through a study of aristocratic manners it is possible not only to trace the development of aristocratic enmity, but also to discover one of the sources of the frustration and alienation in which that enmity was rooted. It will be argued that the court contributed significantly to aristocratic animosity, and that this animosity was connected directly to the rise of centralized monarchical government. Out of that political process came a reorientation of aristocratic values and a new approach to manners. This shift led to a sense of disenchantment, exasperation, and cynicism, from which satire, mockery, and cruelty would flow.

The stress given to manners in the Ancien régime must be seen at least in part as the product of a stratified society. A person's position in the social hierarchy was supposed to determine his conduct and behaviour. The marquis de la Fare, a gentleman at the court of Louis xiv, wrote that everything partook of the spirit of its social state.[1] A contemporary of La Fare, Antoine de Courtin, saw a different spirit in every social class, from the nobility to the peasantry.[2] In a book on manners he revealed the connection that he saw between social class, the spirit which provided a particular class with its most essential characteristics, and the manners that were an outward manifestation of those characteristics. It is not accidental that La Fare was an aristocrat, and Courtin, though a cleric, an aristocrat in social outlook, as both the content of his book and his intended audience make clear. The idea of a connection between class and certain mental characteristics and social manners would obviously be congenial to an élitist grouping, for such a connection both underlined and justified the stratification of society.

While manners will always be important in a society that contains élites, they were particularly important to the seventeenth-century French aristocracy. Maurice Magendie, in his massive study, *La Politesse mondaine*, argues that at the beginning of the seventeenth century the aristocracy was coarse, crude, and unpolished, and in response to this state of affairs books were written encouraging social refinement.[3] But the importance given to manners must also be seen as a response to an economic and political crisis that had profound repercussions on the nobility.

When the crisis began is perhaps not clear, but it was undoubtedly before the sixteenth century. A recent study by Davis Bitton, *The Crisis of the French Nobility*, has shown how the period 1560 to 1640 was a time of grave difficulty for the nobility and that this class responded to political and economic pressures by trying to redefine its role. In an attempt to adapt to the growth of centralized, monarchical government, and to repair economic losses, the nobility proposed several courses of action, including entering state service or commerce, or, paradoxically, being given compensation for not entering commerce and for serving only in the military. Whatever the approach might be, the nobility had to rationalize and defend its case. Nobles could hardly expect to be subsidized for not entering commerce, or to enjoy lucrative political offices, unless they could present a convincing argument for these favours, one that necessarily presupposed their superiority as a class. And because the peasantry was levelling attacks against the nobility it was also necessary to defend existing privileges. Thus, in response to these pressures, the nobility developed an even higher degree of class consciousness.

As Bitton has shown, throughout the period 1560 to 1640 aristocratic moralists tried to equate virtue with nobility. Obviously, if virtue went with noble blood the aristocrat would find it easier to legitimize high reward from the state. Only a few moralists went so far as to find an exact coincidence between virtue and nobility, and others found no necessary connection between the two. Most arguments, however, were compromises between these two extremes: noble birth did not automatically ensure a virtuous nature; rather it had to be realized through virtuous actions; however, it was agreed in general that the aristocrat did tend to possess virtue innately. As Nicolas Faret said, good and evil flow with the blood.[4] A certain L'Alouëtte thought that virtue passed naturally from father to son,[5] while Du Rivault held that the good were born of the good and the virtuous of the virtuous.[6] Du Rivault did not explain the transmission of virtue from father to son solely through heredity; virtue did have a hereditary cause, but it also resulted from education and family tradition, in other words, from factors both genetic and environmental. To account for the occasional bad aristocrat, Du Rivault claimed that such a person was not a true noble, but rather a bourgeois who had recently entered the nobility. Because of his birth and background, he lacked both the natural propensity for virtue of the blood noble as well as the loyalty and honour that went with aristocratic tradition. Obviously, Du Rivault opposed the entrance of bourgeois into the nobility. De Grenaille expressed a similar point of view when he said that a governmental official would preferably come from a noble family, for noblemen were endowed by nature with an air of majesty which commanded respect even in their degradation. And children of the nobility seem to command even in subjection, whereas commoners who are sometimes placed in a position of authority appear to be receiving orders when they give them.[7] Like Du Rivault, Grenaille was critical of bourgeois who entered the nobility because the parvenu aristocrat could not hold an office with the same degree of success as the blood noble. When aristocratic moralists tried to equate virtue with nobility they did so for practical reasons and with their sights set on some gain: if the objective were not offices it was state subsidy. Whatever the end, the nobility rested its case on virtue. According to one train of thought, the noble should have idle time in order to contemplate religion and philosophy, in other words to dwell on serious and virtuous ideas appropriate to his dignity.

The nobility could best protect its interests by serving the state, an undertaking for which few of them were adequately trained. One response to the problem was the compilation of treatises to instruct the aristocrat preparing himself for office. Included in this literature were courtiers' books and treatises on *honnêteté*, both of which assumed that the noble belonged at court, ostensibly to serve the state, and in fact to further his own interests.

Even though the seventeenth-century argument for state service was largely a rationalization, it is an important sign of changing public opinion that such a rationalization was advanced. In a penetrating analysis of *Le Réconfort de Madame du Fresne* (c. 1460), written by Antoine de la Sale, a Provençal knight, Erich Auerbach shows how the feudal ethic emphasized personal honour over public service.[8] La Sale described the dilemma of a seigneur du Chastel, who had either to forfeit the life of his son, whom the English held as a hostage, or to surrender a fortress of which he was the commander. The strategic value of the fortress or its political significance is disregarded; the issues are not public issues, but are the private ones of knightly pride, fealty, personal honesty, and honour.

The feudal mentality had by no means disappeared in the seventeenth century, as Paul Bénichou has shown.[9] Yet, by this time the rise of royal absolutism had made a tremendous impact on the outlook of the French aristocracy. The very existence of royal government, and the obvious advantages to be gained by the aristocracy from serving in that government, largely explains the argument for a service nobility. But, if we are fully to comprehend the aristocratic argument for offices, we must remember that the noble did assume that he was to a unique degree loyal, honourable, and virtuous, and for these reasons best suited to hold office. Also, as aristocrats worked out their case, they learned from classical authors, whose impact in the sixteenth and seventeenth centuries was of course vast. Many of the most influential of these authors argued that the nobility, motivated as it was by civic-mindedness, should be the ruling class. In the opinion of Aristotle and Cicero, to mention only two classical authorities, the noble entered politics not to aggrandize himself, but in order to further the interests of the state.[10]

Classical authors, then, not only helped to rationalize the argument for offices, but also encouraged the nobility to consider government as a responsibility. In *L'Honneste homme*, Nicolas Faret told the noble to study politics, morals, and history, using as his guides Plutarch, Tacitus, Sallust, Livy, and Caesar. From these authors he would learn to subordinate his interests to those of the state, and having done so he was under an obligation to go to court,[11] for only there could he put his virtue to full advantage by giving the prince the wise counsel which he had to offer. In describing the court in first-century Rome, de Refuge pointed out time and again how virtuous courtiers promoted the public weal by exerting their influence in the right way.[12] Pasquier argued that the aristocrat's education should include politics, and that he should study this science by reading classical authors, from whom he would learn not only moral precepts but also practical lessons in the art of government.[13] And, in his opinion, morality and politics were inseparably connected, for only after acquiring the former could the aristocrat practise the latter. In Pasquier's mind, as in Faret's, the aristocrat was under a moral obligation to go to court. Antoine de Courtin, after arguing that the aristocrat should put the interest of the state before his own interest, cited Pericles, Philip of Macedon, Caesar, and Augustus as examples of men who were dedicated to the welfare of the public.[14] In all these manuals the aristocrat was supposed to commit himself to state service, after the fashion of the Greeks and Romans, not for reasons of self interest but from a sense of duty. By taking himself to court the aristocrat was putting to best use both his innate superiority and the loyalty and deeply imbedded sense of responsibility which he assimilated through his family tradition. In this prescriptive pattern of conduct there was a fusion of two sets of ideals: one of feudal honour and duty, the other of classical civic-mindedness. The result, from the noble's point of view, could hardly have been more satisfactory. The noble who held office could see himself as honourable and virtuous; here was a view that perpetuated the feudal tradition of honour, paid homage to the classics, and also took contemporary political realities into account.

Nobles wanted offices, then, for two reasons: to further their material interests and to satisfy their honour. Already in the early sixteenth century the state had so extended its functions at the expense of the nobility that it caused a malaise within the noble class. But if the nobility were to share in and even benefit from the growth of monarchical absolutism by becoming the governing class, nobles could once again find dignity and meaning in their role, as well as solve the economic problems which threatened to destroy their material position. But would the nobility succeed in this political ambition?

With one important qualification, the answer is no. While the twentieth-century historian likens nobility to a corridor through which people pass, the seventeenth-century noble would have preferred another metaphor, that of a room filled with a fixed number of people. The crown, for reasons both political and economic, preferred the metaphor of the corridor. In order to keep the military, sword nobility from becoming too powerful, and also as a desperate financial expedient, the crown chose to sell offices, and in no period as extensively as in the seventeenth century. Since offices frequently conferred nobility it is inaccurate to say that nobles were barred from office. On the contrary, most high offices were filled by nobles, but predominantly by men who entered the nobility from below and through monetary transaction. From the old, blood noble's point of view the crown's policy of selling offices was both perfidious and disastrous.

The extent to which, or exactly when, the 'true' nobility came to see the problem in this light is difficult to say. It is possible to examine attitudes in courtier's books and treatises on *honnêteté*, both of which reflected at least in part the outlook of a certain segment of the nobility. Up to about 1660 and, in some instances even later, courtier's books praised civic-mindedness and exhorted the noble to go to court and serve the state. But eventually, the fatuity of this rhetoric became evident, at least to some nobles, and as a result new attitudes took hold.

The courtier's treatises on *honnêteté* urged the noble to go to court and to serve the state, and were also books of etiquette. In fact, disparate as advice on politics and manners might seem, the two were connected. To obtain a politically important position the courtier had to win the prince's favour, as well as know how to exert influence on the various cliques that were forever taking shape at court. The courtier, then, had to master the art of pleasing, which required *politesse*, tact, elegant conversation, in a word all that was necessary in the way of refinement to move easily and persuasively in this sophisticated social world. Manners did have a serious and practical function. The courtier who was well-mannered could better realize the political ambitions essential to his self interest.

Manners were also important in themselves, serving as a visible means of separating the best society from the coarse, ill-bred, unpolished people. The popularity of books of etiquette in the sixteenth and seventeenth centuries might well have been a response to the crisis of the nobility, which was at once political, economic, and psychological. In perfecting his manners the aristocrat demonstrated his superiority, just as he did by serving the state; again, the connection between manners and state service becomes apparent. What would happen to manners, though, if they were separated from politics?

Interestingly, the answer to this question was in the most famous of all courtier's books, Castiglione's *Il Cortegiano* (*The Book of the Courtier*) (1528), which in French translation went through seven editions in the sixteenth century and which had a considerable influence on virtually every seventeenth-century French courtier's book and treatise on *honnêteté*.

In his fine analysis of *Il Cortegiano*, John S. White tries to explain the 'deep rift' between books 1–3 and book 4.[15] White sees in books 1–3 a pattern of courtly life that was apolitical, but in the later book 4 a new outlook, which, like Machiavelli's *The Prince*, was conditioned by political crisis. While the courtier was to become aware of politics in book 4, and consequently commit himself to patriotism and state service, in books 1–3 the courtier ideal existed only for itself. The courtier of books 1–3 was an aesthetic individualist who formed himself into a work of art. In so doing, he necessarily had to perfect his manners, but this he had to do effortlessly and easily, in a word with the *sprezzatura* of the natural aristocrat.

Sprezzatura, Castiglione said, was essential to true art, 'which does not seem to be art.'[16] Since the mastery of the courtier had to be supremely easy, nonchalant, and graceful, any display of effort was ruinous. Poor, laughable Pierpaolo, for example, danced with stiff legs, never moving his head, studying every step as if he were counting, and looking 'as if he were a stick of wood.' 'What eye is not to see in this the ungainliness of affectation ... ?'[17] Castiglione was disdainful of affectation, which for him was simply bad style. His concept of style included both excellence and contempt for the individual who could not achieve it. The root word of *sprezzatura*, *sprezzare*, means 'to disdain,' or 'to hold in contempt.' Castiglione also used a synonym of *sprezzatura*, *disinvoltura*, which means 'ease,' 'simplicity of manner,' and 'aplomb,' but also 'coolness,' 'cheek,' and 'impudence.'[18] The courtier was easy and graceful in his achievements, a naturally superior being who looked down on lesser beings who could not measure up to his standards.

Manners became a way of setting the courtier apart from the rest of the social order. Characteristically, Castiglione advised the courtier to avoid country festivals, where he would meet people of low birth. Similarly, 'in horseback vaulting, in wrestling, in running and jumping, I should be very glad to have the courtier shun the vulgar herd or at most put in a rare appearance with them ... ' The courtier lived in a world of aristocratic isolation, necessarily artificial and intentionally unreal. Thus, at a masquerade it was possible for 'a cavalier to dress as a rustic shepherd or in some other costume, but astride a perfect horse and gracefully attired in character.'[19] In this passage the courtier became his own apotheosis, but gave the appearance of the opposite. And significantly, the discussion of masquerades followed a conversation on dancing and how to execute difficult steps in 'public spectacles.' The courtier should not attempt more than his abilities allow, lest he lose his dignity and his 'fine and airy grace of movement.' Such concerns evaporated at the masked ball, where the courtier could dance any step he wished, whether difficult or not. The 'freedom and license' of the masquerade, then, allowed the courtier to forget himself in public, and it opened a world of fantasy and unreality. Class-consciousness led, in this context, to a highly refined, escapist ideal.

In France Castiglione's ideal was realized only towards the middle of the seventeenth century. Nicolas Faret certainly read Castiglione carefully, but as a social type his *honnête homme*, compared to Castiglione's courtier, was rather pedestrian. Faret's book, written in 1630, repeated *Il Cortegiano* frequently: the *honnête homme* was preferably a noble, he should practise the profession of arms, play the lute, dance, engage in exercises, read the classics, and cultivate the art of conversation with the ladies. But Faret, committed as he was to both Christianity and the ideal of state service, could not envision life as an elegant ceremony. Castiglione's aestheticism was beyond his reach.

The chevalier de Méré read Castiglione in a rather different spirit from Faret. Méré, as a young man of twenty-one, offered his services to Richelieu, who replied that he considered young people suspect. Shortly afterward Méré participated in a military adventure that turned out badly. Disenchanted by politics, he began to frequent the *précieux* salon of Madame de Rambouillet, whose outlook he appears rapidly to have assimilated, and which, along with his reading of Castiglione, contributed significantly to his notion of the *honnête homme*.

Méré worked out his concept of the *honnête homme* in correspondence beginning in the 1630s, and then in formal treatises published between 1677 and 1700. That he borrowed many points from Castiglione is not exceptional, for Faret and other French writers had also done so. Méré's achievement was that he realized Castiglione's ideal of the aesthetic individual whose style was a reflection of his superiority. His *honnête homme* despised lowness, bad taste, a vulgar and ignoble air, the air of the law court, of the bourgeoisie and of the provinces, the discussion of common subjects, and 'tout ce qui vient d'un esprit mal fait ... '[20] Méré pointed out that one was not an *honnête homme* by métier, but rather by nature, which he augmented by art. But his art was difficult to pin down. His ideal escaped exact definition, and in a well-known discussion of *honnêteté*, he concluded that it was really easier to say what the *honnête homme* should avoid rather than what he should be. Only the natural aristocrat could attain this ideal.

Nevertheless, Méré continually dwelt on the personal qualities and social attributes essential to the *honnête homme*. And in his elucidation of these qualities and attributes he recaptured Castiglione's ideal of the aesthetic being who, in stylizing his life, became detached and aloof, a social being of no practical consequence. Like Castiglione's courtier, Méré's *honnête homme* was a fixture at court. But he was enervated, and 'il y a toujours eu de certains Fainéans sans métier ... '[21] This *honnête homme* was not anxious to govern, his only goals being his own enjoyment and winning the esteem of others. He dressed properly, pleased in conversation, jested lightly, and maintained the proper tone. As he was rather too detached from life to become involved in pursuits requiring active participation, he could only stand apart; he became an actor who enjoyed his role as did a comedian.[22] In this aesthetic, artificial world, both politics and morality became irrelevant. Only style counted. Méré contrasted two types of men he had observed. One was skilled in politics and morality but socially clumsy, while the other mastered only the social arts. The former was seen in improper company, while the latter, whom Méré obviously preferred, was always well received by the right people.[23]

When Méré equated the skilled politician with the social incompetent he showed his contempt for the office-holding class. Here was a group of people who, in his opinion, lacked refinement and sophistication, unlike well-manered natural aristocrats. Obviously true aristocrats would exclude socially clumsy *officiers* from their company. In viewing the office-holding class in this way, Méré was responding to the royal policy of selling offices and creating a new nobility. Having been rebuffed by Richelieu when he offered him his services, Méré blocked out an ambition that he could not achieve and found dignity elsewhere. As the embodiment of *politesse*, in which his pride was necessarily rooted, he could only look down on those lesser creatures who held office. While works in which Méré expressed these attitudes began to appear only in 1677, the date of their composition is uncertain. In any event, they reflect attitudes that began to take shape when he was a young man, during the ministry of Richelieu. Like many of his contemporaries, Méré had grievances against the cardinal, but what is interesting is his way of dealing with them. While most of his peers dreamed of recovering their ancient liberties and moved in a world of extravagant valour, pride, and honour, all of which were tied to the military tradition of the nobility, Méré dedicated himself to the social arts and became the theorist par excellence of *honnêteté*. In doing this he found a new outlet for his pride.

Now we can see the complexity both of aristocratic responses to absolutism and of the role of manners in aristocratic life. Aristocrats could want offices or they could despise those who held them; they could cultivate their manners in order to gain influence at court, and thereby secure lucrative positions, or they could perfect their manners as a substitute for state service. All of these possibilities were present during the ministry of Richelieu, and in degrees that we shall never measure exactly, all were considered and explored. One thing is certain: the final consolidation of royal power under Louis xiv could only bring the problem of manners into ever sharper focus.

Of course, nobles went to court during the reign of Louis xiv in unprecendented numbers, and, as before, in the hope of reward. While

Louis did grant offices to the court nobility, they were only household and not political offices. In so doing he offended and frustrated the nobles, who actually practised the social skills recommended in courtier's books and treatises on *honnêteté* with the intention of winning the prince's favour and thereby benefitting from his generosity. It turned out, though, that the immense effort expended by the courtier in perfecting his social skills was of mixed value, for the arts with which he adorned himself were also useful to the prince. They were a means by which he turned the courtier into an ornamental fixture of little practical significance, a fact of which at least some nobles were perfectly aware. One response to Louis' emasculation of the court nobility was a feeling of resentment, hostility, and cynicism, as shown by this passage from the Sieur de Chévigny's *La Science des personnes de la court* (1706), that describes in bitter irony the position of the courtier under Louis XIV. Everything at court, he wrote, 'dépend de la disposition de l'esprit & du coeur du Prince qui règne. S'il se tourne de côté de la dévotion, toute la Cour est dévote, au moins en apparence; s'il s'abandonne aux plaisirs, aux amusemens, toute la Cour embrasse ce parti avec joie, d'autant plus qu'il est conforme au penchant du coeur.' The courtier's arts required the skills of old along with some made necessary by current reality: 'De la patience, de la politesse, point de volonté; tout écouter, ne jamais rien rapporter. Paroître toujours content. Avoir beaucoup d'amis, peu de confidens.'[24]

In this passage manners have become the instrument not of the aristocrat's perfection, but rather of his degradation. At the beginning of the seventeenth century the aristocracy had hoped to become the ruling class, and from this ambition came a large body of literature that both rationalized the ambition and indicated how it might be realized. In giving advice to office-hungry nobles aristocratic manuals emphasized manners. Both the argument for state service and the stress placed on manners rested on the assumption of aristocratic superiority, and for this reason both helped bring into being a dignified image of the aristocrat. The chevalier de Méré withdrew from politics, expressed contempt for the person who did not, and, as the *arbiter elegantiae* of his day, fashioned a wholly social aristocratic ideal. Méré's *honnête homme* revealed his superiority by refining himself and forming himself into a work of art. But for the Sieur de Chévigny, even manners have become degrading. Méré kept half of the dignified image, but for Chévigny even this was impossible. The result was complete exasperation and frustration, both of which came out in irony, mockery, and satire. Unable to form his world as he wished, Chévigny chose to ridicule it.

It would certainly be incorrect to say that courtiers were merely weak-willed, hypocritical, and pathetic in the manner that Chévigny depicted them. In fact, the aristocracy became more powerful in the eighteenth century, partly through the energy and pragmatism of the court nobility. Still, in spite of the enormous successes that awaited the aristocracy under Louis xv and even more under Louis xvi, Louis xiv's temporary victory over the nobility did make a profound impression on that class, and particularly on the court nobility. It produced a mood of despair and futility and it helped paint the picture of the effete and corrupt courtier. This mood, it is important to emphasize, came from Versailles, and it contributed to a negative view of this social type, as can be seen in authors as different as Saint-Simon and Montesquieu.

Writing in the 1740s, and looking back to the death of the Dauphin in 1711, Saint-Simon described its results on his fellow courtiers. The event at once undermined some cabals and created others, and it made everyone reassess his position now that there was a new heir to the throne. On such an occasion as this courtiers revealed their true character.

Chaque visage vous rappelle les soins, les intrigues, les sueurs employés à l'avancement des fortunes, à la formation, à la force des cabales; les adresses à se maintenir et en écarter d'autres, les moyens de toute espèce mis en œuvre pour cela; les liaisons plus ou moins avancées, les éloignements, les froideurs, les haines, les mauvais offices, les manèges, les avances, les ménagements, les petitesses, les bassesses de chacun ... la satisfaction extrême et inespérée de ceux-là, et j'en étais des plus avant, la rage qu'en conçoivent les autres leur embarras et leur dépit à le cacher.[25] (*Ibid.*, vol. 16, 246).

In another passage, when Saint-Simon said Louis iii, duc de Condé, 'n'avait ni l'injustice, ni l'avarice ni la bassesse de ses pères,'[26] he implied that it was possible to inherit vice, and he went on to say that Condé did in fact have his ancestors' malevolence. It seems that in Saint-Simon's opinion the very blood of courtiers had been corrupted; rather than being genetically superior, courtiers were genetically unsound.

Also writing in the 1740s, Montesquieu described 'le misérable caractère des courtisans' in the following way:

L'ambition dans l'oisiveté, la bassesse dans l'orgueil, le desir de s'enrichir sans travail, l'aversion pour la vérité, la flatterie, la trahison, la perfidie, l'abandon de tous ses engagements, le mépris des devoirs du citoyen, la crainte de la vertu du prince, l'espérance de ses faiblesses, et, plus que tout cela, le ridicule perpétuel jeté sur la vértu ...[27]

Angola, different as it was in tone and purpose from Saint-Simon's *Mémoires* and Montesquieu's *L'Esprit des lois*, did express attitudes that bring to mind passages in these works. Behind the polished, elegant veneer of the courtier was a rotten and morally diseased interior. The scene was a ball, attended by courtiers.

Le bal étoit prêt à finir, les bougies diminuoient, les musiciens, ivres ou endormis, ne faisoient plus usage de leurs instruments. La foule étoit dissipée, tout le monde étoit démasque, le blanc et le rouge couloient *à grands flots* sur les visages *recrépis* et laissoient voir des peaux *livides, flasques et couperosées*, qui offroient aux yeux le spectacle dégoûtant *d'une coquetterie délabrée*[28] (original italics).

The courtiers in *Angola* frequently went to town for amusement, with important social results. In the reign of Louis xiv a social group known as *La cour et la ville* had already taken shape. While it included both bourgeois and nobles, its outlook was clearly aristocratic, and interestingly, its ideal was the courtly ideal of the *honnête homme*.[29] Through this social group we can see how attitudes that originated at court filtered into other social strata and contributed to values that can be called aristocratic. It is not necessary to say that the court played a predominant role in shaping aristocratic values, nor is it possible to list here the attitudes that passed from one social sphere to another. Our point is that the court was the most select group in a society that valued birth and rank, and that attitudes did flow from Versailles to a larger social world. Among the courtly attitudes that entered into the life of the French aristocracy were the cynicism and negativism that reflected one response to the policies of Louis xiv.

We can now turn to eighteenth-century literature that depicted a do-nothing way of life, and that represented the aristocracy, not just the court nobility, as corrupt. The manners that originated at court and moved to Paris contributed to that corruption, and served as a means of separating the aristocracy from the people. Various literary genres portrayed both the manners and their consequences for aristocratic life, but the following discussion will limit itself to the *roman érotique*.

In *Les Egarements de Zéloïde et Amanzarifdine* (1714), Paradis de Moncrif depicted aristocrats who, in order to please others, had to acquire the latest jargon, neglect the ladies just enough, keep informed of all their trifling, romantic incidents and be certain to discuss them, take part in the ladies' pastimes and amusements, and above all spend money lavishly. More trenchant in its satire of aristocratic manners was *Les Egarements du cœur et de l'esprit* (1736–38), by Crébillon *fils*. Descriptions of such an aristocratic lady as Madame de Sénanges revealed the degrading consequences of over-refined manners. This heroine spoke the bizarre language of the court, which was at once old-fashioned and new, and which she uttered in a nonchalant, drawling tone. She affected slovenliness, sometimes thought to be natural. To this exotic lady the innocent hero of the novel was too plain, possessing neither an extravagant tone nor ridiculous manners. Another character in the novel, Versac, undertook the education of the hero. A man of rank and honour, Versac explained, must strive above all to make his name celebrated. This obligated him to understand the norms of society, by which he would be measured. Since in society only fashion counted, it was necessary to study that elusive and arcane science. The man of society would not only seize a fashion during its season of popularity, but also invent the follies that went by the name of fashion. And the best way to learn when a fashion turned stale was to determine when women began to lose interest in it.

Aristocratic manners were satirized in *Angola*, as F.C. Green has argued, through the characters' extravagance.[30] La Morlière's aristocrats had to avoid any of the common, vulgar habits of the bourgeoisie.[31] At the opera it was the fashion to appear blind, to screw up one's eyes, and to use a looking-glass. Prince Angola, who enjoyed perfect vision, followed the fashion in order not to commit a breach of decorum. Later, at a dinner with Zobéïde, Angola revealed his coarseness by eating amply and healthily. The well-bred Zobéïde conducted herself far better, leaving all the good things and eating only entrails, the heads and feet of birds, sucking-pigs' trotters, and a small helping of a sweet dish. For dessert, she drank champagne and Barbados rum, grimacing and complaining that it was too strong while, in fact, she enjoyed it thoroughly.

Joseph, Durey de Sauroy, marquis de Terrail, mocked aristocratic manners in *Le Masque* (1751). Spending an evening at the house of a princess, everyone dressed to the hilt, displaying all the most recent appurtenances such as snuff-boxes made of lacquer, jasper, or costly lapis-lazuli. A fashionable aristocrat had to change snuff-boxes every few weeks, and purchase nothing of lasting value. Utility was irrelevant, and only the bizarre and exotic had appeal. A snuff-box, which dried up its contents and would fall apart in a day, was considered in the best of taste. Not only were such useless objects in the highest vogue, they were almost the sole topic of conversation at this aristocratic gathering.

The *American College Dictionary* describes decadent as a 'falling off or deteriorating,' and this precisely describes manners in the *roman érotique*.

Behind the absurd language and fashions in the *roman érotique* were serious discussions of both in seventeenth-century manuals and novels. Decadence was also seen in the *roman érotique*, in the futility of aristocratic life. The heroes and heroines, having nothing worthwhile to do, became exotic and foolish social ornaments who flitted about without any purpose. In *Angola* the entire court returned to the palace after dinner, where the older men played cards, cheated, and acted overbearingly if they won. The younger men lolled about on sofas with the ladies, whispered into their ears, offered advice to the card-players, and hummed wanton songs that made the ladies tap them with their fans for the sake of appearance. In another description, some aristocrats, who were the cleverest men at court, helped Zobéïde make patchwork screens to be placed beside paunchy grotesques that were the last word in drollery.

How far these passages in *Angola* are from descriptions of well-mannered aristocrats in seventeenth-century novels! Those novels both described and prescribed a social code whose function was to maintain a dignified image of aristocratic life. In that code, manners that for the most part originated at court were not only rooted in the idea of aristocratic superiority; they were also a visible means of demonstrating it. The true aristocrat comported himself in a way that was consistent with his genetic makeup. His refinement stamped him as a man of quality. But in the *roman érotique* manners revealed the aristocrat's feebleness and decadence. This literary genre portrayed characters who were over-refined and weakened by a degenerate social code.

That the *roman érotique* also depicted strong-willed aristocrats who were ironic and vented hostility through barbed witticisms is not surprising. As different as the satirical and aggressive type of aristocrat was from the bloodless and effete type, both derived from the same social conditions. When the sieur de Chévigny mocked the courtier who accepted the meaningless ritual and enforced subservience of Versailles, he was in fact displaying his own anger. Life at court could produce two responses: either it could debilitate the noble who surrendered to a code that twisted politeness into falseness and made servility a social necessity, or it could stir resentment and hostility in the noble whose pride was offended by this degrading way of life.

Mockery was by no means new to Chévigny's *La Science des personnes de la cour*. On the contrary, early in the sixteenth century Castiglione had encouraged the courtier to master the witticism. In doing so he responded to certain conditions at court that made wit a highly developed art. Living in the non-functional, ornamental, make-believe world of the court, Castiglione developed an aesthetic view of life that reflected the futility of that world. Detached from the active life, the courtier lived in a stylized and subjective universe of his own creation. But the need for direct participation in life was too powerful to suppress completely. Since the courtier resented having been driven from the political arena, anger did come to the surface, but it could do so only in ways that were socially acceptable, such as the witticism. The courtier could not achieve real power, but when he unleashed the devastating jest he could gain an ascendancy over his fellows.

Another source of the courtier's wit was the reserve that was an essential component of his style. Acutely aware of his class superiority, he was distant, aloof, and imperturbable. Internal tension mounted since social necessity forced him to stifle his feelings and his spontaneity. Under these circumstances anger had to come out, and it broke through as the destructive joke and the barbed witticism. Interestingly, seventeenth-century manuals urged the aristocrat to control his wit; he should jest in a light and delicate manner. The jest should never offend, and it should be refined. Even if it were part of an attack, it should please more than antagonize. The authors of the manuals appeared to realize how dangerous jesting could be, and wanted to check a harmful urge.

The destructive power of wit is apparent to the reader of Saint-Simon's *Mémoires*. In passage after passage, Saint-Simon described courtiers who made elaborate plans for someone's humiliation. The comte de Tessé, for instance, was what Saint-Simon called the victim of a 'plaisante aventure' arranged by the duc de Lausun.[32] Lausun, affecting an 'air de bonté, de douceur et de simplicité,' asked the comte de Tessé about the hat he was going to wear at a forthcoming inspection. Tessé replied that according to custom a person of his rank had to wear a cap, rather than a hat. However, through trickery and a cunning aside, Lausun convinced Tessé that he should wear a hat. When Louis XIV saw it he demanded to know where Tessé had got it. When he told the king that the hat came from Paris the disingenuous officer incurred the wrath of the monarch. 'Jamais je ne vis un homme plus confondu que Tessé,' wrote Saint-Simon. 'Il demeura les yeux baissés en regardent ce chapeau avec une tristesse et une honte qui rendirent la scène parfaite.'[33] How perfect that Saint-Simon should close the description with this comment, indicating as it does the planning, even artistry, that went into the incident!

In another passage Saint-Simon described a trick that Lausun played on Louis XIV. Lausun learned that the king was sleeping with Madame de Monaco, and that she came to a back door of the royal apartment by means of a concealed staircase. He stationed himself in a privy opposite this door, and looking through the keyhole of the privy, saw Louis put the key on the outside of the door and then enter the room. He slipped out of the privy, locked the door, took the key, and awaited the arrival of Madame de Monaco. She came, looked for the key, and knocked on the door. Louis, waiting on the other side, told her to use the key to get in, she replied that it was nowhere in sight, and after Louis tried unsuccessfully to force the lock, the lovers had to say goodnight. 'Lausun, qui les entendait, à n'en pas perdre un mot, et qui les voyait de son privé par la trou de la serrure, bien enfermé au crochet comme quelqu'un qui serait sur le privé, riait bas de tout son cœur, et se moquait d'eux avec délices.'[34]

Why, it might be asked, did Lausun play this highly dangerous game? In the first place, Saint-Simon said that Lausun himself was in love with Madame de Monaco, so the gamekeeper was punishing the poacher. But Lausun had other grievances against Louis. After secretly promising him an artillery commission, Louis withdrew the offer because the recipient had given away a secret. When Louis announced his decision to revoke the commission, Lausun 's'éloigne de quelques pas, tourne le dos au roi, tire son épée, en casse la lame avec son pied, et s'écrie en fureur qu'il ne servira de sa vie un prince qui lui manque si vilainement de parole.'[35] Since the king had broken his word, deprived him of a position he wanted, and compromised his dignity, Lausun retaliated through a clever ruse. Looking through the keyhole of a privy, he mocked a king whose frustration his artistry had brought about.

The connection between the clever trick and a feeling of powerlessness runs throughout Saint-Simon's *Mémoires*. Another example is the ruse worked by the chevalier de Coislin on his brother, the duc de Coislin. As a younger brother this chevalier lived in near penury at Versailles. Although he never left the court, he made it a matter of principle never to see Louis, even if he had to cross a street to avoid him, giving evidence that he had grievances against his monarch. Apparently the king had chosen not to give him a position. Yet, Coislin did follow his older brother whenever he joined Louis on a royal journey. During one trip this brother, who had a reputation for excessive flattery, heaped compliments on a hostess who was entertaining them. He did so in the evening, and then again even more fulsomely the next morning. The chevalier de Coislin was enraged with his brother over his conduct, and retaliated, as he believed, appropriately. When they finally left and were three or four leagues away he mentioned his brother's flattery, which he said might not have left a favourable impression. The duc could not understand why, because he felt certain his manners had never served him better. The chevalier explained that he was so exasperated that he had 'pousée une grosse selle tout au beau milieu sur le plancher,' and 'la belle hôtesse ne doute point, à l'heure qu'il est, que ce présent ne lui ait été laissé par vous avec toutes vos belles politesses.'[36] Then he and the others present 'rire de bon cœur' at the duke's visible distress. In describing this incident Saint-Simon first made clear the chevalier's penury, then he discussed his hostility to the one person in the world who could have improved his material position and given him a position of dignity, and finally he described an incident on a royal journey. It would not be accurate to say that Coislin was retaliating primarily against the king when he left his 'présent' on his brother's behalf, but his conduct is fully intelligible only if this factor is taken into account. Furthermore, it was the duc de Coislin's excessive flattery, to which his younger brother objected as a man of principle, that brought about the attack. What the chevalier de Coislin thought about courtly manners, at least as practised by his brother, is shown by his behaviour on this occasion.

Not only did Saint-Simon derive vicarious satisfaction from describing nobles who mocked, jested, and ridiculed others, he too poured out contempt and hatred in his character portraits. Such a collection of twisted, demented, crippled, malicious, malevolent people one would hardly expect to find in memoirs depicting the life of the most splendid court of Europe. Lausun was 'plein d'ambition, de caprices de fantaises jaloux de tout, voulant toujours passer le but, jamais content de rien, sans lettres, sans aucun ornement ni agrément dans l'esprit, naturellement chagrin, solitaire, sauvage ... méchant et malin par nature ... '[37]

The duc de Condé, he wrote,

était un homme très-considérablement plus petit que les plus petits hommes, qui sans être gras était gros de partout, la tête grosse à surprendre, et un visage qui faisait peur. On disait qu'un nain de madame la Princesse en était cause. Il était d'un jaune livide, l'air presque toujours furieux, mais en tout temps si fier, si audacieux, qu'on avait peine à s'accoutumer à lui ... Ses mœurs perverses lui parurent une vertu, et d'étranges vengeances qu'il exerça plus d'une fois, et dont un particulier se serait bien mal trouvé, un apanage de sa grandeur. Sa férocité était extrême et se montrait en tout. C'était une meule toujours en l'air qui faisait fuir devant elle, et dont ses amis n'étaient jamais en sûreté, tantôt par des insultes extrêmes, tantôt par des plaisanteries cruelles on face, et des chansons qu'il savait faire sur-le-champ qui emportaient la pièce et qui ne s'effaçaient jamais.[38]

The comte de Gramont 'était un homme de beaucoup d'esprit, mais de ces esprits de plaisanterie, de reparties, de finesse, et de justesse à trouver le mauvais, le ridicule, le faible de chacun, de le peindre en deux coups de langue irréparables et ineffaçables, d'une hardiesse à le faire en public ... C'était un chien enragé à qui rien n'échappait. Sa poltronnerie connue le mettait au-dessous de toutes suites de ses morsures; avec cela escroc avec impudence, et fripon au jeu à visage découvert, et jouant gros toute sa vie.[39]

The importance of these descriptions lies not merely in the recurring theme of malevolent aristocrats who gave vent to anger and frustration through barbed witticisms and cunning strategies, but more so in Saint-Simon's connection of this pattern of conduct with court life. We have seen that both Lausun and the chevalier de Coislin were hostile to Louis XIV, and that their meanness was rooted in that hostility. This pattern runs as clearly as a red thread throughout the *Mémoires*. As La Bruyère viewed the court from the standpoint of an outsider, he could hardly have represented court life as did Saint-Simon. Neither, for that matter, could anyone else, for Saint-Simon is one of the most original of French writers. Still, La Bruyère's view of the court does show considerable agreement with Saint-Simon. In the *Caractères*, courtiers are less overt in acting out their hostilities, but the psychology is basically the same. Courtiers were forced to toady and court favour, they had to dissimulate and disguise passion, and they squandered whatever intelligence they had on futile plans. Not surprisingly, such an existence not only hardened the courtier's heart, but also brought out vice. As candour and frankness were out of place, the courtier was forced to become devious, and so he turned to raillery and witticism.[40]

Just as the *roman érotique* satirized the decadent manners that originated at the court, so too did it treat aristocratic malevolence whose source was the same. Versac, in Crébillon *fils' Les Egarements du cœur et de l'esprit* contended that society associated wit with scandal. More than in any other way the man of *bon ton* was distinguishable by his ability to slander. Scandal could be neither too cruel nor too abstruse (*précieuse*). Even if the well-bred man had not the least intention of mocking, he could not have too scornful an air or too malicious a tone. Such a manner would add to one's power, since it put others on the defensive. Even a man of little merit could inspire fear through scandal and mockery. Aristocrats in erotic novels frequently conducted themselves much as Versac recommended. Scandal was a common subject of conversation, and in moments of hostility characters gave vent to hatred not through passionate outpourings but through barbed witticisms delivered with an excessively polite and complimentary air. Beneath the cultivated language and refined manners of the well-bred aristocrat was a destructive urge and a need to dominate others through cruelty.

Aristocrats in novels were to release their destructiveness by means other than slander: they were to become sadists. Cruelty was to have a sexual dimension, as aristocrats poured their energy into plans and schemes that enabled them to mock, ridicule and destroy their opponents in the game of love. But, since this takes us to the subject of the next chapter, we shall now summarize our findings on manners.

At the beginning of the seventeenth century the French nobility entertained the hope of becoming the ruling class. And of course, there was never any question that anyone else would operate the levers of political power. But it became clear as the seventeenth century unfolded that the old, titled nobility would not occupy high political offices; rather, these would be held by men from the upper middle class who had purchased their way into the royal government. Both courtier's books and treatises on *honnêteté* reveal the disillusionment with which the established nobility, and more particularly the court nobility, regarded this development. After encouraging aristocrats to educate themselves, to perfect their social skills, and showing them how to manœuvre and manipulate at court, manuals began to register an awareness that all this preparation was pointless. Hope gave way to despair, civic-mindedness to a sense of futility, pride to a feeling of degradation. Obviously, the court was not made up entirely, or even largely, of aristocrats who were effete or malevolent as a result of alienation. Yet, the court nobility had been frustrated in its ambition to become the ruling class, resulting in feelings of discontent, anger, hostility, bitterness, cynicism, and destructiveness. This mood was to pass into the society and culture of the eighteenth-century French aristocracy, and was to contribute to the underlying attitudes in the *roman érotique*.

4

Aristocratic perversity
in the *roman érotique*

The eighteenth-century novelist regarded both the Christian idea of love and the carefully cultivated manners in the *nouvelle* as constraining; he ridiculed them, and so enlarged the scope of personal freedom. When heroes in the *roman érotique* rejected the rigid moral and social code that held sway in the *nouvelle* it would appear that they could achieve a higher degree of happiness. However, this was not the case; heroes appearing in erotic novels from the 1730s to the 1780s became cruel, perverse, and sadistic, and dominated by psychic forces too powerful to regulate.

In examining the myth of the evil aristocrat as projected in erotic novels, I should like to illuminate at least one sector of the moral climate that prevailed in France at the end of the Ancien Regime. If we understand how the aristocracy were viewed by the populace we can appreciate certain of their emotions, feelings, moods, and predispositions of thought. This might well be as important as a knowledge of their actual life. To paraphrase G.M. Young, the real, historical importance of the eighteenth-century aristocracy is not how they lived, but how people thought they were living.[1] We shall look first at the picture of aristocratic life in the *roman érotique* then we shall try to discover whether it was an accurate picture; finally, we shall relate our findings to the contemporary population's view of the aristocracy.

In the *roman érotique* life was organized solely for pleasure, which soon led to satiety. *Ennui* was a universal condition, and a source of aristocratic motivation. When all other pleasures paled, aristocrats turned to love. A character in Crébillon fils' *Le Sopha* said 'rien ne nous livre plus aux passions que l'oisiveté.'[2] Clitandre, in Crébillon fils' *La Nuit et le moment*, explained that one lived in society, became bored, and noticed women who were also bored; so one amused oneself by finding women not quite confident of their charms. 'Voilà ce qui fait que, comme vous dites, j'en ai eu quelques-unes.'[3] The hero in *Angola* completed his 'education' only after he reached a state of *ennui*; only then was he prepared to enter into liaisons solely for gratification. A group of aristocrats gathered at the house of a countess in Sauroy's *Histoire d'une fille célèbre* (1782). After-dinner conversation turned on literature, but the metaphysical novels under discussion plunged the company into a 'mélancolie mortelle.'[4] This condition was insupportable to people for whom pleasure was the breath of life. Gaiety replaced melancholy as the conversation shifted to love. A new guest, the Chevalier Doricourt, musketeer and *bel-esprit*, argued that love should be no more than a playful amusement, a passing taste purged of the insipidity of sentiment and the absurdity of constancy. A serious affair, he contended, became boring. The rest of the company was quick to agree with the chevalier's view of love. And well they should, for as the chevalier was soon to learn, he was in a salon whose members alternated in pre-arranged liaisons.

The logic of aristocratic life led to transitory love, and a combination of hedonism and boredom reduced it to momentary gratification. However, love paled when reduced to an arithmetic of pleasures, and this led to another stage in the pattern of aristocratic conduct. Always experiment-ing, aristocrats discovered new means to whet jaded appetites. An abbé in Bibiena's *La Poupée* frequently drank a potion before visiting his mistress. A countess in Denon's *Point de Lendemain!* took her lover to a room consecrated to love. When they reached the altar a mechanical device launched them on to some cushions where they performed their perfidious rite before an altar. An aphrodisiac was necessary before they could repeat their blasphemy. Beyond the jaded appetite of the hedonis-tic and bored aristocrat was the final stage in the logic of conduct: cruelty, perversity, and sadism.

In Bibiena's *La Poupée* (1744) cruelty had become part of sexual be-havior. It could be argued that this work is tied more to the *gaulois* tradition than to the sadistic novel of the late eighteenth century. How-ever, although anti-clericalism and the use of incubi echo an earlier age, the tone of this work is distinctively eighteenth-century, and the calcu-lated destruction of an abbé suggests novels that were to appear later. The egotistical, pretentious abbé thought that Julie could not resist him. Amused, Julie told him to come to her house, where he would find a rope ladder that would take him to her room. On entering he found the room dark, heard sighs, and reached for Julie, who promptly leapt into bed. When he joined her he discovered that she was naked, so he rapidly took off his clothes. But when the abbé began to make love, he realized that his partner was a man. At that moment the room lit up with the blaze of a hundred candles, and the abbé found himself in the arms of a repulsive negro. Julie and her lover, Clitandre, viewed the scene from a hidden alcove, and then directed the servants to blindfold the abbé, change his clothes, and put him on a ladder. Once outside his blindfold was pulled off, and the window was closed, the unfortunate abbé discovered that it was daylight, and he was dressed in an absurd costume that parodied his clerical garb. Worse still, the ladder extended not to the garden from which he first came, but to a main street crowded with traffic. As he descended, he was greeted by a roar of laughter and verbal abuse. To complete his humiliation, a throng of tormentors chased him through the streets to the very door of his house.

A similar incident in Sauroy's *Histoire d'une fille célèbre* often imitates the sequence of events in *La Poupée*. This work, it will be recalled, describes a salon whose members alternated in pre-arranged liaisons. Their lives seemed an unending string of pleasures. After explaining to the Chevalier Doricourt that *'Liberté*, c'est notre devise,'[5] de la Barte invited him to have dinner with her. Then, she added, they would go to the opera, and to Mademoiselle Courtin's for another dinner. The night ended in love that, thanks to the 'divine' Mademoiselle de la Barte's 'ressources,' heightened pleasure to the utmost limits. While it would appear that these aristocrats had turned their *'liberté'* to maximum advantage, it turned out that even a night of successful love did not satisfy. The next day, when the chevalier visited La Barte, she revealed how she had achieved the ruin of an egotistical abbé. She summoned him with an enticing letter and, as they were retiring together told him she would join him in a moment. As soon as he undressed there was a blow on the door and La Barte entered, exclaiming that they were undone. Her brothers had just returned from Versailles. She told the abbé to leave immediately, by a rope ladder that would take him to the ground. But as he began to dress, she knocked the light from the table and ordered him to leave as he was. The abbé found himself on a ladder that hung below the balcony, but failed to reach the ground. He could neither rise nor descend, and he was naked. Servants shone lights on him, emptied chamber pots on his person, mocking him all the while. But the abbé had not learnt his lesson, and allowed La Barte to entrap him again. This time he actually found himself making love to his mistress, but when 'le tems de la catastrophe étoit arrivé'[6] candle-bearers rushed into the room showing the abbé the hideous negress in whose arms he lay. He sprang from the bed only to be chased by tormentors with whips.

When we turn to Laclos' *Les Liaisons dangereuses* we encounter a work of major literary importance; indeed, the only eighteenth-century *roman érotique* that can be called a masterpiece. While *Angola* is a splendid example of its genre (the *conte de fée*), the genre itself was lightweight. Even though both Crébillon *fils* and Denon wrote lucidly and intelligently, and deserve to be read, the erotic novel usually and deservedly occupies the bottom shelf. Its position there might well make this literary genre all the more important to the historian. In the opinion of Daniel Mornet books of the third and fourth order can reveal an age better than the masterpiece.[7] It can be argued that the author of a masterpiece transcends his age because of his genius. While Laclos' genius lifted his novel far above other *romans érotiques*, *Les Liaisons dangereuses* is not different in content from other works in the genre. In fact, it is a culmination of the erotic novel, drawing together many of its themes. Laclos' genius lay in investing those themes with an astringency, a psychological and historical penetration that they had never before received.

With deft and sure strokes Laclos sketched in the historical background of the leading protagonists, the Vicomte de Valmont and the Marquise de Merteuil. Valmont, the 'appui' of an 'illustre' family,[8] entered 'dans le monde, jeune et sans expérience; passé, pour ainsi dire, de mains en mains, par une foule de femmes, qui toutes se hâtent le prévenir par leur facilité une réflexion qu'elles sentent devoir leur être défavorable.'[9] To resist these wanton women would only have made Valmont ridiculous, so he moved with the tide of society and allowed himself to be corrupted. The marquise, though watched over by a vigilant mother, was also influenced by society, which she entered while still a very young girl; endowed with a natural curiosity, she observed *le monde* and soon became interested in love. She married at an early age, threw herself into the futile distractions of society for a few months, then she and her husband retired to the dismal countryside, where she became bored. Already interested in intrigue, she longed to return to Paris, which the death of her husband soon made possible. Before setting herself up in *le monde*, however, the marquise studied manners and morals (*nos mœurs*) in novels in order that she could carry out her ambition.[10] Both Valmont and the marquise were products of their society, and both conformed to a specifically aristocratic pattern of behaviour.

There is in *Les Liaisons dangereuses* the same relationship between man-ners and aristocratic conduct as in other erotic novels. With the notable exception of Madame de Tourvel, whose dress was considered ridiculous and whose innocence and piety rendered her absurd, everyone was in the tip of fashion. Social survival required gallantry, brilliant conversation, wit, perfect etiquette, and propriety of behaviour. But, as in other *romans érotiques*, beneath the veneer of aristocratic elegance was perversity. Social life was a game with clearly defined rules, and the victor, while observing the rules, at the same time used them to further his diabolical designs. This was why the extremely intelligent Marquise de Merteuil studied '*nos mœurs*' so assiduously before setting herself up in society. Having learned 'ce qui qu'on pouvait faire, de ce qu'on devait penser, et de ce qu'il fallait paraître,'[11] the marquise had little difficulty in establishing a virtuous reputation.

The Prévan incident illustrates perfectly how she turned that reputation to her advantage. After learning that Prévan questioned her virtue and hoped to disprove it, the marquise resolved to destroy him. That he also knew society's rules made the game all the more interesting. Anticipating his '*marche réglée*,' the marquise employed a brilliant counter strategy, and, so to speak, stole the march. She knew in advance how he would arrive and bear himself, what tone he would maintain, and how the conversation would go. So she lulled Prévan into a disastrous self-confidence, and then arranged their liaison. He was to have dinner with her and pretend to leave early. Then, after sending away his carriage, he would use a secret stairway leading to the marquise's room, where she would meet him after everyone else had left. When she appeared in a negligée, Prévan wanted to join her in a similar state of undress but, as that would ruin her plan, the marquise quickly inflamed her prey, and used him. Then she rang the bell for help. In burst her servants, who quickly subdued and expelled the intruder. Reports of the outrage were carefully circulated the next day, resulting in an ugly scandal that ruined Prévan's reputation and cost him his commission in the army. The virtuous marquise was greatly affected by the incident, and naturally, received sympathy and consolation.

Valmont's charm, good looks, and wit made him an almost worthy adversary of the Marquise de Merteuil. Such was his appeal that women fell easily into his arms and into his schemes. In a chance meeting, the Vicomtesse de M*** asked Valmont to pass the night at a chateau, which he agreed to do as long as he could spend it with her. Impossible, she replied, since her lover, Pressac, would be there. Until then, Valmont had not really been serious, having intended his comment as a polite formality, but the word 'impossible' aroused him, and the difficult circumstances made the game more interesting. The rules were that the vicomtesse would be in a room directly opposite Valmont, her husband on one side of her, and Pressac on the other. Valmont persuaded the vicomtesse to provoke an argument with her lover and at the end declare that she would not visit him that night. Instead, she visited Valmont. And Valmont's amusement grew when the vicomtesse returned to her room at dawn and discovered that she had locked herself out. He was tempted to watch her face the consequences, but, finding the problem an interesting challenge, contrived instead to get her into the room. In a final manipulation, Valmont effected a reconciliation between the vicomtesse and Pressac, receiving in return grateful kisses from both. Of the two, he enjoyed Pressac's more.

On another occasion, Valmont picked up the gauntlet when he learned that a former mistress, Emilie, was about to spend the night with a wealthy Dutch burgomaster. Valmont persuaded Emilie to make the Dutchman so drunk that he would pass out. Then, having vanquished his enemy, he enjoyed the prize. But this was not enough. Valmont had been pursuing the virtuous Madame de Tourvel, and after describing the campaign to Emilie, he used her back as a desk to write her a double-entendre letter which, couched in reverential, sentimental language, in fact described the affair with Emilie. Treachery was the wit of the Vicomte de Valmont.[12]

Both Valmont and the marquise experienced boredom, sought amusement and diversion, were fashionable and, in a sense, beautifully mannered; both turned to love for distraction, and were anti-romantic in principle; both were cruel. In every detail, this pattern of conduct is typical of the *roman érotique*. The love-vengeance theme, central to *Les Liaisons dangereuses*, had already appeared in earlier erotic novels.[13] But owing to Laclos's realism, and the unique psychological probability of his characters, the love-vengeance theme reached an unprecedented degree of credibility in *Les Liaisons dangereuses*.

The aristocratic schemers in *La Poupée* and *Histoire d'une fille célèbre* indeed manipulated, but the objects they controlled were hardly life-like. Both works included a stock object of ridicule in literature reaching back to the Middle Ages: an abbé, whose absurdity led to his destruction. Owing to Laclos' powerful evocation, the victims in *Les Liaisons dangereuses* were anything but artificial. They were real, and they were virtuous. While it has been said of Cécile that she was basically a sensualist,[14] and that Valmont only helped her to realize her essence, her letter to the marquise, written the morning after Valmont seduced her, weakens that argument. In any event, Valmont systematically corrupted a fifteen-year-old girl who only desired a romance with a young man of her own age. The reader shudders when he learns that Valmont avoided all precautions in order to make Cécile pregnant, that he won an ascendancy over her mind by attributing every vice to her mother, and that he used this mastery to form her habits and conversation. How amused Valmont was to imagine the amazement of Cécile's husband on his wedding night, when his bride would describe everything by its technical name! The contrast between Cécile's artless candour and her shameless language was really incredible. Reflecting on his 'catéchisme de débauche,' Valmont explained that 'il n'y a plus que les choses bizarres qui me plaisent.'[15]

Valmont's seduction of Madame de Tourvel was, if anything, even more perverse. This wife of a robe noble was one genuinely virtuous character in the novel. Indeed, it was precisely her character, in addition to the heroine's beauty, that whetted Valmont's appetite. True to form, Valmont had a carefully devised strategy. Thanks to his charm and attractiveness, Madame de Tourvel did fall in love with him, but so deep was her virtue, that she overcame her passion and continued her resistance. On several occasions Valmont witnessed her agony, torn as she was between love and duty. Seeing her throw herself on the floor in prayer and remorse only made him more ferocious in his pursuit. He was not above lying to a local curé and using him as a witness to his high moral calibre, nor was he above threatening suicide after every other ruse failed. Only when she thought that she had to sacrifice her person in order to save Valmont's life did Madame de Tourvel succumb.

Not only did all *romans érotiques* rest on fundamentally anti-Christian premises, but also, as we have seen, some of them were blasphemous. In *Les Liaisons dangereuses* irreligion reached a higher stage of development. While the hero and heroine who committed their treacherous rite in *Point de Lendemain!* did so in an almost playful spirit, in *Les Liaisons dangereuses* blasphemy was tied to perversity and destructiveness. Valmont made his sacrifice on the Christian altar of Madame de Tourvel, making the desecration all the more sacrilegious.

Homosexuality was a theme in some earlier *romans érotiques*, and also in *Les Liaisons dangereuses*. But most important in the many-faceted perversity of Valmont and the marquise was their need to destroy innocent victims. This destruction was of course sexual. The marquise pointed out that mere seduction was unimportant, and that she attached no merit to the simple domination of others, which required only a handsome figure, grace, wit, and a praiseworthy impudence. She contended that her achievements were a thousand times more illustrious: she was born to avenge her sex and to rule the male sex. 'Ces tyrans détrônés devenus mes esclaves.'[16] Both she and Valmont wrote letters describing their achievements, which became more demonic as the correspondence progressed. As the hero and heroine rolled up victories they found themselves in direct competition with one another. They became more destructive, more diabolical, and then, inevitably, they declared war on one another. Both were generals who strove for *la gloire*. But the hero was not content with victory; he must annihilate the enemy. He was at once a master strategist, a conquering hero, and a sadist.

Obviously any attempt to link the Marquis de Sade's novels to eighteenth century *romans érotiques* must be tenative. Sade was psychopathic and a practising sadist, and his novels were the products of a distorted mind. And yet, there are so many ties between Sade's novels and earlier, erotic novels that we can establish a relationship between the two. As in *romans érotiques*, aristocrats in Sade's novels were hedonistic in outlook; their pursuit of pleasure was mainly erotic; they seduced and corrupted adolescent girls; they appointed rooms specially for love; and they were irreligious and impious. The themes of deviancy, cruelty, and perversity appearing in *romans érotiques* received their apotheosis in Sade's novels. In fact, as we have seen, sadism appeared in *romans érotiques* decades before the Marquis de Sade wrote his first novel, the *Cent Vingt Journées de Sodome* (1785).

Why, then, did aristocratic sexual freedom become so corrupt? In the first place, authors of *romans érotiques* were influenced by the work of others, in their own and in other genres. As one *roman érotique* announced a theme, another would develop and amplify it. The internal logic of conduct in this type of novel leads from boredom to cruelty to perversity to sadism. Moreover, the anti-romantic view of love in the erotic novel must be seen against the background of the sentimental novel. In the 1730s love was treated antithetically in these genres, but the antithesis became even sharper after 1760. From 1740-60 the *roman érotique* reached its highest stage of popularity, and then, as literary tastes shifted, its production declined. After 1760 the sentimental novel became more fashionable, and for that reason it further projected a romantic view of love. Just as this novel treated love tenderly and tearfully, so the *roman érotique* reacted against that treatment by depicting a perverse type of love. During its period of inception the *roman érotique* reflected a consciousness of the classical *nouvelle*, but after three decades or so it tended to become more influenced by the contemporary sentimental novel. In the sentimental novel love dominated the characters and dissolved their identity. They were so overwhelmed by love that they become its victims. Not only was the vengeance theme in the erotic novel an answer to the tyranny of sentimental love, but also the egotism of the perverse and sadistic aristocrat was a rejection of a type of love that dissolved the identity.[17] The Marquise de Merteuil read *La Nouvelle Héloïse* and was herself an anti-Julie.

But novels are not just the products of other novels. To some degree literature also reflects its milieu, so that we must look for a connection between the literary pattern and aristocratic society. There have been efforts to find in novels a fictional representation of the actual life of the French aristocracy,[18] and the assumption behind this argument is that the aristocracy became sick and literature reflected their condition. While any diligent researcher can certainly prove that sadistic characters in novels resembled certain contemporary aristocrats, some deeper digging would uncover similar aristocrats in earlier periods of French history. The pattern of sadism in the eighteenth century novel does not reflect only the depraved morals of the aristocracy.

While it is easy enough to criticize another interpretation of a problem, it is not so simple to advance one that is more convincing or successful. When the problem is so complex as this one, the historian can only try to present an argument that might shed some light on the subject.

There is no way in which an exact, empirical connection between characters in literature and contemporary society can be established, so that it is necessary to find another approach to the problem. I have chosen to construct typologies that, rooted though they are in concrete evidence, make no claim to describe the actual life of a certain number of aristocrats, or for that matter even a particular aristocrat. Still, by putting evidence together into an abstract model and then comparing that model to literature we might see relationships that a strictly inductive method would not reveal.

The theme of my first typology will be what may be termed 'the fantasy of the endless chase.' Since erotic conduct is central to this typology, it is not inappropriate that we turn to Freud for an approach. Freud argued that 'the instincts of love are hard to educate; education of them achieves now too much, now too little.'[19] Our task will be to examine the 'education' of the 'instincts of love' among three aristocratic memoirists, the prince de Ligne, the duc de Lauzun, and the comte de Tilly. While their accounts describe little about their youth, what they do say is interesting. The prince de Ligne was educated by a number of tutors, some Jesuit, some

Jansenist. Under their supervision he discussed Madame Guyon, Féne-
lon, Bossuet, Molina, and Molinos; he read a recent translation of the
Bible; and he learned the catechism of Montpellier. Although Ligne
claimed that for all his ecclesiastical erudition he knew nothing about the
real meaning of religion, there can be little doubt that this training did
have an effect. In his opinion, teachers erred in telling their pupils to
avoid pleasure, to keep away from women, not to fall in love, and never to
miss a mass. This is what he heard from his own tutors, and his experience
was not uncommon. Tutors were typically abbés; schools were run by the
church; and education consequently had religious instruction as one of its
main goals. And there were other ways in which an aristocratic youth
could come into contact with Christian attitudes. The comte de Tilly's
parents did nothing to further his moral progress, and, indeed, his father
set an unedifying example. But he came under the influence of a grand-
mother filled with provincial religious zeal, who ranted against not only
Voltaire, but also Corneille and Racine.

According to Ligne and Tilly, then, the aristocrat could move in a
morally severe world. Whippings were their punishment and conventional, rigid sexual standards were imparted by their tutors or in school.
But the memoirist who wrote of the severity of his education sometimes
also felt an absence of moral direction within the family. Tilly made a
fascinating comment on an incident that occurred when he was nine. His
father noticed that he was sexually responsive to a housekeeper, who
caressed and aroused him. The father told the housekeeper to encourage
the youth and entice him to her sleeping alcove. The next day, with his
father presumably away hunting, Tilly began to make pathetic, immature
advances to the housekeeper. At this point his father burst in and gave his
son a thrashing with his riding whip. Did the father seek to punish the boy
in order to aid his moral progress? Tilly's description indicates not. Tilly
said that he had never known a man to fall in love as quickly as his father
and that even in old age he often took and discarded mistresses. In fact,
Tilly's father seems to have been jealous of his son and to have feared that
he would become a competitor encroaching on his preserves.

The prince de Ligne had, if anything, even worse memories of his
father. 'Mon père ne m'aimait pas. Je ne sais pourquoi, car nous ne
connaisons pas.'[20] When Ligne was about twenty (significantly, he was
uncertain about the year of his birth), his father took him to a house where
there lived a 'quantité de jolies figures épousées ou à épouser.' A servant
told him that his father had arranged his marriage; 'Huit jours après
j'épousai.'[21] The duc de Lauzun said of his marriage (he was seventeen)

that 'mon père s'applaudit de m'avoir donné une femme qui ne m'aimait ni ne me convenait, comme s'il avait uni deux amants qui l'eussent vivement désiré.'[22]

By the time our memoirists married, they had become well acquainted with the ways of love. Lauzun described the role of the duchesse de Gramont in his first premarital experience. Lacking a dowry, this woman had been forced to become a canoness against her wishes. Resentful of the role assigned to her, she manœuvred herself into a more favourable position by establishing a close relationship with her brother, the duc de Choiseul, one that Lauzun suspected was incestuous. While this strategy secured her a position at court, the duchesse de Gramont seems to have been hostile towards marriage even in her improved circumstances. She observed that Lauzun had been smitten by Madame de Stainville when he first saw her on her wedding day, and consequently arranged frequent meetings between them, partly in order to control Lauzun, but also in an attempt to defile the very institution of marriage, which had contributed to her own unhappiness. Shortly after this experience, Lauzun's father arranged his marriage. Resentful and swearing that he would not be married against his will, he quickly established one liaison with an actress and another with a 'jolie fille' he met at the opera ball who 'avait formé la plupart des jeunes gens de la cour, et voulut bien se charger de mon éducation.'[23] By the time the marriage that he had sworn to prevent took place, Lauzun's way of life had already been shaped. His memoirs, like those of Ligne and Tilly, are a catalogue of seductions; life for each of these aristocrats was a continual pursuit of women.

Our task now is to try to explain the libertine way of life common to Lauzun, Ligne, and Tilly. In the first place, we learn from the memoirs that the child did encounter repression. Fathers and tutors punished severely. The child met a different type of repression at school: that of the traditional Christian education. Significantly, an abbé told the prince de Ligne that if he fell in love he would be damned. But, alongside the repression and moral severity was a very different world which the child observed in the life of his parents and their society. This other world was characterized by that very unrestrained sexual freedom which the child had been instructed was evil. Striking a balance between such sharply different moral influences can hardly have been easy. Upon entering adolescence our memoirists went to court. Suddenly women, heretofore largely missing from their accounts, made an appearance. Often they were older women seeking what a Freudian might call inverse Oedipus relationships, whether out of sheer wantonness or in desperate attempts to atone for maternal neglect. By the time these aristocrats married, life had become an endless chase. While they tried to blame their infidelity on forced marriages, the fact is that arranged marriages were but a logical extension of family and sexual attitudes deeply rooted in aristocratic society and culture. The child, long subject to those attitudes, was already fractured by the time of marriage. The acting out of sexual fantasies resulted from problems whose origins went back to childhood.

But what is unique, it might be asked, about this eighteenth-century pattern of aristocratic sexual and marital customs and the related pattern of libertinism? Sidney Painter has described the feudal castle as a large brothel,[24] and undoubtedly this was so for the reasons that we have discussed. In the feudal period, marriages were arranged, and the same view of love and the family was already being formed. In fact, the pattern of aristocratic family life that emerged from the memoirs we have used was, by the eighteenth-century, becoming anachronistic. In his study of the French family, Philippe Ariès saw a large distance between parents and children in the medieval family or, *mesnie*.[25] The *mesnie*, in contrast to the modern conjugal family, contained several familial elements and sometimes several households, along with a host of servants and retainers. In this welter of people the child was easily lost. Further, Ariès argues, there was little idea of childhood, since parents regarded children as small adults and often treated them as such. Then, in the sixteenth, seventeenth, and eighteenth centuries the conjugal family slowly disengaged itself from the various concentric circles surrounding it. Simultaneously, the notion of childhood began to arise. Parents began to treat children as children, solicitude and concern deepened. As the new consciousness of childhood led to a relaxation of punishment in schools and to more closely knit families, children began to move in a world of greater love. Aristocratic family life in the eighteenth century would appear to encourage a greater degree of family unity.

How then, are we to explain the lives of these memoirists? Changes in family life took place slowly, and the elimination of earlier attitudes and customs was by no means completed in the eighteenth century. Old practices lingered beside new ones. Many parents were unable to cope with closer family relationships. Parents were supposed to love their children more, but some of these parents were unable to love. There are concrete historical reasons for the inability of part of aristocratic society to catch up with the new ideas of family and childhood. In the first place, the weight of the past was too great, the old attitudes and customs too deep to overcome completely. Arranged marriages continued to be common throughout the eighteenth century, showing that parents had not yet completely abandoned traditional customs. The society and culture of the eighteenth-century French aristocracy was becoming more humane and loving, but islands and residues of earlier attitudes persisted. The pressures that could result from this type of situation might help explain the behaviour we have observed in these eighteenth-century memoirists. In their own way, they were striving for greater happiness by joining the unending chase. Strangely, they were moving with some of the deeper, and healthier, social forces of the time. In fact, the new solicitude and humaneness might well have made them enter the chase with an ever greater intensity. The desire to be happy drove them forward, but problems rooted in their experience and tied to the shifting values of their society determined the type of happiness they sought. Their culture had not educated the erotic instincts successfully. So divided was that culture between strictness and freedom that these memoirists, though they tried, could not bridge the chasm. Just as their culture was divided, so too were they. The fact that each of them later went through a period of moral reform indicates that they never escaped entirely from the world of moral strictness. Until they could, they acted out the fantasy of the endless chase.

The evidence for my second typology, which may be termed 'the fantasy of free love,' comes from seventeenth-century aristocratic manuals, and in particular from those of the chevalier de Méré. We have seen that Méré created his own aesthetic world; he likened himself to an actor and viewed the real world as a comedy. He constructed his world in an attempt to escape from the discomforting and inequitable atmosphere of the court, and in doing so he responded to internal stresses and strains through psychological withdrawal. As Méré rejected an active type of life and fashioned his own subjective world, he also criticized the Christian view of love and marriage. While his aesthetic view of life did not force him to redefine the role of love, it encouraged him to do so. Werner Sombart argues that the aristocrat is erotic by temperament, and that leisure time is important in shaping that temperament.[26] In Méré there is not only leisure, but also a connected sense of futility. Méré coped with this problem by pouring his time and energy into a refinement of manners, and in doing so he found a way to satisfy his pride. But his redefinition of love shows another response to the problem. Once liberated from the Christian view of love and marriage the aristocrat could find a new outlet for frustration and at the same time fulfill an erotic wish as old as the aristocracy itself.

While Méré indicated the core of that wish, it was only later, and in the more imaginative medium of the novel, that it would be fully developed. In one *roman érotique* after another, love was entirely physical. We have seen that in *Angola* it was necessary for several women to overcome the hero's resistance, but once they did he fell into their way of life. Everyone else in this novel followed the same rules, so that it was important for the hero to follow suit. And basically, this is what happened throughout the *roman érotique*. Any resistance, token or otherwise, was broken down in order that everyone would be a willing partner in the game of love. While Cidalise, in *La Nuit et le moment*, protested when Clitandre joined her in bed, and twice refused to make love with him, thereby making him take her forcibly, she knew the rules of love as well as he. And Clitandre of course understood that to be the case. In spite of ploys, strategies, and endless manœuvring, the participants all knew how the game would end. The plot of the *roman érotique* turned on seduction, and regardless of who seduced whom the lovers had a similar view of love. There could be no barriers, no obstacles; only pleasure counted; and love must never be serious. If the lovers became attached on the human rather than just the physical level their pleasure would be compromised. Since lovers must be free to exercise their prerogative without constraint, affairs were invariably short. So wide was the scope for gratification that heroes and heroines indulged themselves as they saw fit. In doing so they were acting out an erotic wish that was rooted in aristocratic life.

The reasons for aristocratic eroticism are of course complex, but amongst them is the class frustration associated with the rise of royal absolutism. By emasculating the nobility and making then a nonfunctioning, parasitical class the crown created a challenge to which nobles would respond through erotic fantasies. Unable to prove themselves on one field, they would do so on another. At least in part the fantasy of free love was an aristocratic solution to problems rooted in the process of political change. Had the French nobility been able to govern or to serve society it is doubtful that the erotic side of life would have become so important. In order to understand class attitudes and orientations we must look at material conditions. Everywhere in seventeenth-century Europe nobilities were brought face-to-face with new realities. In England the aristocracy gained access to the levers of political power, and in Eastern Europe they became functional, in the strictest sense of the word, as a service nobility. But in France the crown preserved the nobility's privileges while at the same time taking away its functions. Here was a class that had always had erotic propensities, that was now condemned to leisure, and deeply resented its futility. Out of these circumstances came the fantasy of free love.

The third typology, which I shall call the fantasy of world destruction, helps explain the final stage of aristocratic conduct in the *roman érotique*, the stage of cruelty, perversity, and sadism. Central to the first two fantasies was a search for greater freedom, but in some novels aristocrats failed to achieve that goal. While love was only a physical pleasure, and a pleasure that aristocrats enjoyed as they saw fit, they were not really free. Rather, they were driven and possessed by a need not only to seduce woman after woman, but also to corrupt and destroy. The aristocrat wanted to destroy the object that dominated his world.

Interestingly, he schemed, plotted, and employed the clever ruse in much the same fashion as had the courtier. Wit, mockery, and the artistic but destructive stratagem had been one of the means by which the courtier dealt with his world; unable to form it as he wished, he mocked it; unable to achieve real power he used the cunning aside or devastating jest in order to gain a mastery over other courtiers. In Saint-Simon's *Mémoires* we discover such a uniform pattern of demented, malevolent people, such a consistent pattern of conduct, and such exotic, almost incredible character portraits as to tax the credibility. Were these people really as Saint-Simon saw them? Or do we encounter his fantasies instead? Certainly the almost mechanical regularity with which these people crop up, as well as the interminable length of the *Mémoires*, suggests some interesting analogies with pornographic novels. As Steven Marcus has said of that type of novel, it describes not life, but a particular vision of it, and it does so time and again and always in the same way.[27] What is important in Saint-Simon, in this connection, is the complete absence of sexuality. Scabrous he was, but not erotic. And yet, one might suspect that somewhere, down at a motivational level, Saint-Simon's hostility did have a sexual spring. However, this is never evident in his writings. On the conscious level of his thought he was a loyal husband and dutiful Christian.

When we turn to literature, though, the three fantasies – the endless chase, sexual freedom, and world destruction – fuse together to present a pattern of cruelty, perversity, and sadism. Valmont acted out the fantasies of the endless chase and free love, but also gave himself to cunning and clever stratagems that destroyed innocent victims, such as a fifteen-year-old virgin and a virtuous married woman. He was both destructive and a master of the witticism, a man who was demonic but whose social sense was highly cultivated. In fact, there was a connection between these two sides of his being: he represented a type of person whose manners and refinement actually contributed to terrible forces that could only emerge destructively. Manners stifled and smothered him, but there was no healthy outlet for his pent-up energy.

While this pattern of cruelty, perversity, and sadism cannot be applied to the entire aristocracy, or to most or even a large segment of it, I am suggesting that aristocratic life can explain the behavioural pattern. Having established that relationship, let us now return to the novel.

In the *roman érotique* libertinism emerged from the same social conditions as it did in memoirs, and heroes in the novel entered into the chase as relentlessly as did the memoirists. As we have seen, these heroes were bored and they were hardened by aristocratic social style. Hostility developed naturally in this context, and came out as the jest and witticism. Then the three fantasies were united, and the result was perversity and sadism, both of which received their ultimate literary expression in novels written at the end of the Ancien Regime.

How then can we relate the image of the libertine, perverse, and sadistic aristocrat to the contemporary population's view of his class? The comte de Tilly, writing after the Revolution, thought that ill-mannered novels which were once considered in the best of taste had poisoned the thought of the lower classes.[28] Unfortunately, we shall never know to what extent these novels shaped popular attitudes. It is significant that the *roman érotique* was a highly popular literary genre, and it seems probable that ideas in novels would, to some degree, have filtered into society. But the historian can use the *roman érotique* in another, and probably more pertinent way by looking at stereotyped images of aristocrats which appeared elsewhere and which agree, interestingly, with images in the erotic novel.

Take Rousseau, for instance. He came to Paris from Geneva, and turned his intelligence and imagination to good advantage as he began to find a place in the salons. But then, disgusted by what he saw, he symbolically gave up his gold lace, his white stockings, his watch, and his sword, all signs of the aristocratic life into which he had entered. Now, it can be argued that Rousseau reacted this way because he had been a failure in aristocratic society; be that as it may, his response immediately won for him a large following. Many Frenchmen, aristocrats included, agreed with his views. Particularly illuminating is the most popular of Rousseau's works, *La Nouvelle Héloïse*, a novel that prescribed a pattern of aristocratic life conspicuous for its high moral tone. As certain passages show, there was fixed in Rousseau's mind the image of the libidinous and perverse aristocrat. In fact, many writers of the time held this view. Examples are Beaumarchais, Marmontel, Mercier, and Bernardin de Saint-Pierre. Sometimes we find it in Diderot. Indeed, it is common to find such sterotyped thinking in novels written after 1760.

Particularly interesting in this regard are the novels of Restif de la Bretonne, in which virtuous peasants were corrupted by the life of the upper classes when they moved into the cities. Restif did not describe the life of the urban poor as virtuous. These people, like the urban rich, were criminal, but lower-class criminality issued from different circumstances. One cause of crime was grinding poverty; another was a surfeit of wealth and what we have called the fantasy of the endless chase. Restif's novels are autobiographical, and thereby reflect his own experiences and his own response to the life of the upper classes. He came from a peasant family, went to Paris to school, returned to his village, then went to nearby Auxerre, and finally returned to Paris, where he spent the remainder of his life.

How did Restif form his idea of the perverse aristocrat? By direct observation of aristocratic life? By reading erotic novels? Perhaps both. But there is another possible explanation. Every society, to some extent, thinks in symbols and images. And as a result, symbols and images – myths – assume a life of their own. What Restif's novels project, then, and many other novels did the same, was the myth of the perverse and sadistic aristocrat. That such a myth existed on the eve of the Revolution is undeniable. And, undoubtedly this myth derived from the society and culture of the eighteenth-century French aristocracy. The myth helps us to understand how some Frenchmen felt about the aristocracy on the eve of the Revolution. Further, it helps explain the intensity of the anti-aristocratic sentiment that broke out after 1789, which would play an important role in determining the course of the Revolution. Here is a myth which, after having been formed by history, turned around and helped to make history. It was merely repaying a debt.

5

Sentimentalism and moralistic literature

In a thought-provoking article on the love-vengeance theme in the French novel after 1760, J. Robert Loy sees a direct connection between the depiction of love in the *roman érotique* and in the sentimental novel. Loy argues that the cruel and perverse love of the *roman érotique* was a reaction against, and therefore the dialectical opposite of, the ennobling, romantic love of Rousseau and his legion of imitators.[1] While the erotic novel might not have responded fully to the view of love maintained in the sentimental novel until the 1760s, it is important to remember that the origins of both types of novel went back to the 1690s.[2] That each began to develop its own view of love at this time is not accidental, for both rejected the austere concept of love that had held sway in the classical novel. But it is not easy to reject the values of a previous generation; an innovator is connected to the past by his very reaction against it. In both the *roman érotique* and the sentimental novel there was continuity with the seventeenth century, in the former through parody and in the latter through the persistence of *précieux* values in those eighteenth-century salons that helped to nourish the sentimental novel.[3]

While the first instalment of *La Vie de Marianne* did not see light until 1731, and the last (still unfinished) until 1741, Marivaux's idea of *sensibilité* was already apparent in the *Avis au Lecteur* in his first novel, the *Effets surprenants de la Sympathie*, written in 1712.[4] Unfortunately, little is known of the early years of Pierre Carlet de Chamblain de Marivaux (1688–1763). That he was an *habitué* at Sceaux and at the salons of Madame de Lambert and Madame de Tencin is certain, but just when he began to frequent these *ruelles* is unclear. Since Marivaux's approach to love was particularly close to that of Madame de Lambert, it is regrettable that we do not know exactly when he first attended that lady's *mercredis*. Having arrived in Paris in around 1712, he probably wrote the *Avis* to his *Effets surprenants* before coming into contact with her. It would seem that Marivaux arrived at the concept of *sensibilité* independent of Madame de Lambert, and that he was attracted to her salon because he found the ideas there compatible with his own.

Yet, Anne-Thérèse, marquise de Lambert (1647–1733), is important to an understanding of Marivaux's approach to love, and for two reasons: first, Marivaux matured while under the influence of her salon, and secondly, her own writings reveal the continuity between seventeenth- and eighteenth-century ideas which, in part, gave birth to Marivaux's *sensibilité*. To read Madame de Lambert is to perceive the persistence of preciosity in a cultural milieu of which Marivaux was both the embodiment and the leading spokesman.[5]

At times, Madame de Lambert appears to belong entirely to the seventeenth century. In the *Avis d'une mère à sa fille* (1728) she used Augustine as an example of one who rejected love and pleasure, and commented on the dangers of love. 'Si votre cœur a le malheur d'être attaqué par l'amour, voici les remèdes pour en arrêter le progrès. Pensez que ces plaisirs ne sont ni solides ni fidèles; ils vous quittent, et quand ils ne vous feroient que ce mal, c'en est assez ... L'amour, dans les commencemens, ne vous présente que des fleurs et vous cache le danger. Il vous trompe ...'[6] Central to Madame de Lambert's concept of love was her fear of the passions. 'Faites réflexion aux funestes suite des passions; vous ne trouverez que trop d'examples pour vous instruire ... [L'amour] surprend la raison, il jette le trouble dans l'âme et dans les sens; il enlève la fleur de l'innocence, il étonne la vertu, il ternit la réputation ...'[7] In her opinion, to live for pleasure was to descend to futility: 'Quand vous ne vivez que pour les plaisirs ... l'âme tombe dans un grand vide.'[8] True happiness lay not in pleasure, but in 'la paix de l'âme, dans la raison, dans l'accomplissement de nos devoirs.'[9] The moral integrity, high-mindedness, commitment to virtue, and stress on reason prescribed by Madame de Lambert places her in the pattern of Madame de la Fayette and the seventeenth century. Up to a point, the same can be said of this lady's view of love, rooted as it sometimes was in a rejection of both passion and pleasure.

But not all Madame de Lambert's writings reveal such a rigorous moral outlook. Mingled with traditional seventeenth-century attitudes are ideas that connect to new currents of thought. The seventeenth century to which Madame de Lambert was tied was not just austere and pleasure-denying; also, and more importantly, it was the reoriented, secularized, late seventeenth century of Pierre Bayle and Saint-Évremond, of deism, philosophical hedonism, and a lay morality. The very intellectual currents that corroded traditional moral thought after 1660 penetrated the thought of Madame de Lambert, for her moral outlook was conditioned not only by the late seventeenth-century French rationalists, but also by French translations of Shaftesbury that began to appear in 1708.[10] Madame de Lambert projected the same benign view of nature as had the English moralist. It was not the object of morality to destroy nature, but to perfect it, as she wrote on one occasion; on another, she said that the 'cœur ... est la source de l'innocence et du bonheure.'[11]

Nature perfects, and happiness comes from the heart. The two ideas are connected. As Shaftesbury abolished hell, the devil, and the last judgment, he eliminated the external checks formerly used to control man's conduct. Since the universe was well-ordered and harmonious, there were internal means through which moral order was maintained. Man was endowed with a moral sense, and he was innately good. This was what Shaftesbury meant when he said that the 'heart ... must approve in some measure of what is natural and honest, and disapprove of what is dishonest and corrupt.'[12] To be virtuous, then, was only to be 'natural.' And, Shaftesbury continued, 'to have the natural affections, such as are founded in love, complacency, goodwill, and in a sympathy with the kind of species, is to have the chief means and power of self-enjoyment.'[13]

For Madame de Lambert, also, to be moral was to be happy. 'Le bonheur dépend des mœurs et de la conduit ...'[14] In addition to a well-ordered moral life, another source of happiness was the feelings. 'Rien ne rend plus heureux que d'avoir l'esprit persuadé et le cœur touché.'[15] What touched the heart most deeply was love, which was no longer the destructive machine raised by the passions, but rather the warm, beneficent, impulse that pierced the heart and suffused the moral sense inherent in man. She wrote in her *Traité de l'amitié* (1732), 'Le cœur étant fait pour aimer, il est sans vie dès que vous lui refusez le plaisir d'aimer ou d'être aimé,'[16] and in her *Réflexions sur les femmes* (1727), 'l'amour perfectionne les âmes bien nées ...'[17]

Love stirred the feelings, making it essential to the fully developed moral life. Not to experience the warmth of love was to be morally impoverished. This being the case, it was important to study love. 'Puisque ce sentiment est si nécessaire au bonheur des humains, il ne faut pas bannir de la sociéte: il faut seulement apprendre à le perfectionner. Il y a tant d'écoles établies pour cultiver l'esprit; pourquoi n'en pas avoir pour cultiver le cœur?'[18]

Cultivating the heart is a theme which runs through many of Madame de Lambert's writings. This was done not by emotional transports, but rather by using the mind to regulate the warm sensations that radiated the inner person. While Madame de Lambert gave primacy to the sentiments, she did not ignore the rational faculty. In fact, 'La sensibilité secourt l'esprit et sert la vertu.'[19] Love was internal, sentimental, and radiant, but also delicate and appropriate. To cultivate the heart required a taste for delicate sentiments, and a certain attentive politeness.

The position of Madame de Lambert is obviously transitional and intermediate. While the primacy of the heart and feelings anticipated Rousseau and the late eighteenth century, the importance of delicacy and politeness looked back to Madame de Rambouillet, whom this lady admired. Madame de Lambert was tied to the *précieuses*, but hers was a late preciosity that looked upon love as fulfilling, enriching, and morally beneficial. The sensibility of Madame de Lambert was a compound of seventeenth-century preciosity and the benign, hopeful, optimistic, lay morality of the early eighteenth century.

Essentially, Marivaux's concept of love was that of Madame de Lambert. The sensitive heart, through which the warm sensations of *amour* ran, experienced sweet happiness, and the depth of feeling inspired by love enriched the inner life. But, the emotions did not dominate. Rather, they were held under rational control. There was the same balance between *cœur* and *esprit* in Marivaux as in Madame de Lambert.

In Marivaux's most famous novel, *La Vie de Marianne*, Marianne was immediately smitten when she saw Valville in church. This experience occasioned pages of analysis. As soon as the 'flutters of sensibility' (Jamieson's phrase) touched the heart, the mind began to sort out the variety of feelings suddenly let loose. Marianne realized that for a brief moment she had neglected to put her feminine arts on display. So stricken was she by a rush of unknown feelings that she forgot herself; clearly, she understood, she was in love.

Marianne's response upon first seeing Valville is revealing. The awakening of her heart brought her sensibility into play; but at the same time her mind went to work. In thinking about her appearance at the very moment of tender agitation she disclosed her *amour-propre*. Marianne considered pride instinctive: 'Cet orgueil, on ne nous le donne pas, nous l'apportons en naissant ... C'est la nature qui a le pas sur l'éducation.[20] Yet the fact is that Marianne's pride was a construction of her ego, and it enlarged the scope of her sensibility. Her *amour-propre* gave rise to a sensibility of self-love, and thereby permitted her to analyse her feelings as those feelings were aroused by love. Each shift, each development in her romance with Valville, elicited fresh analysis, and this analysis makes clear just how preoccupied Marianne was with herself.

It is equally clear that Marianne was an artful strategist and a coquette. 'Les hommes parlent de science at de philosophie; voilà quelque chose de beau en comparaison de la science de bien placer un ruban, ou de decider de quelle couleur on le mettra!'[21] Obviously, Marianne gave careful attention to her appearance: 'Il me prenait des palpitations en songeant combien j'allais être jolie.' Regardless of the circumstances, Marianne's coquettishness was in evidence. When Valville saw her *en négligé* in a surprise visit to the convent, she realized that her natural charms could serve her as well as the different, cultivated charms of the toilet. But when she dressed for a party she was able to 'avoir de la coquetterie par obéissance.'[22]

In spite of her pride, Marianne was not selfish. Although she took every care to present the right image and to cultivate her beauty, she was not only, or even primarily, self-seeking. In fact, love gave further inspiration to her innate goodness. When it appeared that her marriage to Valville would irretrievably ruin his career, and irrevocably compromise his social standing, Marianne did not hesitate to renounce the marriage, and when Valville later betrayed her, she refused to punish him. Her love was too warm, too pure, too steadfast to be destroyed. Not only did love bring happiness, but it also inspired virtue.

It is important to note that Marivaux never completed *La Vie de Marianne*. As soon as the obstacles to Marianne's and Valville's marriage were removed, Marivaux seems to have lost interest in the story. While he did continue the novel beyond the reconciliation with Valville, the marriage never took place. The last two parts of *Marianne* (x–xi) are, in effect, another, separate novel. Marivaux never picked up Marianne's story where it ended in part ix, and for good reason. As we have seen, his interest was in the development of love and the analysis of sentiment; this meant that he could only turn to adolescent love, and the shafts that could pierce none but the innocent heart of the virgin. When Marianne said 'De quel prix n'est pas une minute au compte de l'amour.'[23] she was describing a sensation that could not be sustained over a long period of time. This, she realized, was why Valville temporarily lost interest in her. 'Son cœur n'est pas usé pour moi, il n'est seulement qu'un peu rassasié du plaisir de m'aimer, pour en avoir trop pris d'abord.'[24]

Because Marivaux was primarily an analyst of love, he did not fully develop moral ideas that were inherent in sensibility. As Vivienne Mylne has pointed out, characters in the novel of *sensibilité* naturally fell into 'good' and 'bad' categories. In order to throw the virtues of the *âme sensible* into bold relief, it was convenient to introduce characters given to meanness and insensitivity.[25] The very nature of sensibility, then, encouraged the novel of *sensibilité* to be didactic. In Marivaux, these didactic tendencies contributed to the emphasis placed upon the moral significance of premarital chastity, and the importance of marriage and the family.

Both are present in *La Vie de Marianne*. That Marianne could ever have given up her virginity before marriage is of course inconceivable. Penniless and forced to live beneath her natural dignity, Marianne nevertheless rejected Climal's offer, the material advantages of which could not have begun to match the moral losses inherent in the type of arrangement that he proposed. Nor is there so much as a hint that Marianne and Valville would ever indulge themselves illicitly. Love directed both Marianne and Valville to marriage.

Equally important in *Marianne* was the way of life connected to the state of marriage. Love, having brought husband and wife together, spun its web through the entire family, holding it together as a coherent, stable unit. Thus, Valville's mother, Madame de Miran, being concerned for her son's material prospects, opposed a romance that could only compromise his interests. But when this solicitous mother met Marianne and recognized not only her deep moral worth, but also the virtuous feelings she inspired in her son, she was forced to lift her opposition. Her son's happiness and well-being came first and, when convinced that she could best achieve these goals by accepting Marianne, her course of action became clear. Immediately, she thought of Marianne as her daughter. Love, having been channelled into a plan for marriage, at once began to cast its net and draw parents and children into a close familial relationship. This meant that Marianne looked upon Madame de Miran as a mother, and always treated her with the gratitude of a loyal and loving child.

But while Marivaux's concept of romantic love led him to idealize premarital chastity, marriage based upon mutual affection, and familial love, he could not give these topics full scope in *La Vie de Marianne*. It would not be correct to say that Marivaux took these themes lightly, and thereby gave them only superficial attention. They were treated seriously, and at considerable length. But regarding love, and the unending analysis of the feelings that attended it, as he did, Marivaux could not see, or chose not to see, the story through to its logical conclusion. Even if he had ended with Marianne marrying Valville, it is difficult to imagine the novel continuing beyond that point. The analysis of the feelings are appropriate to the coquette and the virgin, but to the wife, mother, and housekeeper they are absurd.

In all of Marivaux's theatre, there is but one instance of conjugal love. This was the scene in *La Femme fidèle* (1755), in which the Marquise d'Ardeuil was about to be married, having lost her first husband ten years earlier. However, the husband, who had been captured by Algerian pirates, returned home in disguise on the day of the wedding. When he was certain that his wife still loved him, he revealed his true identity, to her ineffable happiness. Marivaux depicted a different type of familial love in *La Mère confidente* (1735). Angélique fell in love with the well-born but penniless Dorante. Her mother, Madame Argante, had arranged for her to marry melancholic, sullen Ergaste. Having learned of her daughter's romance, she worried about the problems that would result from an unequal marriage, but, at the same time, her main concern was for her daughter's happiness. After meeting Dorante, she was convinced that he was honourable and virtuous, and, since her daughter loved him, she accepted the marriage. This solicitous mother, who cared for her daughter rather than dominating her, was far removed from the disagreeable mothers who generally frequented Marivaux's theatre. In fact, Madame Argante closely resembles Madame de Miran in *Marianne*, which is not entirely coincidental, since Marivaux wrote *La Mère confidente* while working on parts III and IV of *Marianne* in which Madame de Miran appears.

The affinity between *La Mère confidente* and *La Femme fidèle* and newly emerging dramatic genres has not passed unnoticed.[26] Dramatists began in the 1730s to work in a '*genre mixte*,' between comedy and tragedy. This style, called the *genre larmoyante*, was anticipated by Destouches and Piron, realized by P.C. Nivelle de la Chaussée (1697–1754), and, for a time, influenced even one as unlikely as Voltaire.[27] In this genre, sensibility was replaced by sentimentality. Further, the dichotomy between vice and virtue, already present in the literature of *sensibilité*, was allowed to realize to the full its potential for mawkishness. Yet, the themes of the *genre larmoyante* are significant. In particular, La Chaussée depicted domestic life: he took precisely the step that a man of Marivaux's taste and refinement could not. His themes included the libertine husband who returned to his wife, the rich or noble son who was scorned by a poor girl, and the illegitimate son who met his father.[28] In selecting these themes, La Chaussée directed the audience's attention to moral and social problems.

In the 1730s the *genre larmoyante* already was stressing the didacticism and utilizing the domestic subjects that would be of such central importance to the *drame*.

After writing his first *drame*, *Le Fils naturel* (1757), and while working on his second play, *Père de famille* (1758), Denis Diderot (1713–84) wrote an essay, 'De la poësie dramatique' (1758), in which he set forth a rationale for his own dramatic efforts. This essay demonstrates perfectly how self-conscious moralizing had become in French literature at this time. It reveals Diderot's conviction that literature was capable of corrupting an audience: 'Quel art serait plus funeste que celui qui me rendrait complice du vicieux.' And, by the same token, Diderot thought that literature had the ability to inspire virtue: 'O quel bien il en reviendrait aux hommes, si tous les arts d'imitation se proposaient un objet commun, et concouraient un jour avec les lois pour nous faire aimer la vertu et haïr le vice!' When he wrote, 'Poète, êtes-vous sensible et delicat?' he was insisting that a writer must touch the heart to inspire virtue. As in the literature of sensibility, the writer of *drames* could describe the first stirring of adolescent love; but he could also, and with greater effect, set forth conjugal love. 'Croit-on en effet que l'action de deux époux aveugles, qui se chercheraient encore dans un age avancé, et qui, les paupières humides des larmes de la tendresse, se serreaient les mains et se caresseraient, pour ainsi dire, au bord du tombeau, ne demanderait pas le même talent, et ne m'intéresserait pas davantage que le spectacle des plaisirs violents dont leurs sens tout nouveaux s'enivraient dans l'adolescence?' In his own *Père de famille*, Diderot tried to use a domestic subject to convey a didactic message. His theme in that work was 'La fortune, la naissance, l'éducation, les devoirs des pères envers leurs enfants, et des enfants envers leurs parents, le mariage, le célibat, tout ce qui tient a l'état d'un père de famille ...'[29]

The basic plot in *Père de famille* was a romance between well-born Saint-Albin and destitute Sophie. While Sophie's very presence purified and moralized Saint-Albin, Saint-Albin's father, d'Orbesson, opposed the marriage that his son desired. 'Qu'osez-vous me proposer ... Moi, j'autoriserais, par une faiblesse honteuse, le désordre de la société, la confusion du sang et des rangs, la dégradation des familles?'[30] Though d'Orbesson opposed his son marrying beneath his rank, he did believe that love was essential to marital happiness. 'Mariage ... est ... la source des plaisirs les plus doux. Où sont les exemples de l'intérêt pur et sincère, de la tendresse réele, de la confiance intime, des secours continus, des satisfactions reciproques, des chagrins partagés, des soupirs entendus, des larmes confondues, si ce n'est dans le mariage? Qu'est-ce que l'homme de bien préfère a sa femme? Qu'y a-t-il au monde qu'un père aime plus que son enfant? ... O lien sacré des époux, si je pense à vous, mon âme s'échauffe et s'élève! ... O noms tendres de fille, je ne vous prononçai jamais sans tressaillir, sans être touché!'[31]

Diderot solved the problem of d'Orbesson's opposition to the marriage by a *coup de théâtre*. It turned out that Sophie was not a seamstress, but the daughter of a provincial aristocrat whose charitable deeds angered his relations, and whose death left his family destitute. Learning this, d'Orbesson approved the match. The play ends with him invoking a blessing on his worthy son and the virtuous girl he was about to marry. 'Approchez, mes enfants ... Une belle femme, un homme de bien, sont les deux êtres les plus touchants de la nature ... Mes enfants, que le ciel vous bénisse, comme je vous bénis! Le jour qui vous unira, sera le jour le plus solennel de votre vie. Puisse-t-il être aussi le plus fortuné!'[32]

Jean-Jacques Rousseau (1712-78) achieved the same moral programme in the novel that Diderot recommended for the theatre. Unlike Marivaux, Rousseau extended the action in *La Nouvelle Héloïse* (1760) beyond the stirrings of adolescent love. Julie was married at the end of part III, approximately half-way through the six-part novel. In describing marriage and domestic life, Rousseau might well have been influenced by Diderot. In April 1757, at which time he was writing a novel about passionate, romantic love, and did not have in mind a finished design,[33] Rousseau showed the first two parts of *La Nouvelle Héloïse* to Diderot. Then, six months later, Diderot showed Rousseau 'le plan du *Père de Famille*.' This would have been at the very time that Diderot was writing the essay, 'De la poesie dramatique' (might it have been a version of this essay that Rousseau read?) in which he prescribed the role that marriage and domestic life should occupy in the *drame*. Almost certainly Diderot discussed these ideas with Rousseau.

While the relationship between Rousseau and Diderot was soon to rupture, at this time they were on favourable terms. And they had much in common. Already in 1756 Rousseau had planned to write a work on associationist psychology, titled *La Morale sensitive, ou le matérialisme du sage*. Though Rousseau abandoned the project in 1759, he did, in fact, adhere to the same empirical doctrines as Diderot; just as Diderot drew moral implications from an associationist psychology, so too did Rousseau. Both introduced into literature fetching scenes that would inspire a love of virtue and abhorrence of vice. Given this outlook, it is not surprising that *La Nouvelle Héloïse* contains a series of domestic tableaux whose function was to edify the reader.[34] By concentrating these tableaux most heavily in parts IV–VI, Rousseau was only working out an approach inherent in his theory of learning. The elements from which Rousseau would fashion the moralistic tableaux in *La Nouvelle Héloïse* were present in his mind before he began to write the novel; that these tableaux appeared most frequently in the last three parts might be attributed partly to the influence of Diderot. In any event, Rousseau decided to extend his novel beyond marriage, and to describe married life. Like Diderot, he was transforming the subject of the literary form in which he was working. In the development of the French novel this was a turning point of the first importance.

The marriage that Rousseau portrayed with such care and detail in *La Nouvelle Héloïse* can only be described as strange. Julie and Saint-Preux were deeply and passionately in love; they experienced all the sublime feelings of *amour romantique*; and, being virtuous, they wanted to marry. Saint-Preux, however, was a tutor, and Julie was the daughter of a proud and strong-willed baron. Baron d'Étanges planned to marry his daughter within her rank, and furthermore he hoped to repay a debt to an old friend, Wolmar, who years before had saved his life; he planned for Julie to marry Wolmar. Rousseau described this ambition as both cruel and unnatural, and he encouraged the reader to sympathize with Julie's and Saint-Preux's tragic dilemma. But he did not remove that dilemma. Rather, the baron did prevail, Julie did marry Wolmar, and Saint-Preux was pushed close to insanity. And then, in a curious turn, the scene shifted to Wolmar's estate, where Julie had become a mother and was, in a sense, happily married. She lived in continual guilt, however, over her one lapse from virtue when she and Saint-Preux had become lovers. Wolmar, who knew about the affair, and understood how Julie punished herself for its memory, decided to bring Saint-Preux into his household as a tutor for his children. And Saint-Preux did come, in part IV, thus beginning a relationship *à trois* that would scarcely seem appropriate to a happy and stable domestic life.

Rousseau completed the third part of *La Nouvelle Héloïse* in the spring of 1757, planning only a concluding fourth part. But just then there occurred what F.C. Green has called 'Rousseau's one and only great passion.'[35] Sophie, the comtesse d'Houdetot, arrived at the Hermitage, where Rousseau was staying, in May, 1757. For Rousseau, it seems, she became a living Julie. In any event, Rousseau was soon head over heels in love, and in a summer evening he and Sophie re-enacted the scene in *La Nouvelle Héloïse* in which Julie's kiss intoxicated Saint-Preux with happiness. But, remembering her lover after kissing Rousseau, Madame de Houdetot said 'mon cœur ne sauroit aimer deux fois.' As Rousseau described the scene: 'quel embrassement! Mais ce fut tout.'[36] When Sophie's lover Saint-Lambert, came to the Hermitage, the three entered into an arrangement à trois similar to the one Rousseau would create in his novel. Sophie established a relationship with Rousseau from which physical love was absent. Curiously, Julie also created a Platonic relationship with her lover, Saint-Preux.

Does it not seem at least somewhat surprising that a *philosophe*, a friend of Diderot and d'Alembert, would advocate such an ethereal type of love? In order to understand this facet of Rousseau's thought it is necessary to turn, not to the Enlightenment, but rather to particular circumstances in Rousseau's life. The *Confessions* cannot, of course, be taken as an accurate record of his life. But they do reveal his subjective state; further, they reveal his painfully earnest attempt to understand how he came to be the person that he was. In the company of women he was deeply, physically uncomfortable. The urinary malady, to which he was forever referring in the *Confessions*, became particularly acute in time of emotional stress. When faced with a crisis his body itself rose up in rebellion. 'This infirmity was the chief reason that kept me away from social groups, and prevented me from being in a room with women.'[37] Aware of the intensity of his inhibitions, and, in particular, his fear of the opposite sex, Rousseau attempted, at the beginning of the *Confessions*, to explain them. It seemed to him that his education had been of the strictest sort. 'Si jamais éducation fut modeste et chaste, c'est assurément celle que j'ai reçue. Mes trois tantes n'étaient pas seulement des personnes d'une sagesse éxemplaire, mais d'une réserve que depuis longtemps les femmes ne connaissaient plus ... une fort bonne servante y fut mise à la porte, pour un mot un peu gaillard qu'elle avait prononcé devant nous.'[38] Rousseau thought that such strict standards twisted his outlook. 'Non seulement je n'eus jusqu'à mon adolescence aucune idée distincte de l'union des séxes; mais jamais cette idée confuse ne s'offrit à moi que sous une image odieuse et dégoutante. J'avais pour les filles publiques une horreur qui ne s'est jamais effacé; je ne pouvais voir un débauché sans dédain, sans effroi même: car mon aversion pour la débauche allait jusque-là, depuis qu'allant un jour au petit Sacconex par un chemin creux, je vis des deux côtés des cavités dans la terre où l'on me dit que ces gens-là faisaient leurs accouplements. Ce que j'avais vu de ceux des chiennes me revenait aussi toujours à l'esprit en pensant aux autres, et le cœur me soulevait à ce seul souvenir.'[39] Reflecting further, Rousseau scrutinized his 'temperament combustible' and the 'sotes fantaisies' and 'érotiques fureurs' that were rooted in his being. From the conflict between his natural ardour and his inhibitions came timidity, passivity, masochism, and exhibitionism, all of which he found repelling. But the conflict that led to his fantasies eventually persuaded him of his innate goodness. By recognizing and admitting the aberrations into which he had fallen Rousseau reveals a deep need to convince himself and others that he had another, higher side. In the conflict raging within, the morally elevated Rousseau had to triumph. He described this process: 'Je n'ai pas laissé de jouir beaucoup à ma maniere; c'est à dire, par l'imagination. Voilà comment mes sens, d'accord avec mon humeur timide et mon esprit romanesque, m'ont conservé des sentimens purs et des mœurs honnêtes par les mêmes goûts qui, peut être avec un peu plus d'effronterie m'auroient plongé dans les plus brutales voluptés.'[40] By channelling his eroticism into his 'imagination,' and by giving scope to his 'être sensible' and 'esprit romanesque' Rousseau was sublimating; Platonic love came to his assistance, and helped him to structure his fantasies.

Julie, then was a construction of Rousseau's fantasy life. She was a means by which his higher side demonstrated its superiority. By creating such a perfect heroine Rousseau was revealing his own basic goodness. As he said in the *Confessions*, 'on ne pouvoit prendre un intrest si vif à l'Héloïse, sans avoir ce sixième sens, ce sense moral dont si peu de cœurs sont doueés, et sans lequel nul ne sauroint entendre le mien.' Then, in an illuminating passage, Rousseau said 'Ce qui me rendit les femmes si favorables fut le persuasion où elles furent que j'avois écrit ma propre histoire et que j'étois moi-même le Héros de ce roman.' To this assumption, Rousseau replied 'on se trompoit en pensant qu'il avoit fallu des objets réels pour les produire.'[41]

In fact, though, Rousseau was Saint-Preux. And Saint-Preux's function was the same as Julie's: to lay bare the author's own inner person. It was necessary, however, since Rousseau was aware of the two sides to his personality, that his fictionalized self would assume a different moral shape from Julie. As perfection itself, Julie helped Saint-Preux aspire to a level of moral purity that was within his reach but to which he could not rise by himself.

Thus, while Julie and Saint-Preux shared a perfect love, there were clear-cut differences between them. Especially in the first two parts they did appear, at times, not to have been morally apart. As Julie said, 'Nos âmes se sont, pour ainsi dire, touchées par tous les points et nous avons par tout senti la même cohérence.'[42] In fact, though, Julie was much the stronger of the two, and she had a far more elevated concept of love than Saint-Preux.[43] As a girl, Julie had received exacting moral instruction. 'J'ai été élevée dans des maximes si sévères qu l'amour le plus pur me paroissoit le comble de déshonneur.' This made her afraid of love and hesitant to allow her feeling for Saint-Preux to rise to the surface. 'L'excessive défiance de moi-même augmenta mes allarmes.' But the 'générosité' of her tutor showed her fears to be groundless. 'Expérience' taught her that her 'cœur trop tendre' did need love: but this love was Platonic. 'Mes sens n'ont aucun besoin d'amant.' Realizing this, a life of calm happiness opened up before her. 'Sortie de cette profonde ignominie où mes terreurs m'avoient plongée, je goûte le plaisir délicieux d'aimer purement ... A peine puis-je en concevoir un plus doux, et l'accord de l'amour et de l'innocence me semble être le paradis sur la terre.'[44]

Julie naturally wanted to help Saint-Preux achieve a similar state of happiness and perfection. 'Ah mon ami, que ne puis-je faire passer dans votre âme le sentiment de bonheur et de paix qui règne au fond de la mienne! Que ne puis-je vous apprendre a jouïr tranquillement du plus délicieux état de la vie! Les charmes de l'union des cœurs se joignent pour nous à ceux de l'innocence: nulle crainte, nulle honte ne trouble notre félicité.'[45] In addressing herself to Saint-Preux in this way, Julie admitted the difference between herself and her tutor. Saint-Preux was impetuous, impassioned, and, when seized by love, frenzied and incoherent. 'Oui, chère Amante, il me semble que mon amour est aussi parfait que son adorable objet; tous les désirs enflammés par vos charmes s'éteignent dans les perfections de votre âme, je la vois si paisible que je n'ose en troubler la tranquillité. Chaque fois que je suis tenté de vous dérober la moindre caresse, si le danger de vous offenser me retient, mon cœur me retient encore plus par la crainte d'altérer une félicité si pur.'[46]

While Julie did yield, just once, to Saint-Preux, she was not passionate by nature, and her loss of virginity was followed by remorse. 'Ce doux enchantement de vertu s'est évanoui comme un songe: nos feux ont perdu cette ardeur divine qui les animoit en les épurant; nous avons recherché le plaisir et le bonheur a fui loin de nous ... Un feu pur et sacré brûloit nos cœurs; livrés aux erreurs des sens, nous ne sommes plus que des amans vulgaires.'[47] Of course, marriage could have legitimized Julie's and Saint-Preux's love, but the truth is that the hero and heroine were basically different. Already, in letter 50, long before she married Wolmar, Julie said that lovers 'ne désirent pas; ils aiment.' The flame of true love 'honore et purifie toutes ses caresses, la décence et l'honnêteté l'accompagnent au sien de la volupté même ...'[48] To such a Platonic spirit as this Saint-Preux could never have been an adequate mate, not the Saint-Preux who wrote, 'ce corps si délié qui touche et embrasse ... quelle taille enchanteresse ... au devant dux légers contours ... ô spectacle de volupté ... je vous vaise mille fois!'[49] Wolmar, on the other hand, was a man of serene passions and natural coolness. Only a man of his detached, dispassionate nature could have made Julie happy, and Wolmar did. Writing to Saint-Preux, Julie explained that given a free choice, 'ce n'est pas vous que je choisirois, c'est M. de Wolmar.'[50]

In settling into marriage, Julie was able to implement her views on love. She was not sensual and could not have entered into even marital love with the same ardour as Saint-Preux. Indeed Julie said: 'L'amour est accompagné d'une inquiétude continuelle de jalousie ou de privation, peu convenable au mariage, qui est un état de jouissance et de paix. On ne s'épouse point pour penser uniquement l'un à l'autre, mais pour remplir conjointement les devoirs de la vie civile gouverner prudemment la maison, bien élever ses enfans.'[51] Julie's indifference to marital love, which was rooted in her earlier concept of Platonic love, helped her to perpetuate her moral ascendancy over Saint-Preux after he entered the Wolmar household. Saint-Preux was happy to live in Julie's shadow, and indeed he found comfort there. Her example helped him to regulate his ardour.

It has been argued that by identifying himself with Saint-Preux, Rousseau was at once admitting his own impassioned nature, the weakness to which that nature gave rise, and his psychological need for a person stronger than himself to provide moral leadership. At the same time, the fictionalized Rousseau reveals the innate virtue of the author. But the hero needed the assistance of another, more perfect person, to preserve that virtue. Just as Rousseau submitted to Sophie, so too did Saint-Preux submit to Julie. By idealizing Platonic love and marriage Rousseau was prescribing a pattern of moral conduct of which he himself was incapable, which is hardly surprising. It is difficult to imagine a father and husband breaking into Rousseau-like rhapsodies over the beauties of domesticity. The departure that Rousseau made in *La Nouvelle Héloïse* was made by a man who looked at a way of life that to him was forever closed.

But *La Nouvelle Héloïse* was not merely a crystallization of Rousseau's fantasies. In that case Rousseau would have been irrelevant to the eighteenth century, and to a study of the French novel. Rousseau did not think in a vacuum, but was very much in contact with current developments in thought and in literature. Indeed, his importance, at least in the novel, lies not so much in innovation as in the systematic development of an earlier approach. We have seen that Diderot applied domestic themes to the theatre, and that he discussed his plans for the *drame* with Rousseau. In writing a domestic novel Rousseau was not just doing for the novel what Diderot had done for the theatre; he was adding another dimension and a higher degree of logical consistency to the romantic approach to love.

In Marivaux, the lovers were in love with love. To be in love was to be suffused by sweet sensations; but it also involved an analysis of those sensations. Love brought both heart and mind into play. The result was a constant dialogue between the two, from which came an ever-continuing refinement of love. To be refined, in this sense, was to be *sensible*; and, as s we have seen, *sensibilité* was appropriate to the virginal stirrings of adolescent love. To the tedium and humdrum of married life, it was not appropriate. This being the case, Marivaux did not complete *Marianne*. His sensibility led him into frequent moralizations, many of which were eulogies of marriage and family life. But Marivaux could not complete his novel; he could not imagine Marianne as a housewife.

Rousseau's achievement was that he found a consistent way to extend the action of *La Nouvelle Héloïse* beyond marriage. While not a 'born novelist' (the term is F.C. Green's), Rousseau was a remarkably perceptive thinker. In writing *La Nouvelle Héloïse*, he comprehended the problem of romantic love in its totality, and he discovered a way to bring its antithetical elements together. He did so, first, by intensifying the effects of love. Love did not radiate as much as it ravished; it did not glow as much as it burned. But, as before, it brought the rational faculty into play. A similar dichotomy between *cœur* and *esprit* was present in Marivaux and Rousseau, but in *La Nouvelle Héloïse* intelligence served a new function. By intensifying the effects of love, Rousseau placed new demands upon the intelligence, whose purpose was to study the moral side of love.

Saint-Preux said in letter 10 that 'le feu coule dans mes veines.'[52] As we have seen, he was continually being carried away by passion, brought face-to-face with the abyss. Julie too, as she said in letter 4, was 'entraîner dans l'abîme,'[53] but once there she stopped and retreated. Aware of the destructiveness of passion she brought hers under control by discovering Platonism. Before she married Wolmar, she said that lovers 'ne désirent pas, ils aiment.'[54] Yet, this was a different type of Platonism from that of the seventeenth-century novel, for it still gave wide scope to the romantic soul. Julie did say that love alone could gratify all the desires, but she had in mind a type of love that would bring together two beings in a union that was at once sentimental and pure. Furthermore, since the erotic side of love was denigrated, Rousseau discovered a way to build a bridge across the marriage ceremony and to extend the action of his novel into married life. In working out this approach Rousseau could write a novel about both romantic love and conjugal life. Julie's solution to the problem of romantic love was the foundation on which she built her marriage.

Finally, we return to the opening subject of this chapter: the dialectical relationship between the anti-romantic love of the *roman érotique* and the romantic love of the sentimental novel. Rousseau did work out the inner logic of sentimental love; but his innovation in the novel, and Diderot's innovation in the theatre, must be seen as well against the background of erotic literature. When Diderot said that literature could corrupt he was, perhaps, commenting upon the *roman érotique*. And the production of *romans érotiques*, as Mornet has shown, was greatest during the period 1740–60.[55] In a genre that Mornet calls *romans et contes licencieux*, twenty-four of the forty-four titles published between 1740 and 1780 appeared between 1745 and 1751. The popularity of erotic literature was greatest just before Diderot and Rousseau enlarged the didactic element which had always been inherent in the literature of romantic love. Looking further into Mornet's bibliography, we discover three new categories: the sentimental novel which was influenced by Rousseau (12 titles); the sentimental novel in which Rousseau's influence is predominant (17 titles); and novels imitating the title of *La Nouvelle Héloïse* (7 titles).[56] In reorienting the novel Rousseau helped to popularize a literature idealizing both romantic love and the Christian idea of love and marriage.

6

Marriage and moralistic literature

In order to grasp fully Rousseau's views on marriage it is useful to look not only at *La Nouvelle Héloïse*, but also at *Emile* (1762). While the central theme of the latter work was education, marriage also received serious treatment. Indeed, Rousseau's views on education were directly related to his approach to marriage. The core idea of *Emile* is that education should prepare a youth for life, and for Rousseau no sector of life was more important then marriage. Thus, the novel ends with Emile's marriage to Sophie. In both of his novels, Rousseau prescribed a pattern of conduct that would contribute to marital stability and happiness. The anguish that followed Julie's and Saint-Preux's single lapse from virtue indicates the importance that Rousseau attached to premarital chastity. In *Emile* the hero's tutor protected his chastity by taking him from the corrupt life of the city, whose gilded surfaces suggested seduction, to the healthier environment of the countryside. Here Emile would see vice, but the crude vice of peasants that would repel more than attract him. Also, a tutor could exercise greater control over his pupil in a village, as there would be fewer distractions, and everyone would be eager to assist the master in the instruction of his disciple. The purpose of these lessons was to impress Emile with the evil of debauchery and to show him that health, strength, courage, virtue, love itself – all that was essential to man's well-being – depended on premarital chastity.

Emile's tutor, in addition to instilling sound principles in his pupil, took every possible precaution to keep him even from thinking about sex. The best diversion was hard work. 'Il lui faut une occupation nouvelle qui l'intéresse par sa nouveauté ... Les langueurs de l'amour ne naissent que dans un doux repos; un violent exercice étouffe les sentiments tendres.'[1]

Emile's tutor was a constant companion, who strove to protect the youth from himself as well as from others. His policy was never to leave him, day or night, to share his room, never to let him go to bed until sleepy, and to let him rise as soon as he awoke. However, Emile did ask questions about sex. They were answered briefly and truthfully, but as far as possible the ever-present tutor kept him in a state of pure innocence.

Les termes grossiers sont sans conséquence; ce sont les idées lascives qu'il faut écarter ... Je ne vois qu'un bon moyen de conserver aux enfants leur innocence; c'est que tous ceux qui les entourent la respectent et l'aiment. Sans cela, toute la retenue dont on tâche d'user avec eux se dément tôt ou tard; un sourire, un clin d'œil, un geste échappé, leur disent tout ce qu'on cherche à leur taire ... Il y a une certaine naïveté de langage qui sied et qui plaît à l'innocence: voilà le vrai ton qui détourne un enfant d'une dangereuse curiosité.[2]

Rousseau stressed both male and female chastity in order to promote marriages based on unswerving fidelity. A debauched youth could hardly be expected to correct in marriage the vices with which he had already become familiar. Emile had to avoid youthful promiscuity in order to prevent adultery; having kept his chastity intact, he would remain loyal to his wife. In *La Nouvelle Héloïse*, Julie lost her innocence, not promiscuously, but as the result of her love for Saint-Preux, whom she had hoped to marry. Nevertheless, she felt that she and Saint-Preux had sullied themselves by their lapse, and she never forgot it. Her single lapse from virtue fortified her desire to be a good, absolutely loyal wife to her husband, to whom she wanted to make amends for her loss of virginity.

In treating love and marriage with the utmost seriousness in *Emile* and *La Nouvelle Héloïse*, Rousseau's purpose was to elevate a union between two people who, since they were bound together by mutual affection, were assured of happiness together. In *Emile* Rousseau wrote: 'Qu'en lui peignant le mariage, non seulement comme la plus douce des sociétés, mais comme la plus inviolable et le plus saint de tous les contrats, on lui dise avec force toutes les raisons, qui rendent un nœud si sacré respectable à tous les hommes et qui couvrent de haine de malédictions quiconque ose en souiller la pureté.'[3]

It was because Rousseau placed such emphasis on the marital state that he opposed arranged marriages. In order for husband and wife to live happily together, they should love one another, and should therefore be allowed to make their own decision about marriage. A father who committed his child to a marriage with a stranger for reasons of social or material advantage was creating a situation that would probably result in disinterest, unhappiness, and a weakening or breaking of the marital tie.

Rousseau conveyed this message in different ways in both *La Nouvelle Héloïse* and *Emile*: in the former the misguided father brought misery to his daughter by committing her to a marriage of convenience; in the latter the kind and benevolent father believed that his daughter should have the right to choose her own husband, since it was she who would have to live with him. Julie gave vent to her anger and frustration when she was required to marry Wolmar. She felt she had been traded like mere merchandise, and she considered her father cruel, unnatural, and unrelenting.

It was Bomston, a generous, liberal, English aristocrat who criticized marriages of convenience most sharply. He took up Julie's and Saint-Preux's cause and unsuccessfully tried to get the baron d'Étanges to accept Saint-Preux as his son-in-law. In a letter to Julie's friend, Claire, he wrote that, in his opinion, the decision to marry was the most sacred of all engagements, and should be made from free choice. All laws that constrained it were unjust, all fathers who dared to force or break it were tyrannical. This chaste tie of nature should be subject to neither paternal nor state authority. The child, whose only guide was love, might choose badly, but the father, whose decision was determined by the opinion of others, would make a worse choice. If an inexperienced daughter wanted advice, her father should give it. Indeed, it was his duty to say 'c'est un fripon,' or 'c'est un homme de sens,' or 'c'est un fou.'[4]

But after hearing his advice, the daughter should make her own decision.

A counterpart to Bomston was Sophie's father in *Emile*, who also viewed marriage sensibly. He told his daughter that since she was approaching the age of womanhood, it was time to consider marriage. There were two ways, he explained, of entering that state: the natural method, meaning that husband and wife chose one another; and the accepted custom, which was for parents to arrange marriages. Of these, the former was vastly preferable. The surest way to marital happiness was for the couple to be in love before entering wedlock, which they should do of their own free will. 'C'est là le droit de la nature, que rien ne peut abroger: ceux qui l'ont gênée par tant de lois civiles ont eu plus d'égard à l'ordre apparent qu'au bonheur du mariage et aux mœurs des citoyens.'[5]

Rousseau sought to ennoble the state of marriage by every possible means. Here was an institution so manifold in its benefits both to society and to the individuals who enjoyed its blessings that it was worthy of the highest respect. It was not just a socially useful institution, but also a sacrament. Before her marriage, Julie had contemplated an adulterous union with Saint-Preux, but upon taking her marriage vows she underwent a moral transformation. In spite of the fact that Julie married, not the man she loved, but a virtual stranger old enough to be her father, the marriage ceremony impressed her so profoundly that she at once abandoned her adulterous thoughts and swore to be faithful to her husband. She found this easy, since the ceremony gave her an instinctive understanding of right and wrong; the marriage ceremony contributed to her moral salvation. Her crisis dissolved and peace descended upon her as she realized her true purpose in life: to subordinate her own interests (her passion for Saint-Preux) to those of her husband and the new condition into which she was entering.

Rousseau contended that marriage could engender deep happiness, but if husband and wife did not conduct themselves properly bitter unhappiness could be the result. The physical side of marriage should be handled with the closest circumspection. Since frequent relations could lead to disinterest, the husband and wife should avoid satiety; those who tired of the pleasures permitted by marriage might fall into adultery, which would jeopardize the marriage. This was no problem for Julie, who held a Platonic view of love, or for Wolmar, who was rational and dispassionate by nature, and whose years had stripped him of ardour. Moreover, Rousseau had equipped Julie with a philosophy of life that would safeguard her from engaging in any excesses, sexual or otherwise. 'Elle sent en paix cette volupté suprême, elle ne se refuse aucune de celles qui peuvent s'associer avec celle-là; mais sa manière de les goûter ressemble à l'austérité de ceux qui s'y refusent, et l'art de jouir est pour elle celui des privations; non de ces privations pénibles et douloureuses qui blessent la nature et dont son auteur dédaigne l'hommage insensé, mais des privations passagères et modérées, qui conservent à la raison son empire ... Elle prétend que ... prévenir toujours les désirs n'est pas l'art de les contenter mais de les éteindre.'[6]

Emile and Sophie were mutually attracted by youthful love, so satiety could become a problem for them. Emile's tutor showed the young bride and groom how they could enjoy 'dans la vieillesse le charme de la première union.'[7] If love were to retain its freshness, neither party should make selfish advances, and neither should consider love a prerogative; Nature herself decreed that a married couple should make love only when it was mutually desired. In marriage, hearts were bound, but bodies were not enslaved; fidelity was owed, but not submission. Even the slightest favours should be considered as gifts. With tact and delicacy, one could determine the other's feelings. By waiting until the opportune moment, there would be no possibility of giving offence, and satisfaction would be mutual. Were Emile and Sophie to follow this advice, they would avoid satiety: their love would remain fresh, and the basis of their happiness solid.

It was not only to protect the love of husband and wife that Rouseau urged such measures, for, in his opinion, the real function of marriage was to have and raise children. As soon as husband and wife became mother and father, they assumed a new set of obligations that were of the greatest importance. They could no longer think exclusively of their own happiness; they must provide for the moral welfare of their children, both by example and instruction. The family should consist of a close network of personal relationships that would bind all its members together. In an ideal relationship, the parents would dedicate themselves to the proper moral upbringing of their children, and the children in return would become models of filial devotion.

Rousseau closed *Emile* with a eulogy on domestic virtue, as the husband of a few months entered the room of his tutor, saying, 'Mon maître, félicitez votre enfant; il espère avoir bientôt l'honneur d'être père. Oh! quels soins vont être imposés à notre zèle ...'[8] But Rousseau's views of the family were developed most fully in *La Nouvelle Héloïse*, in which it was his intention to describe the responsibilities of both children and parents. Even when her father made her marry against her wish, Julie remained both grateful and loyal. At first her response was one of bitterness, but then, as she reflected on all that her father had done for her, and as her daughterly affection came to the surface, she was overcome by a sense of devotion. 'Père barbare et dénaturé! mérite-t-il ... quoi, mériter? c'est le meilleur des pères.'[9] Thus, Julie declined when Bomston offered her sanctuary with Saint-Preux on his English estate. She loved her parents too much to injure them; as their daughter she could not neglect their feelings: 'J'abandonnerois impitoyablement ceux par qui je respire, ceux qui me conservent la vie qu'ils m'ont donnée, et me la rendent chère; ceux qui n'ont d'autre espoir d'autre plaisir qu'en moi seule? Un père presque sexégénaire! une mère toujours languissante! Moi leur unique enfant, je les laisserois sans assistance dans la solitude et les ennuis de la vieillesse, quand il est temps de leur rendre les tendres soins qu'ils m'ont prodigués?'[10] Julie was heartbroken when her mother died, and throughout her married days demonstrated continual concern for her father. This became apparent at the end of the novel, when she became ill after rescuing one of her children from a lake. As she lay on her deathbed, some of her last thoughts were about her father. She feared the distress her death would cause him, and lamented the inevitable loneliness of his old age. 'Hélas, dit-elle, que deviendra-t-il après moi? A quoi tiendra-t-il? Survive à toute sa famille! ... Quelle vie sera la sienne?'[11] The gratitude and devotion Julie felt for her father served as a model for her own children to emulate, and therefore helped to perpetuate family unity. In loving and caring for her children she was meeting a responsibility that contributed not only to the happiness of her own family, but also to the well-being of society, 'Julie a un père qui s'inquiète du bien-être de sa famille; elle a des enfans à la subsistance desquels il faut pourvoir convenablement. Ce doit être le principal soin de l'homme sociable, et c'est aussi le premier dont elle et son mari se sont conjointement occupés.'[12]

Rousseau sketched a series of tableaux in La Nouvelle Héloïse whose underlying theory of associationist psychology was to edify the reader. In one domestic scene, Julie worked at her embroidery as two girls busied themselves weaving lace, and her two boys took turns identifying pictures in a book of prints.

It is to Rousseau's credit that he resisted the temptation to lump his characters into 'good' and 'bad' categories. Each person in La Nouvelle Héloïse has a problematic side. Rousseau developed his views on marriage by positive means, pointing out the importance of correct moral education and stable, responsible domestic life. But to the second-rate author it was tempting to moralize by contrasting vice and virtue. There was a suggestion of that approach in Marianne; in the Contes Moraux (published in 1761; written originally in the Mercure after 1757) by Jean-François Marmontel (1723–1799) the 'good' character was commonly pitted against the 'bad'.

In 'La Bonne mère,' Emilie was conscientiously raised to marriageable age by her mother, who believed that she should select her own husband. She was therefore free to choose between the two suitors. The first, to whom she was initially most attracted, was the vainglorious but handsome marquis de Verglan, who was 'doué de la plus jolie figure. Son miroir et les femmes le lui avoient dit tant de fois, qu'il avoit bien fallu le croire. Il s'écoutoit avec complaisance, se voyoit avec volupté, se souroit à lui-même, et ne cessoit de s'applaudir ... Il savoit par cœur tous ces petits propos de toilette, tous ces jolie mots qui ne disent rien. Il étoit au fait de toutes les anecdotes galantes de la Ville et de la Cour.'[13] Verglan's views on marriage became apparent in his praise of the baron d'Hauberive and his wife, who had tired of one another and taken lovers. The four members of this civilized arrangement were friendly and on the best of terms, which Verglan considered an intelligent procedure, and whose merits he pointed out to Emilie:

On parle du bon vieux temps ... que l'on me cite un example des mœurs de nos pères, qui soit comparable à celui-ci. Autrefois une infidélité mettoit le feu à la maison; l'on enfermoit, l'on battoit sa femme. Si l'époux, usoit de la liberté qu'il s'étoit réservée, sa triste et fidèlle moitié étoit obligée de dévorer son injure, et de gémir au fond de son ménage, comme dans une obscure prison. Si elle imitoit son volage époux, c'étoit avec des dangers terribles. Il n'y alloit pas de moins que de la vie pour son Amant et pour elle-même. On avoit eu la sottise d'attacher l'honneur d'un homme à la vertu de son épouse ... En honneur, je ne conçois pas comment dans ces siecles barbares on avoit le courage d'épouser. Aujourd-hui voyez la complaisance, la liberté, la paix régner au sein des familles. Si les époux s'aiment, à la bonne heure; ils vivent ensemble, ils sont heureux. S'ils cessent de s'aimer, ils se le disent en honnêtes gens, et se rendent l'un à l'autre la parole d'être fidèles. Ils cessent d'être amans, ils sont amis. C'est ce que j'apelle des mœurs sociales, des mœurs douces.[14]

Upon hearing these perverse views on marriage, Emilie began to incline toward the other candidate, Belzors, who, of course, disagreed with Verglan. An arrangement such as the one favoured by Verglan would mean that:

la sainteté inviolable des nœuds de l'hymen fait la sainteté des noeuds de la nature. Souviens-toi, mon ami, que s'il n'y a plus de devoirs sacrés pour les Epoux, il n'y en aura guère pour les enfans. Tous ces liens tiennent l'un à l'autre. Les querelles du ménage étoient violentes du tems de nos pères; mais la masse des mœurs étoit saine ... la plaie se resermoit, aussi-tôt. Aujourd'hui c'est un corps languissant ... nous n'avons pas l'idée de ces joies pures et intimes que goutoient deux Epoux au sein de leur famille, de cette union qui faisoit les délices de leur jeunesse, & la consolation de leurs vieux ans.[15]

The proper conception of marriage presented by Belzors obviously prevailed.

In 'La Mauvaise mère' Madame de Carandon completely spoiled one of her sons, whom she called Monsieur l'Etang, at the expense of the other, named Jacquant. To get rid of Jacquant, she sent him to school, at which he excelled. When he graduated, his mother suggested that he enter the church or the army, since she could not give him any financial assistance. Instead, Jacquant secured passage on a ship to the West Indies, where his intelligence and industry enabled him to prosper and buy a plantation. Then, he received news that his mother was on her death bed. She had given most of her fortune to Monsieur l'Etang, so that he could make a favourable marriage and secure a good position in society. He and his wife soon went their separate ways and he found himself making love to ladies of easy virtue, on whom he squandered most of his money. When it was all but gone he made a frantic attempt to recover it by a fling at the gaming table, losing the little that remained. When his mother appealed to him for desperately needed financial assistance he had to tell her that he could not give it, and indeed needed help himself. Grief-stricken and disillusioned by this unhappy news, Madame de Carandon lapsed into that critical state of which Jacquant had been informed. This good son sold his property and left his fiancée, herself a plantation owner, to whom he promised to return with all possible dispatch as soon as he had provided for his mother's needs. The following scene took place when Jacquant appeared at his mother's bedside.

Ah! mon fils: dans quel moment venez-vous revoir votre mère? votre main va lui fermer les yeux. Quelle fut la douleur de cet enfant si pieux et si tendre, de voir cette mere qu'il avoit laissée au sein de luxe & de l'opulence, de la voir dans un lit entouré de lambeaux, & dont l'image souleveroit le cœur, s'il m'étoit permis de la rendre. O, ma mere! s'écria-t-il, en se précipitant sur ce lit de douleurs: ses sanglots étoufferent sa voix, & les ruisseaux de larmes dont il inondoit le sein de sa mere expirante, furent long-temps la seule expression de sa douleur & de son amour. Le Ciel me punit, reprit-elle, d'avoir trop aimé un fils denaturé, d'avoir ... Il l'interrompit: tout est réparé, ma mere, lui dit ce vertueux jeune homme, vivez: la fortune m'a comblé de biens; je viens les répandre au sein de la nature: c'est pour vous qu'ils me sont données. Vivez: j'ai de quoi vous faire aimer la vie.[16]

Madame de Carandon recovered, went to the West Indies with her son, and lived a happy existence with him and the faithful woman who had awaited his return, and whom he married upon his arrival. The bad son paid the price of his profligacy and debauchery by dying of syphilis.

In summing up Rousseau's and Marmontel's treatment of marriage, it should be noted that the social context differs. Julie, Wolmar, and Emile are all aristocrats, while the 'good' characters in Marmontel's *Contes* are often bourgeois. Marmontel not only described bourgeois characters, but also emphasized the moral significance of belonging to that class. In 'La Bonne mère' Belzors won Emilie because his view of marriage was more virtuous than that of the marquis de Verglan. 'La Mauvaise mère' was bad because she tried to establish one of her sons in aristocratic society, and in so doing only corrupted him. Her other son, whom she neglected, was industrious and therefore succeeded in life, both morally and materially. The story ended with the hero entering into the state of marriage. As a rule in these *Contes Moraux* to be happily married was to be bourgeois; and to realize the bourgeois way of life was to be virtuous.

Marmontel was writing his *Contes Moraux* at the exact time that Rousseau wrote *La Nouvelle Héloïse*. These works represent a similar view of love, marriage, and the family. Yet, the social setting of one is aristocratic, of the other, bourgeois.

7

The social context
of moralistic literature

Historians have long assumed that after 1789 the bourgeoisie became the dominant political class. As dust was still settling from the Revolution, François Pierre Guizot saw in the political and social upheaval that had just ended a transfer of power from the nobility to the bourgeoisie. In a more rigorous and systematic fashion Karl Marx was to reach a similar conclusion, as would such distinguished twentieth-century historians as Albert Mathiez and Georges Lefebvre. Since the Revolution has generally been considered bourgeois, it is only logical that historians would emphasize the rise of the bourgeoisie during the Ancien Regime. And, in the field of literature, it is tempting to describe as bourgeois the considerable output of moralistic literature in the pre-Revolutionary period, particularly since shifting literary fashions seem to coincide with the political pattern. Aristocratic, erotic literature flourished during the mid-eighteenth century, from 1740 to 1760, when the Ancien Regime still stood on foundations that at least seemed stable. But thereafter, as cracks in those foundations became clear, literature appeared which condemned abuses in aristocratic life, and the moralistic orientation of which undoubtedly anticipated the Republic of Virtue. What could be more natural than to interpret this literature as bourgeois, especially since it tended to idealize middle-class life. And yet, plausible and attractive as the thesis is, I believe that what happened was quite different. I shall first discuss the connection between social class and *sensibilité* (the stylistic matrix of most moralistic literature), then look at the social argument in the most widely-read and influential novel of the late eighteenth century,

La Nouvelle Héloïse, and finally examine the factors that brought into being a type of literature that idealized the bourgeoisie.

Sensibilité did not rise in a middle-class milieu, but rather in the cultured, elitist salons of the early eighteenth century. While the social composition of these salons was not entirely noble, in both tone and values they were predominantly aristocratic. Furthermore, the emergence of *sensibilité* must be seen as a reaction against the values that held sway within aristocratic society during the second half of the seventeenth century, particularly from 1660 to 1690. During that period, when classicism reached its highest stage of development, the ego was considered hateful. A compassionate spirit like La Fontaine could allow his pity to be directed only towards the animals in his fables. In Racine's tragedies, since only the sublime sufferings and achievements of the great found expression, the audience had no opportunity to commiserate with its contemporaries. The one passage in French literature from this period that seems unequivocally to express compassion arguably does not. This is the passage in La Bruyère's *Caractères* describing the misery of the peasantry. According to Geoffrey Atkinson, La Bruyère, too, was hard of heart, and wrote this passage not from sympathy, but as a veiled attack on the maladministration of public affairs under Louis XIV.[1]

The lack of compassion in aristocratic society during this period was an aberration. It was, among other things, in direct conflict with the ancient aristocratic tradition of *noblesse oblige*. Both medieval and Renaissance literature had described lordly beneficence. Protestant writers of the sixteenth century had emphasized mercy, toleration, and kindliness. But to the society of 1660–90 the emotions were suspect. This helps to explain the reappearance of compassion in the early eighteenth century: to value the feelings was to react against the ban placed on them during the classical period. Also, to rehabilitate the feelings was to return to the earlier tradition of *noblesse oblige*. From this standpoint, the ready reception given to *sensibilité* in France can more easily be understood: the moral framework of *sensibilité* put man in a more favourable light, and it provided a means by which the emotions, long obstructed, could once again flow. The social context in which compassion became fashionable in the early eighteenth century was aristocratic.

It is this way that Marivaux should be seen. As an *habitué* of Madame de Lambert's salon, his novels not surprisingly expressed the same interest in compassion that the marquise herself demonstrated in her writings.[2] In a 1722 number of the *Spectateur français* Marivaux described the plight of a girl who went to Paris:

I am a girl of good family; my father held a rather important post in the provinces. He died three years ago ... and left my mother a widow with three daughters to care for, of whom I am the eldest. After selling what we had left, my mother and I came to Paris to hasten the settlement of a lawsuit which, if successful, would re-establish us ... Those who should be expediting it neglected to do so, because we have no funds with which to pay. Finally, Sir, the poverty-stricken state into which we have fallen, added to the grief, the foul air, and darkness of our quarters ... have made my mother despair ... a rich townsman offers me all possible help. But what help, Sir! It would save my mother's life; it would everlastingly dishonour mine. This is my present state; can any be more terrible?

To this suffering the *Spectateur* replied:

Every decent man will feel how the words of this girl affected me ... Just Heaven! What are the designs of Providence in the mysterious distributions it makes of wealth! Why does Providence seem prodigal of riches with men who are devoid of feeling, born hard and pitiless, whereas it is sparing of riches with those who are generous and compassionate, hardly according them the absolute necessities? Since this is the way it is, what is to become of poor wretches who find no help either in the abundance of the former or in the compassion of the latter.[3]

The plight of the girl in this story was very like that of Marianne, although she had no mother when she went to Paris; she, too, was offered financial assistance under terms that would have dishonoured her forever. Marianne did secure the assistance of kind, beneficent people, most of whom, incidentally, were aristocrats. Though Madame Dutour, the *marchande* with whom she stayed for a while, looked down on Marianne because of her birth, and at times treated her badly, Madame de Miran was deeply moved by the heroine's suffering and virtue. In this lady's generous heart there was no greater pleasure than lending assistance to one who so deserved it. And Madame de Miran, in addition to being compassionate and generous, was also a loving and responsible parent. Not only did she try to secure her son's happiness, but also, and instinctively, she looked on Marianne as a daughter. This aristocratic lady was both beneficent and an ideal example of maternal solicitude. In his description of her, Marivaux reflects the moral orientation of the aristocratic society in which he himself moved.[4]

Rousseau, too, prescribed a moral programme which might be termed aristocratic. The setting of parts iv–vi of *La Nouvelle Héloïse*, in which Rousseau described an ideal household, was the estate of Monsieur de

Wolmar. In this novel, Rousseau represented aristocratic life as he thought it ought to be. The simplicity, virtue, and responsibility of the countryside replaced the extravagance, vice, and frivolity of the town. At the Wolmar estate the furnishings were simple and useful, and convenience was preferred to display and luxury. The entire house and grounds were redesigned to eliminate needless decoration and to provide maximum utility. The Wolmars did not lease their land, but chose instead to farm it themselves. Running his estate took up much of Monsieur de Wolmar's time, and contributed to his pleasure as well as to his profit. Since his estate was large and intensely cultivated, Monsieur de Wolmar hired workers from the local area, thereby winning their loyalty. In order to increase production, he visited his workers almost every day, sometimes more often. Another means of encouraging industry was to establish two wages, the first based on local custom in the area, the second, a bonus to reward workers displaying extra initiative. Such measures worked to everyone's advantage: profits and wages rose, productivity increased, and the nation was better provided with foodstuffs.

Julie lent her support to the smooth operation of her husband's estate. Her objective was the same as Wolmar's: to win the affection of the workers, and to shower them with favours that would encourage them to be more enterprising. She often accompanied her husband on his tours, and every week she distributed coins to the workers who, in Wolmar's opinion, had been most industrious. These monetary favours made the other workers try to emulate the recipients. More important than gifts of money was Julie's personal concern for the workers. She considered all of them her children, and made an effort to learn of their affairs and interests, giving advice and reconciling differences. The workers naturally responded warmly to Madame de Wolmar's favours and concern.

When Monsieur de Wolmar would bring home in the evening an old peasant he had met on his tours, Madame de Wolmar would show him every kindness. At dinner she would listen to the old man prattle on about his youth, his family, his work, and so on. After dinner whe would find some object to give to him as a present for his wife or daughter. This would impress the younger members of the peasant's family, who did not resent not being invited themselves since it was age that had been rewarded. Indeed, the entire family considered it an honour for the Wolmars to have singled them out for special attention.

In a telling comment, Rousseau wrote that the benevolence of the Wolmars helped to knit the bonds of society betweeen people of different rank. The maxim of the heroine was never to encourage anyone to change his social position, and to do all that was possible to make everyone happy in his own estate. In her opinion, disorder and inequality would result if men strove after positions in society appropriate to their particular talents. 'Un Prince ira-t-il se faire cocher, parce qu'il mène bien son carrose? Un duc se fera-t-il Cuisiner parce qu'il invente de bons ragoûts?'[5]

The social unit that Rousseau described might well have derived from Plato.[6] As in *The Republic*, that unit was organic, with higher and lower parts, and the head was the landowner. By describing an ideal aristocratic household and estate, Rousseau consciously idealized rural society. Repeatedly he insisted extravagance, vice, and frivolity were urban, while simplicity, virtue, and order were rural. In the *Contrat Social* he contended that democracy was better suited to the peasantry than to the urban rabble, and in *Emile* he wrote that 'Men were not designed in ant-heaps ... The closer you pack them the more they spoil ... Towns are the sink of the human species.'[7] It seems, according to a passage in the *Lettre à D'Alembert*, that rural society should avoid all contact with the city. Describing the neighborhood of Neufchâtel, he wrote that 'No carpenter, locksmith (etc.) ever entered the country; they have no need of specialized craftsmen, each is his own craftsman ... Indeed they even make watches; and, incredible as it may seem, each united in his own person the various professions which watchmaking, and its very tooling, seem to require.'[8] Rousseau's ideal society, as described in *La Nouvelle Héloïse*, was 'that of villager in a free state.'[9] It is not surprising that among Rousseau's lesser literary efforts were two peasant novels, of which only fragments remain, *Les amours de Claire et de Marcelin* and *Le petit Savoyard ou la Vie de Claude Noyer*. Both were written about 1757.

If Rousseau had been asked if he were writing rationalizations for a conservative and repressive social order he would certainly have replied in the negative. And yet, according to Barrington Moore Jr he was doing precisely that. Moore contends that idealizations of rural society have been commonplace at least since the time of Cato the Elder, and their function has been to mask extortions worked on the peasantry. In order to justify arrangements favourable to the landowning class, rural life is described as an organic whole, organic because of its connection with the soil. Obviously, such a way of life is described as 'better,' and, in fact, moral regeneration is a common theme in the idealization of ruralism.[10]

The idea of regeneration presupposes moral decay, and throughout what Moore calls 'Catonism,' there are protests against urbanism, with which decay is associated. That urban growth in the eighteenth century was considerable is a well-known fact. From 1726 to 1789 the population in cities of 50,000 or more rose by about 30 per cent, while that in cities of 20,000 or more rose by almost 20 per cent.[11] During this same period French foreign trade increased by 900 per cent. Directly connected to the urban growth in eighteenth-century France was an unprecedented prosperity. This being the case, it is not surprising that idealizations of rural life would extol the virtues of frugality and simplicity. The country noble often looked at urban life with a mixture of suspicion and resentment. Indicative of this outlook is the the following satire of the urban noble in the Marquis de Mirabeau's *L'ami des hommes ou traité de la population* (1756):

They [the provincial nobility] are not be be compared with us [the urban nobility], because we know the rules of the theatre, the essential difference between Italian and French music; we know geometry or take our course in botany or anatomy; we know each other by our carriages, by varnish, by snuffboxes, by Chinaware; we are ignorant neither of vanity nor of intrigue, nor of the art of business, nor of demanding charity, nor, above all, of what is the relative value of silver and silver plate. They, on the contrary, make their entire science consist of seven or eight articles: to respect religion, not to lie, to hold their tongue, to do nothing base, to suffer no insult, to ride well, to fear neither famine nor thirst, and to shoot a pistol.[12]

What this passage reveals is the highly self-conscious rural outlook that was certainly important among a large segment of the eighteenth-century French aristocracy. One facet of this outlook was hostility to urbanism; another was a more practical interest in farming techniques. According to a bibliography written in 1810, twelve hundred books on agronomy appeared in the eighteenth century, as compared to one hundred and thirty in the seventeenth century and one hundred in the sixteenth century.[13] The increased production of agricultural books from the sixteenth through the eighteenth century reflects a growing economic awareness among the landowning class. After a severe seigneurial crisis in the fourteenth and fifteenth centuries, of which one consequence was the fragmentation of landed estates, landowners in the sixteenth century endeavored to reconstitute their estates. This they did with considerable success, over a period of time of three centuries. The greatest advances were made in the eighteenth century, and particularly after 1750.[14] In addition to enlarging their holdings, landowners applied new farming methods. Thus, the increase in books on agriculture. Rural society in the eighteenth century not only fashioned a distinctive outlook, in which anti-urbanism was a leading element, but also applied new techniques to the organization of the estate and to the exploitation of the soil. Out of these developments came a socially conservative mentality and material changes prejudicial to the interests of the peasantry.

Now Rousseau, let it be repeated, did not intend to justify the repression of the French peasantry. On the contrary, the central thrust of his position was the amelioration of that class, with which so many of his sympathies lay. The organic society favoured by Rousseau was rooted in social and economic differences, but held together by a spirit of equity. Nevertheless, the superiority he attributed to rural life was fundamentally conservative. As we have seen, Rousseau's ideal 'democracy' was not only rural, but also self-sustaining. Since the manufactures needed by rural society were produced locally, no recourse to the cities was necessary. As Rousseau was suspicious of cities and all that they represented, it is not surprising that of the two most famous states in classical Greece, Sparta and Athens, he favoured Sparta. While Athens was urban and 'modern,' Sparta was rural and 'conservative.' Sparta, far more than Athens, was aristocratic. As a moralist, Rousseau prescribed a way of life favourable to the interests of the second estate. Directly connected to his idealization of rural life was the attention that he gave to the family and to beneficence. By emphasizing the family, Rousseau reflected a point of view that had emerged from within aristocratic society[15] and his stress on beneficence placed him in the tradition of *noblesse oblige*. Rousseau's achievement, then, was to bring together important elements of aristocratic morality and to give them a rigorous and systematic treatment. These elements had been present before, but in Rousseau they achieved a more forceful expression and, owing to his popularity, they reached a larger audience.

While Rousseau did not idealize the bourgeoisie, other authors did. There can be no question that French writers attempted to dignify middle-class life by introducing a new type of hero, the merchant. The appearance of Diderot's 'bourgeois' *drames*, *Le fils naturel* and *Père de famille*, heralded a succession of plays attempting to show the middle class in a favourable light. Before examining the emergence of the *drame*, however, it will be useful to see how literary criticism has tended to interpret this dramatic genre.

In a standard work on the *drame*, *Le Drame en France au* XVIIIe *siècle*, Emile Gaiffe defines it as follows: 'un spectacle destiné à un auditoire bourgeois ou populaire et lui présentant un tableau attendrissant et moral de son propre milieu.'[16] Here was a theatre designed for the bourgeoisie, Gaiffe argued, and representing the morals of that social class. While Gaiffe was by no means a Marxist, his view of the *drame* is basically compatible with the Marxian interpretation. We have seen that G.V. Plekhanov argued that there were 'causal ties between *being* and *consciousness*, between the technique and the economics of society on the one hand, and its art on the other,'[17] and that he used the *drame* as proof of his theory. Now Gaiffe did not make the connection, as did Plekhanov, between the 'economics of society,' ('consciousness') and artistic and literary expression, but his view of the *drame* does seem to support this interpretation. Certainly if a type of theatre written for the bourgeoisie and representing the life of their class favourably were to emerge, it would appear that the bourgeoisie was eager for it. And if members of this class wanted to see the theatre praise their virtue and importance, then almost by definition they reached a new level of class-consciousness. This is what Plekhanov stated explicitly, and it is what Gaiffe implied.

In our attempt to explain the appearance of 'bourgeois' literature we shall for the moment leave aside the question of whether or not it resulted from a new self-awareness among the middle class, and instead look at stylistic change that preceded it. Innovative as writers were who idealized the bourgeoisie, they probably could not have done so had it not been for earlier departures from literary convention. Or, to put the matter differently, authors who introduced bourgeois heroes belonged to a pattern of literary change that reached back to the 1720s and 1730s. As with so many developments in eighteenth-century French literature, it is necessary in discussing this change to return to the classical tradition of the previous century. From the serious novel of the seventeenth century, bourgeois characters were rigidly excluded, and in the more serious of the dramatic genres, tragedy, heroes and heroines were princes and princesses or gods and goddesses. In both the novel and the theatre language was abstract, having been cleansed of common language. The lofty heroes of Racine expressed themselves only in the most elevated phrases which alone were worthy of their noble thoughts.[18] These sublime characters dwelt only on an exalted level, a level which to them was natural. So removed were they from the common race of men that details of everyday living, such as sleeping, eating, and drinking are all but missing. While bourgeois characters did, of course, appear in the comic theatre of the seventeenth century, Molière avoided any 'realistic concretizing' (Auerbach's term). Moreover, the bourgeois in the comic theatre, the 'bourgeois de qualité,' was an object of ridicule, since he aspired to a rank and way of life that was alien to his nature and background.[19]

In order for bourgeois characters to find a place in French literature it was necessary to break from the conventions of classicism, and this is precisely what happened. The anti-classical stance of the first half of the eighteenth century is apparent not only in a literature of libertinism and sensibility, but also in the vogue of orientalism. It shows up, as well, in a quite different context, in the recognition given to the moderns. In such a milieu as this the gods have fallen, and mere men have risen in their place, men of feeling, fallible and compassionate. It has been argued that these men no longer had to be aristocrats, and that French literature was 'democratized' in the first half of the eighteenth century.[20] If so, the appearance of 'bourgeois' literature would fit into a pattern of change that was already well established. It did indeed fit, but the pattern was by no means 'democratic.'

The heroine of *La Vie de Marianne* was an orphan. She lived in the home of a *marchande*, Madame Dutour, and was acutely conscious of her humble social position. It was this very consciousness that revealed Marianne's social outlook. She always clung to the possibility that by birth she was aristocratic, which indeed seemed probable given the circumstances of her parents' death. Marianne sensed the innate difference between herself and the mean-spirited people of Paris, whom she did not hesitate to denounce. And the people did appear common in *La Vie de Marianne*, as the argument between Madame Dutour and the cab driver makes clear. That Marianne would never have demeaned herself by quarreling over a fare is obvious. This girl of impeccable refinement was really only at ease among such good people as the aristocratic Madame de Miran. What drew Marianne and Madame de Miran toward one another, in addition to their refinement, was their sensibility, because sensibility, no less than refinement, revealed the ideal attributes of the aristocrat. While Marivaux introduced a heroine who, in the technical sense was not aristocratic, this heroine did not bear the stamp of the people, in style or in outlook. Marivaux did not create a 'democratic' literature, but he did depart from classical literary conventions. He introduced an anti-classical heroine, an orphan, and his sentimentalism marked a turning-away from the stylistic canons of an earlier generation of writers.

It is important to realize, then, that even though Marivaux extended the social framework of *La Vie de Marianne*, he did not criticize the aristocracy, nor did he elevate the people. And a new type of theatre, the sentimental *comédie larmoyante* of Nivelle de La Chaussée, maintained an elite social framework. The plays of this author, which appeared in the 1730s and 1740s, represented the life of the upper classes. His theatre was anything but 'democratic.' La Chaussée's innovation is that he depicted the misfortunes and sufferings of contemporary Frenchmen rather than gods and goddesses or heroes and heroines drawn from the classical past.

When we come to the *drame*, we encounter a theatre which resembles Marivaux's novels in that the social framework was not exclusively aristocratic. In his *Sylvie* (1742), Landois had called for a theatre in which the characters would have 'un peu plus de rapport avec celle des spectateurs.'[21] With the *drame*, which Diderot introduced in 1757, a theatre that had such an objective was officially launched. According to treatises on the *drame* written by Diderot, Beaumarchais, and Mercier, this type of play should depict men from all classes,[22] and it should edify all society.[23] In order to learn from a play, the audience must identify with the characters. The characters, then, no longer spoke in 'heavy and laboured' alexandrine meters, but in prose. Furthermore, the pomp of the classical hero had become objectionable: 'All the [classical] heroes walked with big strides, lifted high their heads ornamented with floating plumes, held themselves stiff and rigid; they spoke, or rather they bellowed through the speaking tube of the poet.[24] Having disposed of the stately, aristocratic, classical hero, the author of the *drame* could reconstruct the social context of his dramatic genre.

It is possible to extract passages from the *drame* which seem to justify Gaiffe's claim that the social context of this theatre was bourgeois. To cite just two such passages: in *Philosophe sans le savoir* (1765), by Michel Jean Sedaine, Monsieur Vanderk defended the merchant who, in his opinion, had not been sufficiently appreciated:

Quel état que celui d'un homme qui, d'un trait de plume, se fait obéïr d'un bout de l'univers à l'autre! ... Il a signé, cela suffit ... ce n'est pas un peuple, ce n'est pas une seule nation qu'il sert, il les sert toutes et en est servi; c'est l'homme de l'univers ... la guerre s'allume, tout s'embrase, l'Europe est divisée; mais ce négociant anglais, hollandais, ruse ou chinois, n'en est pas moins l'ami de mon cœur; nous sommes, sur la surface de la terre, autant de fils qui relient ensembles les nations, et les ramènent à la paix par la nécessité du commerce.[25]

And the reader of *Les deux Amis* (1770), by Pierre Augustin Caron de Beaumarchais (1732–99), encounters an even more vigorous assertion of the merchant's worth. No other member of society contributed as much to the state's economic vitality as he:

Je fais battre journellement deux cents Métiers dans Lyon. Le triple de bras est nécessaire aux apprêts de mes soies. Mes plantations de Muriers et mes Vers en occupent au tant. Mes envois se détaillent chez tous les Marchands du Royaume ... Et tout l'or que la guerre disperse, Messieurs, qui le fait rentrer à la paix? Qui osera disputer au commerce l'honneur de rendre à l'Etat épuisé le nerf et les richesses qu'il n'a plus? Tous les Citoyens sentent l'importance de cette tâche: le Négociant seul la remplit. Au moment que le Guerrier se repose, le Négociant a le bonheur d'être à son tour l'homme de la patrie.[26]

When we turn to the *Contes moraux* of Marmontel we encounter a similar idealization of middle-class life. Belzors, in 'La Bonne mère,' presented a concept of marriage that, because of its morality, won the love of Emilie. This character, since his name had no particle (in contrast to his rival, the Marquis de Verglan), appears to have been bourgeois. This might account for the fact that 'la nature avait été dirigée au bien dès l'enfance, jouissoit de l'avantage inestimable de pouvoir s'y abandonner sans précaution & sans contrainte.'[27] In 'La Mauvaise mère,' as we have already mentioned, Marmontel described the widow of a wealthy bourgeois who squandered all of her wealth on a son to whom she gave the aristocratic name, Monsieur l'Etang. The other son, who remained true to his bourgeois origins, was industrious and enterprising. Because he prospered he was able to rectify the wrongs of his brother by coming to the assistance of his mother. Marmontel's point is clear: the son who made a practical use of his energy and intelligence not only succeeded in the material sense, but also grew into a morally fit human being. 'L'Ecole des pères' makes the same point. The wife of a merchant considered her husband's occupation degrading and unworthy of her son. Since the son's fortune was secure, he should know how to 'en jouir noblement.' She therefore decided that she 'ne falloit jamais vivre avec ses égaux.'[28] By the time he was nineteen he had taken the name Monsieur de Volny, possessed a mistress whom he kept in an apartment, and he maintained elegantly dressed lackeys and a superb equipage. However, when his mother died, his frivolous and corrupt way of life came to an end: his father compelled him to enter the family business. In time he came to understand the merit of commercial life and was morally transformed. To be a merchant was to be virtuous.

While each of these examples represented an attempt to idealize the bourgeoisie, in fact such was not quite the case. The heroes in both *Philosophe sans le savoir* and *Les deux Amis* were not bourgeois, but rather nobles who had entered commerce. And, as John Lough has shown, the *drame* did not succeed in creating a literature that was middle class in the strict sense of the word.[29] The characters in this literature were, by and large, either aristocrats, or persons living on the fringe of the aristocracy. Authors sometimes introduced characters who seemed unaristocratic and from humble origins; then, in a dramatic turn, it was usually discovered that they did come from virtuous and worthy families of the provincial nobility who had fallen on hard times. An example was the heroine in Diderot's 'bourgeois' play, *Père de famille*. The heroine was an aristocrat; so too was the hero's father, M. D'Orbesson. Or, an author might not depict the social framework exactly. In his *drame*, *Beverly* (1768), Saurin did not specify the standing of his characters, but when the hero received 3,000,000 livres he proposed to buy back

cet antique héritage
Par mes pères transmis jusqu'à moi d'âge en âge,
Que j'ai vendu presque pour rien.[30]

The hero of this so-called 'bourgeois tragedy' engaged in a duel, and was an officer in the army. When we come to the Marquis de Longueil's *L'Orphelin anglais* (1769) we encounter a play in which a leading character was a commoner. In this work, set in England during the reign of Edward III, a carpenter's daughter, Mistress Molly, was married to another carpenter, Thomas Spencer. But it turned out that Spencer was actually the son of the Count of Gloucester, and in the final scene the king, touched by the heroine's self-sacrifice, elevated her to the nobility. In the dénouement, therefore, the commoner became an aristocrat. These examples, and others that could be cited, demonstrate that the *drame* did not depart very far from the classical literary propriety that required an aristocratic social framework. The *drame* did not succeed in its attempt to idealize the bourgeoisie, nor, as Lough has shown, was it presented to middle-class audiences. In fact, the social composition of audiences was substantially the same in the 1760s as in the 1660s.

But in Marmontel's 'La Bonne mère,' 'La Mauvaise mère,' and 'L'École des pères,' characters who actually belonged to the bourgeoisie were idealized. Marmontel's reason for idealizing these characters is important. He did so because he wanted to depict merchants who practised the virtues of thrift and industry, and received the material benefits of their efforts. In 'L'École des pères' Marmontel made the particular point that the son of a bourgeois ought not to enter into a life of aristocratic leisure and self-indulgence, but rather ought to learn his father's business. This theme did not appear accidentally, but in response to a debate in contemporary France over a project to create a commercial nobility.

By an interesting coincidence, in 1757, the very year in which Rousseau was working on *La Nouvelle Héloïse* and his two peasant novels, in which Diderot wrote *Père de famille*, and in which Marmontel began to publish his *Contes moraux* in the *Mercure*, the crown proposed the creation of a new class, a *noblesse commerçante*. This proposal, repeated in 1767, was not new. In fact, the monarchy had for centuries been aware of the value of commerce to the state. As early as the fifteenth century, royal preambles had proclaimed the value and honour of commerce.[31] Louis XI opened trade 'by sea, land, and inland waterways' to the nobility, in an attempt to draw them into the commercial life of France. But the creation of a *noblesse commerçante* required the co-operation of the bourgeoisie as well as that of the nobility. Under the plan the nobles could enter commerce without fear of derogation while bourgeois could be ennobled in return for services rendered to the state. The *Code Michau* of 1628 made overseas trade compatible with nobility, and at the same time conferred the privileges of nobility upon traders who would maintain merchant ships of two or three hundred tons for five years. Then, in 1701 the government issued an edict that opened up wholesale trade to the nobility and provided for the ennoblement of a sizeable number of merchants. Yet, a *noblesse commerçante* was not created at that time, nor would it be in 1757 or 1767.[32] Opposition was too great. Not surprisingly, nobles feared a plan which they believed threatened them with absorption by the bourgeoisie; to embrace the commercial life was to lose what was most esteemed among the nobility: the honour which was the exclusive attribute of the warrior class. Interestingly, merchants also opposed the plan for a *noblesse commerçante*. It was possible for well-to-do bourgeois to move into the nobility, by purchasing governmental offices conferring noble status. But the bourgeoisie, though ambivalent, tended to uphold the traditional, stratified social order. They did so because they esteemed the nobility, and wanted only the opportunity to become nobles themselves.

Now we can see how the proposal for a *noblesse commerçante* sheds light on 'bourgeois' literature. At least in part this literature supported the government's proposal, by dignifying bourgeois who served the country thereby increasing its wealth, and by portraying nobles who entered commerce. A year before the plan for a *noblesse commerçante* was introduced, Abbé Coyer wrote a treatise on the subject (entitled *La Noblesse commerçante*, 1756), a work which elicited considerable debate,[33] as did the actual proposal of 1757.[34] The merits of the merchant, on which the prosperity of France was thought largely to rest, were being discussed and enumerated at the very time that 'bourgeois' literature appeared. Without the departure from classical literary conventions this literature could hardly have taken shape, but these conventions had been discredited, and writers began, tentatively, to dignify the bourgeoisie.

In order to answer the question of whether the literature reflected a new sense of bourgeois class-consciousness, it is useful to look at the purpose for which it was written. This intent was didactic: to encourage the noble to enter commerce, or to persuade the merchant to recognize the dignity of his estate and improve himself both materially and morally, an improvement which would benefit his country. To write with such a purpose was to introduce into 'bourgeois' literature a tedious string of moralistic tableaux. We have seen that didactic scenes appeared in the literature of *sensibilité* in the first half of the eighteenth century, and that their function was to realize the moralistic possibilities of sensibility. The writer of 'bourgeois' literature adopted both this orientation and the affecting scenes that went with it. The result was a literature of propaganda.

The most perspicacious 'bourgeois' writers were well aware of its defects. In his *Essai sur le drame* (1767), Beaumarchais wrote that the 'drama which appeals to our emotions [and] concerns our daily lives is different. If loud laughter is the enemy of reflection, compassion, on the contrary, brings silence. It harbours us, it isolates us from everything. He who weeps at a spectacle is alone.'[35] By 1775 Beaumarchais had changed his mind: the *drame* was boring and there was 'no middle ground between comedy and tragedy.' His two *drames* were 'monstrous productions'; he would turn now to comedy. 'Ridiculous citizens and unhappy kings – there is your existing and possible theatre ...'[36] Diderot, the inventor of the *drame*, was no less conscious of its aesthetic failings. In his masterpiece, *Le Neveu de Rameau* (1762), which he did not publish, he had one side of himself enter into discussion with the other. The Bohemian was poised against the man of virtue.[37] The *toi*-Diderot revealed a world of nonconformity and 'shameless' freedom which was a 'living denial' of the moralistic world of the tendentious *moi*-Diderot. As Goethe said of *Le Neveu de Rameau*, it 'explodes like a bomb in the middle of French literature.' Among the rubble was the *drame* and its programme for an idealized bourgeois literature.[38]

Diderot's self-consciousness is an important key to the bourgeois literature which, in part, was his own handiwork. He was a propagandist, and he knew it. Diderot looked on the bourgeoisie as an outsider, although as a cutler's son he was himself bourgeois. But his ethic was not middle class, at least according to its usual descriptions.[39] Nor was Diderot aristocratic in outlook. He was an intellectual, and his literature was in large part a product of his ideology: as a *philosophe*, he would help reform society. His attempt to create a bourgeois literature stemmed from that ambition.

It is also safe to say that Diderot had internalized certain of his family's values, and it is reasonable to call these values middle class. To the extent that he did so his 'consciousness' was bourgeois. And this 'consciousness' undoubtedly contributed to his didactic literature, and particularly to *Père de famille*. To say this is not to say that such a work as *Père de famille* reflected the 'rise of the middle class' or a change in the 'economics of society.' Rather, it means that Diderot's father succeeded, up to a point, in his attempt to mould the values of his son after his own. But the Bohemian Diderot proves that *père* Diderot's success was at best only partial, for if Diderot supported middle-class morality in *Père de famille*, he made devastating attacks on it in other works.

In fact, there was no literature in eighteenth-century France that emerged spontaneously from what sociologists call the 'bourgeois spirit,' or that derived from what Marxists contend was a 'rising middle class.' In order to find an eighteenth-century literature that did reflect a bourgeois 'consciousness' it is necessary to turn to England. Robinson Crusoe is the perfect example as the novel of homo economicus. Not only did Defoe's hero pursue money but he also instinctively imposed order and stability upon nature. He did this as a living embodiment of economic individualism. In terming money 'the general denominating article in the world,' Defoe revealed the same outlook as that of his hero. *Robinson Crusoe* is a novel in which middle-class values have been internalized.

It is possible, then, to find an eighteenth-century literature which reflects what Plakhanov called a 'causal tie' between 'consciousness' and the 'economics of society.' But even here it is necessary to make some qualifications. *Robinson Crusoe* does not reflect only the 'rise of the middle class,' or a new stage in the history of capitalism. In order to understand the hero's ethic it is necessary to look to the Reformation, and more particularly to Puritanism, of which he was in many ways a product. Of course, the history of Puritanism was, to a degree that we shall never determine exactly, bound up with that of capitalism. But the point is that the hero's 'consciousness' is a product of his religious background as much as of the 'economics of society.' To a degree, then, Plekhanov's approach is valuable. As long as it looks for connections between social life and literature it makes an important contribution to literary criticism. But it establishes too narrow an analytical framework when it stresses the connection between 'consciousness,' the 'economics of society,' and literature.

When the 'rise of the middle class' is also thrown in, analysis gives way to dogmatism.

It is simply incorrect to see the middle class 'rising' from the Age of Reformation through the Age of Enlightenment, and the Revolution as a culmination of that social process. Marc Bloch has argued that Étienne Marcel, a fourteenth-century bourgeois who for a time headed the Estates General, and in that position set himself up as an enemy of the nobles, would have become a noble himself had he lived in the time of Louis XIV.[41] This implies a higher degree of middle-class consciousness, and also a keener hostility towards the aristocracy, in the fourteenth than in the seventeenth century. If anything, the aristocracy became more successful in imposing its values on the rest of society, and particularly on the bourgeoisie, during this period of four hundred years. And those values persisted tenaciously in the eighteenth century. To understand why this was so is to understand French history, and is a necessary preliminary if we are to explain the so-called 'bourgeois' literature that appeared in the eighteenth century.

The social organization of France played a critical role in preventing a 'spontaneous' bourgeois literature from developing. In England the highest stratum of the nobility, the peerage, entered and played a leading role in commerce, industry, and real estate at least as early as the seventeenth century.[42] Undoubtedly, the entrance of the highest nobility into these activities helped remove their fears of being socially misplaced. In the more stratified society of France, commerce and industry were thought to be degrading by both the aristocracy and bourgeoisie. This hindered the bourgeoisie from internalizing a middle-class ethic. In France under the Ancien Regime the bourgeoisie wanted most to purchase land[43] and offices,[44] particularly offices conferring titles of nobility, and to marry their children into the nobility. Obviously, the bourgeoisie tended to accept the social superiority of the aristocracy. It is not surprising, therefore, that they tried to emulate the aristocratic way of life. To the extent that eighteenth-century French literature reveals an internalized bourgeois outlook, this is the one which emerges. By prescribing the life of *tendresse* and refinement so admired by the bourgeoisie Marivaux was far closer to the realities of bourgeois life than was Diderot or Marmontel.

When, in the late 1750s, French literature did begin tentatively to idealize the bourgeoisie, its moral programme included compassion and a lofty view of marriage and the family. Moralistic tableaux, by affecting the reader, persuaded him of the importance of these virtues. Both the moral programme and the use of tableaux originated in the aristocratic literature of *sensibilité* in the first half of the eighteenth century. Not even the morality of 'bourgeois' literature was distinctively bourgeois. The single innovation of this literature was a hesitant attempt to dignify middle-class life, and this was merely an attempt, largely futile, to reorient the outlook of a class that above all prized landed property and the status that went with it.

In conclusion, the didacticism that was part and parcel of the literature of *sensibilité* did not have its roots in bourgeois society, but rather it emerged from an elitist, aristocratic milieu. Even the hero of the 'bourgeois' Revolution, Jean-Jacques Rousseau, wrote novels that idealized an organic, traditional society. While Rousseau did attack aristocratic morals, he did not condemn the nobility; on the contrary, his prescriptions for moral change within the aristocracy could only buttress the existing, stratified social order. To see in Rousseau the harbinger of a capitalistic, bourgeois world is to miss the point of his novels altogether. The thrust of Rousseau's novels, on which his fame largely rested before 1789, was to inject new life into the old order, not to destroy it. And even the literary idealization of the bourgeoisie in the second half of the eighteenth century did not result primarily from economic change, nor reflect a reorientation of the bourgeoisie.[45] In part, it issued from a propaganda campaign in which the government and intellectuals endeavoured to vitalize the economic life of France. To the extent that eighteenth-century French literature reveals internalized bourgeois values, that literature was sentimental, and its values were refinement, delicacy, *tendresse*, and compassion, all of which were aristocratic. If the commercial revival did elicit a literary response, it was probably conservative. The appeal to the simple life was not new in eighteenth-century literature, but it flourished as never before,[46] and for that reason might well reflect the rise of a rural and anti-capitalist outlook.

8

Social discontent
in French literature

While French literature from 1760 to 1789 did not mirror a rise of bourgeois social values, it did at times reflect bourgeois hostility toward a stratified social order, and in that sense it anticipated the Revolution. As Elinor Barber has shown, the bourgeoisie's feeling towards the social order was ambivalent, but they tended to accept it as long as it allowed them to move in the direction of noble status. When this became more difficult they became frustrated, and at this point the literature adopted a theme of protest against the social order. French literature had, however, criticized abuses of aristocratic life before bourgeois hostility came to the surface. From Marivaux in the 1730s, to Rousseau in the 1760s, moralistic literature often condemned corrupt aristocrats, though not the principle of aristocracy. By the 1770s, writers were attacking a society that they considered to be unjust and oppressive.

Jacob, in Marivaux's *Le Paysan parvenu* (1735–6), began his life story by saying: 'J'ai pourtant vu nombre de sots qui n'avaient et ne conaissaient point d'autre mérite dans le monde que celui d'être nés nobles, ou dans un rang distingué. Je les entendais mépriser beaucoup de gens qui valaient mieux qu'eux et cela seulement parce qu'ils n'étaient pas gentilshommes!'[1] When he became wealthy, Jacob went to Versailles. 'Je n'ai jamais oublié cette scene-là; je suis devenu riche aussi, et pour le moins autant qu'aucun de ces mesieurs dont le parle, et je suis encore a comprendre qu'il y ait des hommes dont l'âme devienne aussi cavalière que je le dis là, pour celle de quelque homme que ce soit.'[2] Jacob was angered by neither the idea of nobility, nor by the privileges of that class, but by the contempt with which he was viewed by some aristocrats. He did not condemn the social order, nor denounce the aristocracy. On the contrary, he accepted aristocratic values, and purchased a sword himself when he became prosperous. On encountering a skirmish with swords in which a gentleman was engaging three opponents, he hastily joined the underdog, crying 'Courage, monsieur, courage!' In his desire to live nobly, he dressed elegantly, employed a cook, and behaved generously.

Marivaux simultaneously idealized and criticized aristocratic life. Throughout his work there was an assumption that abuses had crept into gentle society. In *La Double inconstance*, the Seigneur said that 'L'ambition, c'est un noble orgeuil de s'élever.' When Arlequin remained unimpressed by this argument in favour of pride, the Seigneur showed his meanness by replying that a noble was 'plus craint de [ses] voisins.'[3] In the *Ile des exclaves* (1725), two nobles landed on an island governed by slaves, and when they were discovered, were placed under the authority of their servants. The servants jumped at this opportunity to unburden themselves of their pent-up grievances: 'Voilà de nos gens qui nous méprisent dans le monde, qui font les fiers, qui nous maltraitent, et qui nous regardent comme des vers de terre.'[4] Marivaux was not condemning aristocratic honour, nor was he arguing for democracy. He was simply stating that a noble title did not justify arrogance and unfairness. Marivaux's ideal, the *honnête homme*, was not only polite and refined, but sincere, kind-hearted, and generous as well.

We have already seen that the idea of the *honnête homme* lost much of its traditional moral content after 1660. Decency and kindliness were retained, but Christian morality was not followed in the manner of the *honnête homme* of the early seventeenth century. While Marivaux did not criticize the concept of the *honnête homme*, even in its 'relaxed' eighteenth-century form, he did censure another social type, the *petit-maître*. When this term first came into use (probably during the Fronde), it had a military connotation, but by the 1680s the emphasis on valour that had been attached to it gave way to an emphasis on gallantry. The same shift in moral orientation that produced the new type of *honnête homme* also produced the dandy. The crystallization of the dandy as a social type represents a sharper departure from traditional aristocratic morality than was the case with the 'relaxing' of the *honnête homme*. Moreover, while the term *honnête homme* continued to have a favourable meaning, *petit-maître* implied social criticism.

By the time of Marivaux's *Le Petit-maître corrigé* (1734), some thirty plays had depicted this social type.[5] The hero of Marivaux's play,

Rosimond, was a provincial noble who went to Paris, became debauched, and then returned home. His mother had arranged for him to marry Hortense, the daughter of a neighbouring count. Rosimond was basically good, and was attracted to Hortense, but before he could marry her, he had to abandon his corrupt way of life. He disdained marital love, and so Hortense postponed the marriage. Then, as a result of an intrigue carried out by Rosimond's Parisian mistress and her gallant friend Dorante, the engagement was broken and Rosimond disowned. All that was left to him was moral reform, which meant a softening of the heart. He had learned the artificial manners of Paris: now he must forget them. As his love for Hortense increased, his innate goodness emerged, and his artificiality dissolved. A moral, loyal heroine was the instrument by which this petit-maître was corrected.

The reform of the petit-maître was the subject of the Confessions du Comte de *** (1742), by Charles Pinot Duclos and of the Histoire de la félicité (1751), by Abbé Voisenon. In each of these works the hero adopted the artificial ways of corrupt people, but beneath the super-sophisticated veneer of the petit-maître, was a kind heart. Once that heart was touched, artificiality was replaced by moral goodness. This brings us back to the moral significance of sensibilité : to feel and to sympathize was the result of innate goodness. In fact, the emergence of sensibilité must be seen as part of a reaction against manners that were thought to be overly sophisticated, and morals that were thought to be cynical and implies a criticism of a certain segment of aristocratic society. The whole thrust of Marivaux's moral position was to correct abuses, not to lay the foundations for a new social order.[6]

Rousseau took the same position, in both La Nouvelle Héloïse and Emile. In Emile the hero was sent to the country for his education so that he might escape the corruption of the beau monde and the miserable lackeys who were exceeded in decadence only by their masters. Much of the stage of La Nouvelle Héloïse is set in the countryside, again revealing Rousseau's contempt for a society perverted by artificiality. This society was not exclusively aristocratic. It was simply urban, and what Rousseau despised most about it was its acceptance of certain aristocratic values.

Several letters written by Saint-Preux in Paris describe the tyranny of aristocratic life. The robe noble assumed the air of a cavalier, the financier imitated a seigneur, the bishop spoke the language of a gallant, even a simple artisan tried to behave like an homme de Palais.[7] Whatever fashion was taken up at court was immediately adopted throughout Paris. People of all classes wore the same clothing, which would have made it difficult to distinguish a *duchesse* from a *bourgeoise* had not the former discovered arts that the latter would not have dared to imitate. The incessant pursuit of fashion led to overrefinement. 'Leur parure est plus recherchée que magnifique.'[8] A Parisian lady appeared to be more phantom than real. '[Son] hauteur, son ampleur, sa démarche, sa taille, sa gorge, ses couleurs, son air, son regard, ses propos, ses manières, rien de tout cela n'est à elle, et si vous la voyiez dans son état naturel, vous ne pourriez le reconnoître.' Such artificial people considered their graces seductive, and their art of pleasing perfection itself, whereas the truth was that they received people with shocking rudeness, their coquetry was repulsive, and their manners completely without modesty.

Parisian morals were as corrupt as Parisian manners. The scourge of 'tous ces gens si dissipés [était] l'ennui.'[10] Women preferred to be amused rather than loved. In fact, the words love and lover had been banished from intimate vocabulary, and the order of the natural sentiments had been reversed. Girls could not love: this right had been reserved for married women – as long as they did not love their husbands. Adultery was considered normal, but not even illicit relationships were sincere. A '*liaison de galanterie*' hardly outlasted the first visit, and since husbands and wives scarcely knew one another, it was little wonder that parents were strangers to their children.

Interestingly, in spite of his condemnation of contemporary manners and morals Rousseau held an idealized view of aristocratic life, and he attempted to rehabilitate an earlier aristocratic pattern of ethical conduct. By scraping away the crust of artificiality that had grown around the *honnête homme*, he hoped to restore a useful social ideal. Thus, he criticized mockery as the 'poison du bon sens et de l'honnêteté.'[11] When Rousseau recommended a 'certaine *disinvoltura* qui n'est pas *dépourvue* de grâces,'[12] he had in mind the seventeenth-century concept of the *honnête homme*. His own society, so devoted to secret liaisons, was no longer *honnête*. 'Amour' required modesty, but 'la pudeur [était] en dérision.'[13] In idealizing modesty, Rousseau again acknowledged his indebtedness to the seventeenth-century view of *honnêteté*. 'Quel charme peut avoir une vie privée à la fois d'amour et d'honnêteté?'[14]

Rousseau's desire to revive the early concept of *honnêteté* was shared by Diderot, Helvétius, Voltaire, Vauvenargues, D'Alembert, and Duclos.[15] Their attempt to reform aristocratic behaviour was an admission of abuses in the aristocratic way of life. In fostering the return to seventeenth-century *honnêteté* these reformers voiced the need for change, but their acceptance of the existing social order was still intact. In spite of criticism in literature of their contemporary way of life, the eighteenth-century aristocracy did not come under widespread attack.

There were, however, a few sharp and embittered attacks on upper society, especially in the literature of the last decade of the Ancien Régime. Probably the best known example of social criticism is Beaumarchais' *Le Mariage de Figaro* (written in 1778, first performed in 1784). In this play Figaro, an energetic servant, became discontented with his aristocratic employer, and with the principle of nobility. On several occasions he gave vent to his anger by asserting his own superiority.

LE COMTE Un réputation détestable!

FIGARO Et si je vaux mieux qu'elle. Y a-t-il beaucoup de seigneurs qui puissent en dire autant?

LE COMTE Cent fois je t'ai vu marcher à la fortune, et jamais aller droit.

FIGARO Comment voulez-vous? la foule est là: chacun veut courir: on se presse, on pousse, on coudoie, on renverse, arrive qui peut, le reste est écrasé?[16] ... Parce que vous êtes un grand seigneur, vous croyez un grand génie! ... Noblesse, fortune, un rang, des places, tout cela rend si fier! Qu'avez-vous fait pour tant de biens? Vous vous êtes donné la peine de naître, et rien de plus. Du reste, homme assez ordinaire; tandis que moi, morbleu! perdu dans la foule obscure, il m'a fallu déployer plus de science et de calculus, pour subsister seulement, qu'on n'en a mis depuis cent ans à gouverner toutes les Espagnes.[17]

Figaro went beyond denouncing the principle of legal privilege; he also attacked a legal system which favoured the nobility. The law was 'indulgente aux grands, dure aux petits.'[18] He attacked censorship, which prohibited *roturiers* from being critical of existing conditions, or even from writing about subjects of interest to them. 'J'écris sur la valeur de l'argent et sur son produit net: sitôt je vois du fond d'un fiacre baisser pour moi le point d'un chateau fort, à l'entrée duquel je laissai l'espérence et la liberté.'[19] And, in a particularly devastating passage, Figaro attacked the very substructure of the Ancien Régime: 'L'usage ... est souvent un abus.'[20]

As Kenneth McKee has shown, there were several anticipations of Figaro's diatribes in the theatre of Marivaux.[21] Another Figaro type was the hero in Diderot's novel, *Jacques le fataliste* (written in 1773, published in 1796), who also dominated his aristocratic master. However what separated Figaro from the characters of Marivaux and from Jacques was his rage, which was, to a large extent a reflection of Beaumarchais' own anger. Beaumarchais, born in Paris in 1732, was a watchmaker's son. He invented a new type of watch escapement, and when it was pirated he published a grievance in the *Mercure* that brought him to the attention of the court. He made watches for Madame de Pompadour and Louis xv and styled himself watchmaker to the king. He cut an assured figure at Versailles, and moved easily and surely up the social ladder. He obtained a court office, made a socially advantageous marriage, and assumed the aristocratic name of de Beaumarchais. However, when he tried to purchase the office of secretary to the king, which would have conferred nobility, a court cabal blocked the transaction. Clearly, Beaumarchais started out as a socially ambitious commoner who dearly wanted to become an aristocrat.[22] That his ambition was thwarted contributed directly to his own hostility, and to his projection of it through Figaro.

Beaumarchais' frustration at court was no historical accident. It resulted from social and political forces that eventually contributed significantly to the destruction of the ancien Regime. We have seen that the French bourgeoisie accepted the social order since they could themselves move into the nobility. The society of France was stratified, but an ambitious bourgeois could cut through the legal line that separated the third estate from the second. An office conferring nobility had been the commoner's passport to an elitist world, but towards the end of Louis xv's reign, it became more difficult to obtain.[23] The nobility tried, with considerable success, to seal off the avenues through which the bourgeoisie had for centuries moved into their ranks. The two French nobilities, robe and sword, had joined forces in the first half of the eighteenth century, and together had waged a campaign to protect their own interests.[24] In order to hinder the encroachments of the mobile bourgeoisie, the nobility thought it necessary to monopolize high offices, and to prevent the sale of offices conferring nobility. Both strategies were carried out with substantial success, and as a result members of the bourgeoisie who hoped to become aristocrats found it more and more difficult to do so. When it became impossible, social discontent came to the surface.

This discontent is best revealed in *Paul et Virginie* (1787), by Jacques Henri Bernardin de Saint-Pierre (1738–1814). Romantic and adventurous, Bernardin de Saint-Pierre did not embark on the road to Versailles. Instead, he travelled widely, visiting at various times Malta, St Petersburg, Warsaw, Dresden, and Berlin. He went to Turkey, which he considered to be the finest country in the world. The exotic island of Mauritius, where he lived for three years, and which was then known as 'Île de France,' was the setting of *Paul et Virginie*. Two mothers, Madame de la Tour and Marguérite, and their children, Paul and Virginie, lived there amidst benevolent nature, in isolation from France and its decadent society. Every contact with France had brought distress to these virtuous women. Madame de la Tour, who belonged to a powerful aristocratic family, had married a commoner and been disowned as a result, so she went to Île de France. She was joined there by Marguérite, a young peasant woman from Brittany who had been seduced and betrayed by a noble who had promised to marry her, and whose child she was about to bear. Madame de la Tour also was pregnant, so the two women, feeling that they had been drawn together by fate, decided to live in adjacent huts and raise their children side by side. 'L'une se rappelant que ses maux étaient venus d'avoir négligé l'hymen, et l'autre d'en avoir subi les lois: l'une de s'être élevée au-dessus de sa condition, et l'autre d'en être descendue; mais elles se consolaient en pensant qu'un jour leurs enfants, plus heureux, jouiraient à la fois, loin des cruels préjugés de l'Europe, des plaisirs de l'amour et du bonheur de l'égalité.'[25] These two women duly gave birth to their children: Marguérite to Paul, and Madame de la Tour to Virginie. Both grew up strong and healthy, enjoying opportunities unknown to Europeans. 'Vous autres, Européens, dont l'esprit se remplit, dès l'enfance, de tant de préjugés controires au bonheur, vous ne pouvez concevoir que la nature puisse donner tant de lumières et de plaisirs. Votre âme, circonscrite dans une petite sphère de connaissance humaines, atteint bientôt le terme de ses jouissances artificielles: mais la nature et la cœur sont inépuisables.'[26]

The only traces of corruption on the island were two Europeans, a vicious plantation owner, and the governor, who sent Virginie back to France against her will in answer to her aristocratic aunt's request that she return to her own country to enjoy the benefits of a superior civilization. Of course, the girl was completely unprepared for the hypocrisy and corruption she encountered in France, and she returned to Île de France. In contrast to the corrupt plantation owner and the decadent governor of the island were the innocent natives.

On Île de France, Paul met an old man who told him about the hopeless corruption of wealthy French society:

Ils sont la plupart usé sur tous les plaisirs, par cela même qu'ils ne leur coûtent aucunes peines. N'avez-vous pas éprouvé que le plaisir du repos s'achète par la fatigue; celui de manger, par la faim; celui de boire, par la soif? Eh bien, celui d'aimer et d'être aimé ne s'acquiert que par une multitude de privations et de sacrifices. Les richesses ôtent aux riches tous ces plaisirs-là en prevenant leurs besoins. Joignez à l'ennui qui suit leur satiété, l'orgueil qui naît de leur opulence, et que la moindre privation blesse, lors même que les plus grandes jouissances ne le flattent plus. Le parfum de mille roses ne plaît qu'un instant ; mais la douleur que cause une seule de leurs épines dure longtemps après sa piqûre. Un mal au milieu des plaisirs est pour les riches une épine au milieu des fleurs. Pour les pauvres, au contraire, un plaisir au milieu des maux est une fleurs. Pour les pauvres, au contraire, un plaisir au milieu des maux est une fleur au milieu des épines ... Mais ces extrêmes sont également difficiles, à supporter aux hommes, dont le bonheur consiste dans la médiocrité et la vertu.[27]

Furthermore, the nobility oppressed the bourgeoisie:

LE VIEILLARD O mon ami! ne m'avez-vous pas dit que vous n'aviez pas de naissance ?

PAUL Ma mère me l'a dit ; car, pour moi, je ne sais ce que c'est que la naissance. Je ne me suis jamais aperçu que j'en eusse moins qu'un autre, ni que les autres en eussent plus que moi.

LE VIEILLARD Le défaut de naissance vous ferme en France le chemin aux grands emplois. Il y a plus : vous ne pouvez même être admis dans aucun corps distingué.

PAUL Vous m'avez dit plusieurs fois qu'une des causes de la grandeur de la France était que le moindre sujet pouvait y parvenir à tout, et vous m'avez cité beaucoup d'hommes célèbres qui, sortis de petits états, avaient fait honneur à leur patrie. Vous vouliez donc tromper mon courage ?

LE VIEILLARD Mons fils, jamais je ne l'abattrai. Je vous ai dit la vérité sur les temps passés ; mais les choses sont bien changées à présent : tout est devenue vénal en France ; tout y est aujourd'hui le patrimoine d'un petit nombre de familles, ou le partage des corps. Le roi est un soleil que les grands et les corps environnent comme des nuages ; il est presque impossible qu'un de ses rayons tombe sur vous. Autrefois, dans une administration moins compliquée, on a vu ces phénomènes. Alors les talents et le mérite se sont développés de toutes parts, comme des terres nouvelles qui, venant à être défrichées, produisent avec tout leur suc. Mais les grands rois qui savent connaître les hommes et les choisir sont rares. Le vulgaire des rois ne se laisse aller qu'aux impulsions des grands et des corps qui les environnent.

PAUL Mais je trouverai peut-être un de ces grands qui me protégera ?

LE VIEILLARD Pour être protégé des grands, il faut servir leur ambition ou leurs plaisirs. Vous n'y réussirez jamais, car vous êtes sans naissance, et vous avez de la probité.

PAUL Mais je ferai des actions si courageuses, je serai si fidèle à ma parole, si exact dans mes devoirs, si zélé et si constant dans mon amitié, que je mériterai d'être adopté par quelqu'un d'eux, comme j'ai vu que cela se pratiquait dans les histoires anciennes que vous m'avez fait lire.

LE VIEILLARD O mon ami! chez les Grecs et chez les Romains, même dans leur décadence, les grands avaient du respect pour la vertu; mais nous avons eu une foule d'hommes célèbres et tout genre, sortis des classes du peuple, et je n'en sache pas un seul qui ait été adopté par une grande maison. La vertu, sans nos rois, serait condamnée en France à être éternellement plébéienne. Comme je vous l'ai dit, ils la mettent quelquefois en honneur lorsqu'ils l'aperçoivent; mais, aujourd'hui, les distinctions qui lui étaient réservées ne s'accordent plus que pour l'argent ...

PAUL Que je suis infortuné! tout me repousse.[28]

How interesting, and revealing, that the most outspoken criticism of French society in eighteenth-century literature expressed rage over the closing of the avenues of social mobility! Even as he condemned 'corrupt' France, Bernardin de Saint-Pierre looked back with at least a touch of nostalgia to an age when the king favoured men of merit and gave them the honour that was their due.

9

Erotic love in
eighteenth-century painting

Love, marriage, and the family were represented in eighteenth-century French painting in much the same fashion as in literature, although this is not to say that artistic and literary conventions coincided. Looking first at the depiction of erotic love in art, we discover three genres. The first, the pastoral genre, or *fête galante*, had no exact counterpart in literature, and neither did mythological paintings of gods and goddesses in love. But the third genre, bedroom art, represented love as entirely physical, and frequently portrayed intrigue and infidelity in much the same manner as the *roman érotique*. In this chapter the sources and development of these three genres will be examined. Since eighteenth-century artists innovated little in the mythological genre, we can concentrate on the representation of love in pastoral and bedroom art.

By creating what was almost a new type of pastoral art, the *fête galante*, Antoine Watteau (1684–1721) became an artistic innovator of the first rank. It is interesting that Watteau seems to have understood his own importance. In one of his latest and most glorious works, L'Enseigne de Gersaint (1720), two workmen watch as a third puts a painting into a box for shipment. An elegant lady, a client of the art shop shown in the painting, is also looking on. Why do these people pause to study the boxing of a picture? The answer lies in the subject: Louis XIV, as solemn and majestic as the age over which he presided. In consigning Louis XIV to a crate, Watteau indicates his own position. More than any other artist, he created a style that departed from the formal, academic, classical art to which the Sun King gave his official stamp of approval. Thus, as the lady looks at Louis over her shoulder she extends her hand to a gentleman who will lead her to the sales counter where other clients are scrutinizing a painting of nudes in a pastoral setting. In this work, and in the paintings on the walls above, glowing colours enhance the voluptuousness of the nymphs and goddesses. Mars has left the field to Venus. The refinement of the *fête galante* has replaced the grandiloquence of an earlier generation.

Once again, we encounter the dialectic of style. On one side was classicism, on the other, rococo. In a sense, the rococo can be seen as a victory of colour over design, of *rubénisme* over *poussinisme*, and Watteau acknowledged his debt to Rubens by showing some of his works on the walls of Gersaint's shop. But Watteau did not need to revive Rubens because that had been done before he ever set brush on canvas. Members of the Academy had championed the great Flemish artist as early as 1671, and by 1699 the *rubénistes* had achieved a secure position.

Under Louis xiv the 'official' style of the Academy, besides emphasizing design over colour, was grand, majestic, pompous, elevated, and sonorous in its rhetoric, and especially appropriate to noble subjects. Owing to the close connection between the Academy and the crown, it is not surprising that historical subjects were given official encouragement. The heroic achievements of the past were considered proper for the age of the Sun King. Classical mythology and classical history provided a vast store of subjects worthy of embellishing the palaces of Louis xiv. A fine example of official painting is Alexandre et Porus (before 1673, Plate 1) an immense (15 feet by 41 feet) tableau by Charles Le Brun, the head of the Academy.[1] It shows the annihilation of a rival army by Alexander's warriors, mounted on magnificent horses. Like supermen, they hack and slay, creating a sea of carnage. Officers glower solemnly at the scene, and in front of them is Alexander, in a shaft of light that focuses attention upon his person. Seated on a calm, even serious horse, Alexander extends a well-muscled, magnanimous arm to Porus, his defeated and injured rival. Porus, a brave warrior himself, looks at Alexander with a mixture of awe and reverence. He has met his master, and knows it.

Historical subjects did not disappear from rococo art, but they received less attention and were painted in a different style. The anti-classicism of the rococo is most apparent, however, in the *fête galante*. When Watteau was asked by the Academy to present a work that would change his status from associate to member, he executed L'Embarquement pour Cythère (actually, the departure from Cythera). When it approved this work in 1717, the Academy gave official sanction to the *fête galante*.

The pastoral theme was, of course, one of the oldest in European literature. It had been used in the mime before the time of Theocritus.[2] Virgil dispensed with the realistic descriptions of nature which had been present in Theocritus, and conjured up instead 'an imaginary realm of perfect bliss.'[3] In the ideal, bucolic world imagined by Virgil shepherds enjoyed the fruits of an endlessly bountiful nature. Such a careless existence was filled with leisure, and leisure was the occasion for love. The sweetness and sensuousness of Virgil's Sicilian groves contributed to the refined eroticism that runs through the *Eclogues*. Virgil was still read in the Middle Ages, and contemporary poets did write pastoral verse, but in a style that suited their purpose. Claudian (fifth century) tied nature to love, but Christian poet that he was,[4] wrapped his writing in allegory in using the pastoral theme to achieve his didactic objective. By the thirteenth century, the pastoral was joined to courtly-chivalric style, and this new literary mixture became a device to free eroticism from the rigid and conventional doctrines of courtly love.[5] Then, in Honoré d'Urfé's pastoral work, *L'Astrée*, love became the central theme of the French novel. While it had been prominent in earlier novels, it did not dominate the literature until the seventeenth century.

The pastoral subject had a somewhat different history in painting than in literature. In France, bucolic motifs were common in the seventeenth century. Two of Poussin's most famous works, both entitled Et in Arcadia Ego (1630 and c. 1650), captured Virgilian nostalgia by showing classical figures standing pensively by the tomb of a departed friend. In Apollon amoureux de Daphné (1664, Plate 2) Poussin treated love in a pastoral setting, but the underlying subject of this work, which is highly philosophical, is life and death. Throughout his pastoral paintings Poussin took his subjects from the Bible or from classical history and mythology.

A work that anticipates Watteau's *fêtes galantes* more closely than Poussin's pastoral painting, although it is earlier and contains no specific reference to love, is Giorgione's Fête champêtre (before 1510, Plate 3). This painting has a sense of freedom but the setting is without specific classical allusion. Two the four figures are nudes, and two are Venetians. The pastoral theme is only partly present in Rubens' Garden of Love (1632–4, Plate 4), yet for our purpose this is an extremely interesting work, and one that was definitely known to Watteau. Rubens depicted love in a garden, and the lovers are his own contemporaries. Indeed, the couple standing on the left is Rubens himself and his second wife. Rubens extends his hand to his wife, and a putto pushes her toward him and love. Behind

Rubens an amorous couple lies on the grass, and a lady and gentleman enter the garden from a stairway. They do not yet hold hands, but the enchantment of the garden should soon bring them together. At the centre of a shrine to love stands a statue of a god and goddess, which is in marked contrast to the delicate, courtly, considerate figures in the garden. The ample thighs of the goddess are matched by the backside of the god, whose male shape represents the elemental life force of nature, which is further evoked by the dynamism of the composition.

It is clear that in turning to the *fête galante* Watteau drew from many sources. The pastoral tradition in literature had always been associated with love. In French painting love was also connected to the pastoral tradition, but the lovers were gods and goddesses. It was in Italian and Flemish painting that pastoral love was de-mythologized, and in Rubens, signs of both Watteau's colourism and certain of his motifs are present.[6] The reclining couple in the Garden of Love could almost be by Watteau.

Yet how different is the over-all effect of the 'Garden of Love' from Watteau's *fêtes galantes*. Looking at the Assemblée dans un Parc (c. 1717, Plate 5) for instance, we see one couple strolling, arm-in-arm, with heads turned toward each other. To their right are reclining figures. Men reach out towards passive or gently resisting ladies and in the background romantic couples surround the base of a tree. Any of these couples could be from the Garden of Love, but neither the mood nor the atmosphere is the same. A soft languor pervades the work; all is calm and reposed. There is none of the dynamism of Rubens, and none of the sexuality suggested by the shrine of love statue. Watteau's refined way of depicting love is nowhere more apparent than in his reception piece, L'Embarquement pour Cythère (1717, plate 6), in which the sun is setting at the end of the day, and the lovers must leave Cythera. A gilded boat is prepared to carry them back to reality. One couple rises from the turf, and another, already moving toward the boat, glances backward, nostalgically, at lovers seated with Cupid below a rose-decked statue of Venus. Cupid tugs at the lady's dress, indicating that she too must depart, and her downturned face is sad. Reality cannot match the bliss and beauty of the enchanted isle of love.

How did Watteau develop his poetic conception and artistic representation of perfect love? It would seem that finally, after 1700 years, Virgilian love had received pictorial expression. As in Virgil, Watteau's stylized landscape and languid atmosphere provide the ideal setting for love; it took a great poet-painter to capture on canvas the vision of one of the great pagan poets. Yet, Watteau's *fêtes galantes* are unmistakably

French, and to understand this artist is to understand in precisely what sense they are French. In the first place, the *fête galante* must be seen as part of a widespread cultural reaction against the heroic, pompous age of Louis xiv. In creating a new way of representing love Watteau developed an art that was anti-classical, in the sense that it was a reaction to the official style long championed by the Academy. The Academy had given its support to the *grand goût*; Watteau turned away from the grand style, and in so doing worked in a genre, the *fête galante*, which was appropriate to the delicacy and refinement of his artistic sensibilities. When Venus occupied the field left vacant by Mars, she was as perfect in her femininity as her predecessor was in his martial masculinity. Watteau realized his vision of love not only because he was a great poet, but also, and more concretely, because he was French and because he belonged to a culture that, in rejecting the values and style of an earlier generation, was creating its own forms of artistic expression. One of the most characteristic of these forms was the *fête galante*. Watteau did not evoke Virgilian love because he had read and understood Virgil; on the contrary, his biographer, the Comte de Caylus, found it necessary to apologize for the poverty of his education.[7] Watteau's vision was the product of a combination of his own genius and the cultural background against which his art must be viewed.

Since Watteau's work was so characteristically French it might seem contradictory that he sometimes clothed his figures in the Italian costumes of the *Commedia del' Arte*. But it was not. After long popularity and success, Louis xiv banned the Italians in 1697. According to Saint-Simon, the Italians were given to near obscenity and impiety, and even went so far as to mock Madame de Maintenon in a play entitled *La Fausse Prude*. When the Italian troop returned to Paris after Louis' death a number of French authors wrote plays for them which were far more innovative than those written for the *Comédie française*. In comedy, playwrights who reacted against tradition gravitated towards the *Italiens*. They initiated a rehabilitation of the passions and of the view that man was entitled to happiness, a large part of which was love. The type of love depicted by this theatre was *sensible*, sincere, and a delicate blend of *cœur and esprit*. The main elements of Marivaudian love were present in comedies written for and performed by the *Italiens*; and, in fact, Marivaux himself wrote largely for this performing group.[8]

Indeed, Marivaux and Watteau touched at many points. In portraying the first stirrings of love, Marivaux revealed the movement of the heart, and the rationale behind it. A balance between *cœur and esprit* was ideally suited to Marivaux's purpose: he was above all interested in nascent love, the gentle awakening appropriate to the virgin. Watteau's artistic temperament led him to portray nascent, *sensible* love as well. In his *fêtes galantes* the stirrings of the heart are warm and sweet, but always measured. A lover's outreached hand meets gentle resistance, and when he is received it is because of his delicacy. When a couple recline on the turf they share a happiness that is emotional rather than physical. Watteau struck the same balance as Marivaux; for each, love was refined and delicate.

We have seen that Marivaux had connections with the *précieuses*, which were reflected in his view of love. The same was true of Watteau.[9] The lovers who must leave Cythera are nostalgic; the poignancy that pervades the Embarquement stems from the knowledge that reality is less attractive than the enchanted isle. Reality is not perfect, and neither is real, physical love. In refining love Watteau looked back to the seventeenth century, and particularly, to the *précieuses*. Like Marivaux, Watteau was a member of the late *précieux* salon of Madame de Lambert.[10] He was another transitional figure who turned against the heroism, pomp, and formalism of the *grand goût*. He created a new style by eliminating all coarseness from love and purifying it. In developing his style Watteau simultaneously reacted against, but remained connected to, the seventeenth century. French culture contributed to the development of Watteau's art. It provided a style which an innovator would reject and at the same time a path along which he would move, and it was followed by both Marivaux and Watteau.

French artists worked in the pastoral genre throughout the eighteenth century. They tended to depict love in a refined and delicate way, in the manner of Watteau. The *fêtes galantes* of both Pater and Lancret reflect Watteau's direct influence on these artists. François Boucher (1703–70), a far more independent spirit, imprinted his own personality on his Berger et bergères (n.d., Plate 7), which could hardly be more delicate. Indeed, Boucher gives the lovers almost the appearance of porcelain. There is no coarseness in the Berger et bergères nor in the marvellous Grasse Panels (1771–3, Plates 8–11), by Jean-Honoré Fragonard (1732–1806). In La Poursuite a boy, flower in hand, chases a girl, and in L'Escalade she receives him willingly as he joins her in a garden. La Déclaration d'amour shows the girl reading a love letter as her beau lays his head upon her shoulder, and in L'Amant couronné she holds a wreath over his head, acknowledging his victory. Amorous suggestions abound in these four paintings. They portray the stages of love from pursuit to victory, with statues of Cupid and Venus encouraging the couple along the path of love. But there is nothing physical or even remotely coarse about the

Grasse Panels. Nature is highly stylized, the trees resemble fountains, and the lovers seem equally imaginary. The girl in La Poursuite is obviously posed; she is not really running from the boy, but moving across a stage in a patently theatrical gesture. In fact, this painting is analogous to a play, even more to a comic opera. Fragonard's depiction of love has all the conventionality of an aria, and none of the realism of physical love. The Grasse Panels reveal the way in which a great painter accepted the limits of an artistic convention and, at the same time, placed upon the convention the stamp of his own genius.

It is interesting that in their pastoral paintings neither Boucher nor Fragonard departed from the refinement associated with the pastoral genre since the time of Watteau, for both artists were masters of erotic suggestion, if not direct statement. The delightful girl in Boucher's Femme nue étendue: Louise O'Murphy (1751, Plate 12) lies stomach down on a couch, her legs apart. This position, often painted by Boucher, evokes a sensuality lacking in the more typical frontal pose. Kenneth Clark has shown that in antiquity the back view of the nude symbolized lust, and that before the eighteenth century it was seldom represented.[11] In Boucher's mythological paintings, such as Léda et le cygne (c. 1740, Plate 13), this position appears less erotic than in Femme nue étendue because the nude is stylized. Clark contends that Boucher reduced his nudes to useful, highly conventional formulae. But in Femme nue étendue Boucher turned from mythology to the bedroom and he rendered the female anatomy in a convincing way.[12] The combination of pose, realistic depiction, and bedroom setting make Femme nue étendue an erotic painting; the girl in this work is more naked than nude.

When Fragonard worked in the mythological genre, as in La Bacchante endormie (c. 1770, Plate 14), he accepted the conventions long associated with the painting of nudes. This goddess is ravishingly beautiful, but she is a poetic vision more than a living person. The naked girl in La Dormeuse (c. 1770, Plate 15), resembles the goddess in La Bacchante. She too, is asleep, and her head is tilted in a similar manner. But stylization and conventional posing have disappeared from this work. The brushwork is specific, highlighting surface lines and anatomical parts which were smoothed over in La Bacchante. Moreover, the girl's bed is rumpled. Like Boucher's art, Fragonard's became erotic when he turned from mythology to the bedroom.

By about 1760 a new genre appeared in French painting, as artists began to depict real people engaged in love in contemporary surroundings. To show the actuality of love it was necessary to depart from artistic conventions that encouraged stylization, and emphasis came to be placed on frivolous incidents that would occur in real life. In portraying the game of love, artists had ample opportunity to raise a smile or elicit laughter. The bedroom art (for this is what we shall call the genre, even though it is not entirely accurate) of the period 1760–89 is light, amusing, and witty.

The usual setting is the boudoir, though sometimes a barn or a peasant's dwelling. In Fragonard's L'Armoire (before 1778, Plate 16) a peasant boy has been caught with his girl friend. Parents and a younger sister and brother stare at the embarrassed couple, a dog is barking, and the bed is rumpled. It might well be an actual peasant scene. L'Armoire is not a condemnation of peasant morality, but rather a humorous representation of embarrassed lovers, and a witty commentary on the pastoral genre. Unlike the ethereal love of the *fête galante*, love in L'Armoire was realistic.

For Fragonard, rural life resembled life in town: people everywhere knew love. Yet, as he showed in his depiction of the boudoir, the social context of love did differ. In Le Baiser à la dérobée (c. 1788, Plate 18) a boy steals a kiss from a girl, whose mother is seen conversing with friends in another room. The scene has shifted to a bedroom in Le Verrou (c. 1772, Plate 17), as the boy reaches for the latch to prevent the struggling girl from leaving the room. The tasteful and costly clothing and furnishings in these works indicate social refinement and an upper-class setting.

The *petits-maîtres* also represented upper-class love. They were not considered the top artists of the day, did not receive big commissions, and with a few exceptions, were not members of the Academy. They were mainly designers, working in media such as pastel and gouache rather than oil. Many of their originals were copied by engravers, and it was through prints that they were best known. Often these prints were used as illustrations for books.

There is a significant connection between book illustration and bedroom artists. It would appear that themes from the *romans érotiques* provided the subject matter for bedroom art, even if it were not specifically intended to illustrate scenes from novels. That the popularity of erotic literature contributed to the emergence of bedroom art is not surprising. Because of the traditional subject of the novel, it was relatively easy for the eighteenth-century author to describe the game of love. Novels had always treated love, intrigue, and adultery. Such a work as La Princesse de Clèves already contained many of the elements of the *roman érotique*, and, in a sense, the eighteenth-century novelist had only to elaborate the theme of the classical *nouvelle*. Of course, he wrote with different assumptions and with a new purpose, thereby transforming his subject, but there was continuity from the *nouvelle* to the *roman érotique*. However there is no such continuity between the representation of love in seventeenth-century painting and the bedroom art of the eighteenth century. When the seventeenth-century artist portrayed love, his context was historical or mythological, and for this reason he left a legacy in the form of artistic conventions that the eighteenth-century artist could not easily inherit. In order to represent love in a contemporary context it was necessary to invent a new genre, and this was done at least partly through the influence of literature. The bedroom art of 1760–89 represents the very type of love that had already achieved a high level of popularity with the reading public.

In both the *roman érotique* and bedroom art the boudoir was furnished with sumptuous beds, couches, erotic statuary, and paintings designed to arouse the passions. Such a work as Le Carquois épuisé (undated, Plate 19), by Pierre-Antoine Baudouin (1723–69) could easily portray the bedrooms in La Morlière's *Angola*. Another work which brings *Angola* to mind is La Toilette (1775), by Sigmund Freudeberg (1745–1801). Just as a novel was used to titillate *Angola's* hero, so was the lady in La Toilette aroused by the novel she was reading. In Le Roman dangereux (c. 1777, Plate 20), by Nicolas Lavreince (1737–1807), a scantily dressed lady lies suggestively in bed. Beside her is a book, and a man sneaks up behind her, ready to take advantage of the novel's effect. Frudenberg's Le Boudoir (1775) shows a similar situation.

As in literature, the amorous relationships depicted by the *petits-maîtres* invariably take place outside marriage. In two works by Lavreince, both entitled Le Lever, a woman is dressing in her bedroom. In the first of these works (n.d., Plate 21) a servant girl seems alarmed as she hands a note to her mistress. The suggested intrigue is emphasized by the presence of a man at the door. In the other Le Lever (n.d., Plate 22) a lady dresses before her lover, the condition of the bed indicating that they have just arisen. A pendant to this work, Le Repentir tardif (n.d., Plate 23), shows that the lover has betrayed his mistress. She holds her head in anguish as he begs her forgiveness. A very different approach to extra-marital love is seen in Baudouin's Le Fruit de l'amour secret (before 1767, Plate 24), in which a baby is being taken from the lovers who brought about its existence.

An obvious case of marital infidelity is seen in Baudouin's witty L'Epouse indiscrète (engraved 1771, Plate 25), in which the indiscreet wife watches her husband pursuing another lady. Two of Lavreince's pictures show the planning and implementing of an infidelity. In Le Billet doux (1777, Plate 26) a husband secretly takes a note from his mistress as he stands dutifully behind his wife, who is reading a book. The outcome is seen in L'Heureux moment (1777, Plate 27), in which the lovers are together. She is partly undressed, holding the note, and he kneels beside the bed on which she reclines. Another two-picture sequence, La Marchande de lunettes and Le Rendez-vous (both 1774), by Jean Baptiste Le Prince (1733–1781), shows a merchant selling telescopes to an elderly customer. First the merchant falls in love with his customer's young wife, then, with the husband asleep, they arrange a rendezvous. Two other works showing the deception of an older husband are Le Vieillard jaloux (n.d., Plate 28), by Louis Leopold Boilly (1761–1845), and Les Deux baisers (1786), by Louis Philibert Debucourt (1755–1832).

Frudeberg designed a series of illustrations for a lavish book published in 1774, the *Monument du Costume*. Four of the series, Le Bain, La Visite inattendue, Le Boudouir, and La Soirée d'hiver, treat the theme of deception. As in many instances, there is no way of ascertaining the nature of the inconstancy. Inscriptions state that the lady in Le Bain is a woman of quality, and that she adores the man who sent her the *billet doux* she is reading. The man who sent it is a lover, since an accompanying comment states that women are constant only in their inconstancy. These lines sum up one of the principal themes treated in the art of the *petits-maîtres*. Certainly marital infidelity, and undoubtedly a betrayal of even one's lover, find pictorial expression in their works. It might well be the latter kind of promiscuity that Freudeberg is depicting in La Visite inattendue. One lady has tried to escape quickly from a compromising situation as another enters the room. A dog is barking at the dress of the lady who is fleeing. The man, who was of course also compromised by the discovery, seems more amused than distressed. He seems to be experienced at intrigue, knowing that relationships are easily arranged and dissolved. Experienced women also are seen in intrigues and initiating in the making of love. In L'Attente (n.d., Plate 29) by Jean Schall (1752–1825), it is a woman whose room is sensuously decorated, and who lies thinly clad on her bed, apparently awaiting her lover. Love is typically shown as a passing fancy. To judge by the frequency with which marital infidelity was amusingly portrayed by the *petits-maîtres*, there was no reason why marriage should be a basis for constancy.

The *petits-maîtres* treated love as ephemeral and depicted it with considerable frankness. In two pictures by Jean-Baptiste Mallet (1759–1835), both undated, but probably from the 1780s, Le Déjeuner (Plate 30) and

Le Baiser (Plate 31), a third person watches a couple as they make love. Even franker is his Le Déjeuner du matin (n.d., Plate 32), which shows an almost naked woman half-sitting on her lover, her legs crossed and stretching across his. The third person, a servant girl or friend, calmly stirs a hot drink. Certainly one of the frankest pictures of the eighteenth century is Les Soins discrets (Plate 33) by Lavreince, which shows two women lying face down on a bed. An older woman, a servant, gives an enema with a curative clyster. This subject, depicted with slightly erotic overtones in seventeenth-century art, was treated far more daringly in the eighteenth century and became the occasion for lewd suggestion.

In conclusion, in both *fêtes galantes* and bedroom art there are links with literature. The refined love of Watteau resembles Marivaux's interpretation, and the bedroom art of the *petits-maîtres* parallels the *roman érotique*. Indeed, the connection between bedroom art and the erotic novel appears to be closer than mere analogy. Owing to the conventions of painting, there were no direct artistic sources for the bedroom genre of 1760–89, although in literature the very themes that the *petit-maîtres* were to depict had become commonplace. In fact, the *roman érotique* was most popular immediately before the appearance of bedroom art, from which it seems safe to conclude that the popularity of erotic literature helped to provide a new orientation in the artistic representation of love. Furthermore, in settings that were obviously contemporary, both erotic novels and bedroom art showed the upper classes in relations which were both inconstant and adulterous.

10

Didacticism in
eighteenth-century painting

There were two genres of eighteenth-century French painting that represented family life positively, and in both, the role of love and marriage was antithetical to that in bedroom art. While artists working in both genres saw the family as a source of stability and happiness, they arrived at this moral position by different technical means; they reflected different artistic, literary, and ideological influences, and they produced for different markets.

We shall call the first of these genres the 'realistic family scene.' So perfectly does Le Bénédicité (1746, Plate 34) by Jean Siméon Chardin (1699–1780) represent the genre that we can concentrate our discussion upon this one work. Chardin has shown a modest-looking bourgeois mother serving lunch to her two children. She wears a hat, a plain brown dress, and a grey apron. The dress comes to the top of her neck and is designed to conceal her figure, giving her an appearance that is prim in every way. Her manner is calm and a little serious as she places a bowl before the younger of her children, a son, and looks down at him. He returns the look and holds his hands together as he says grace, while his sister watches attentively, making certain that he makes no mistakes. In this wonderful work Chardin has caught a moment in the daily life of a bourgeois family that is at once trivial and significant. It is trivial because it is in no way out of the ordinary, nothing more than a common, everyday event. What makes it significant is the concern of the mother and manner in which the children respond to it. That the boy saying grace returns his mother's look indicates he is performing a daily ritual, and the sister's attention to every word reveals her integral role in the ritual. This mother and her children are held together in a warm, harmonious relationship, and by portraying it Chardin has invested domestic life with a quiet, unimposing dignity.

On all sides of the three figures in Le Bénédicité are household objects which contribute to the realism of the work. A musical instrument lies on the floor next to the boy's chair, and on the chair is a drum. There is a copper stove on the floor. Eating utensils lie on the table beside the plain dishes in which lunch is being served; bottles line a wooden shelf, and a dish and pitcher sit on top of a sideboard. The numerous household utensils in this scene contribute easily and naturally to the domesticity of the subject. But Chardin was also primarily a genre painter. He turned to nature for inspiration, and was never interested in the high rhetoric still encouraged by the Academy. Having been received into the Academy for his reception pieces, La Raie and Le Buffet, Chardin was designated as a specialist in animals and fruits, a minor genre that denied him the prestige enjoyed by artists working in more important subjects, such as history. This does not seem to have bothered him. There is an amusing story about how Chardin began to paint the human figure. It appears that he was astonished by the prices that a fellow artist, Aved, could refuse for his portraits. When Aved quipped that a portrait was more difficult to paint than a sausage, Chardin took the remark as a challenge, and by 1733 started to paint the human figure. During the period from 1733 to 1752, while painting domestic scenes, Chardin continued to work in still lifes, and after 1752 devoted most of his efforts to that genre. One of the great family painters started and ended his career as a painter of still lifes.

Since Chardin apparently turned to the depiction of the family only by accident, it may seem unnecessary to look for influences. And yet, there were some. The key is Aved, the painter who directed Chardin to the figure. Aved spent some time in Holland, and his paintings have a Dutch appearance. It was through his influence that Chardin became aware of the seventeenth-century Dutch masters. How closely Chardin studied Dutch painting is unknown, but the connection is there, and it is unmistakable. By turning to Holland for inspiration he was being true to himself because the same sensitivity to nature and appreciation of the common, every-day side of life that was the natural gift of Rembrandt and Vermeer was Chardin's as well. And just as Rembrandt and Vermeer must be seen as part of a middle-class culture, so too must Chardin be seen as a representative of the middle-class life of eighteenth-century France. More specifically, Chardin reflected the orientation of an element of the

French bourgeoisie that was content with its lot and found dignity in it.[1] Chardin's identification with the bourgeoisie was direct, non-ideological, and a natural product of his own orientation. Unlike Boucher, who was well received at court, favoured by both Madame de Pompadour and Louis xv, and known for his libertine habits,[2] Chardin remained a loyal husband and dutiful father, and undoubtedly found meaning in the modest way of life which he represented with such consummate artistry.

Marvellous as Chardin's paintings of domestic life are considered today, they were more or less ignored by the artistic establishment of eighteenth-century France. The only official commission which Chardin received (in 1764) was a set of three overdoor panels for the chateau of Choisy, Les Attributs des sciences, des arts, et de la musique. The highest price paid for a Chardin during the artist's lifetime was 1500 *francs* for La Serinette.[3] The customer was none other than Louis xv: but, significantly, Louis purchased the painting through Charles-Nicolas Cochin, a close friend of Chardin. In contrast, Boucher received frequent royal commissions, and on one occasion was paid 1,500 *francs* for a mere paper doll. And yet, neglected as Chardin was by the establishment, a large market did exist for his work. It was possible to reach that market only through prints: Le Bénédicité was one of the most frequently engraved of all eighteenth-century paintings. While there is no record of Chardin's still lifes having been reproduced, his domestic scenes were frequently printed by engraving, etching, black-manner printing, lithography, and woodcuting. Among Chardin's engravers was the expert Lépicié, but fine as his prints were, they fetched only modest prices. About the top price paid for Chardin prints was 1 *livre*, ten *sols*, compared with the average selling price of about 6 *livres* for prints of the *petits-maîtres*.

Who, then, purchased Chardin prints, and who favoured the *petits-maîtres*? Vovelle and Roche have studied bourgeois families who lived off investments (rather than working in a trade or profession; these were, in the opinion of the authors, the true bourgeoisie) in the Marais, a section of Paris.[4] They usually derived most of their income from *rentes* which yielded a return of about 10 per cent. They have been divided by wealth into five categories, with the lowest having assets of 500 *livres* or less and the highest, 20,000 *livres* or more. Only those in the top category would have had annual incomes of over 2000 *livres*. Life among the bourgeoisie studied by Vovelle and Roche was not extravagant. Most enjoyed only a bare minimum of comfort. Only 25 per cent had domestic help, and none, with two exceptions, had more than one domestic. The value of household furnishings seldom exceeded 2000 *livres*, and among these furnishings art objects were seldom found. Here is a class that could not easily afford luxury expenditures. For even the bourgeois with an income of about 2000 *livres*, a print costing 6 *livres* would have absorbed more than one day's income, and for those of more limited means such a purchase could have been prohibitive. Undoubtedly, then, the price range of prints took into account differences of income, and it seems safe to argue that the relatively modest cost of Chardin prints reflects the market for which those prints were intended. By the same token, the popularity of erotic art must have been greatest among buyers who enjoyed relatively high incomes.

The production of Chardin prints indicates the existence of an element in French society which reponded favourably to his representation of family life. A buyer of modest means could empathize with Chardin's domestic scenes and their realism was immediately intelligible, even to unsophisticated buyers. Their figures 'speak the same language' as the modest bourgeois, and they move in the same surroundings. The effect of Chardin's realism was to make such a work as Le Bénédicité accessible and attractive to an element of French society that was more or less free from social pretensions.

Before we turn to the second genre of domestic painting, which we shall call the sentimental family scene, we shall make some comments on realism. In both eighteenth-century art and literature, the social context of realism tended to be popular rather than aristocratic. The very function of the realistic novel, according to F.C. Green, was 'the reproduction of *unidealised* nature.'[5] In contrast to the 'realistic' novel was the 'idealistic' novel, which depicted the beautiful, the perfect, and, in the social sense, the aristocratic. Of course, such an 'idealistic' novel as La Vie de Marianne did describe the life of both low and high society, and in so doing it mixed genres. Yet, Marivaux did not depart from the literary proprieties which required the novelist to idealize aristocratic society. In fact, it was precisely in the most 'realistic' scene in La Vie de Marianne, the argument between Madame Dutour and the cab driver, that the coarseness of the people was most apparent. But realism in literature was not limited to scenes from novels that otherwise idealized aristocratic life. Even though, in the opinion of the literary establishment, the novel should reflect an idealized view of life, there was a steady undercurrent of realism in eighteenth-century French literature.[6] There is in this undercurrent an interesting analogy with Chardin. As in Chardin, the social context of the realistic novel was popular, and the function of realism was to project an every-day, concrete image of life. To this realism the 'cultured' and 'enlightened' classes did not tend to respond, in either art or literature.

This gap between realism and the dominant standards of taste influenced the work of the best-received and most influential painter of sentimental family scenes, Jean-Baptiste Greuze (1725–1805). L'Accordée de village (1761, Plate 35) contains many of the elements of Chardin's Le Bénédicité. It too is a family scene and, as in Le Bénédicité, the social context is popular rather than aristocratic. Further, L'Accordée is filled with concrete details, such as chickens, a tattered basket, a rifle, an open closet, and dishes, which give a 'realistic' impression. And yet, if we are to follow Green, this is not a realistic painting: it is not a 'reproduction of *unidealised* nature.' Rather, it is a self-conscious attempt to dignify a virtuous family. In painting a betrothal, Greuze showed a solemn and deeply significant event, one that profoundly affected the entire family. A gray-haired father speaks of the importance of marriage to his future son-in-law, who holds the marriage portion in his left hand. The son-in-law listens carefully to the old man whose words undoubtedly refer to the happiness as well as the responsibilities of marriage. The rest of the family pays close attention to the important event: a younger sister weeps as she rests her head on the fiancée's shoulder; the mother grasps her daughter's arm, suggesting her love and how much she will miss her; and the daughter responds to her sister's and mother's affection by leaning away from her fiancé, and toward them. In doing so, she underlines the modesty that is apparent in her innocent, almost bashful expression. The only evidence of love for her fiancé is the light touch of her fingers on his hand.

L'Accordée, then, is not a representation of the everyday side of family life, but rather, it is an idealization of family life. And this is not just our interpretation. It represents the opinion of none other than Diderot. By coincidence, Chardin's Le Bénédicité was shown in the same Salon (1761) as L'Accordée de village. Diderot's response to these works is extremely interesting. Of the former, Diderot wrote, 'C'est toujours une imitation très-fidèle de la nature, avec le faire qui est propre à cet artiste; un faire rude et comme heurté; une nature basse, commune et domestique.'[7] Then Diderot commented on Chardin's position in the Academy, and the intelligence with which he talked about painting. At the end of the discussion he said that Chardin was original 'dans son genre,' that the genre was well suited to engraving, and that having once seen a family painting of his, one has seen them all. Diderot's honesty forced him to recognize Chardin's technical skill, although he was basically uninterested in him.

About Greuze, however, Diderot was highly enthusiastic. In contrast to the fifteen lines devoted to Le Bénédicité in the Seznec and Adhémar edition of the Salons were the one hundred and twenty-three lines given to a discussion of L'Accordée. Diderot wrote of this work that 'Le sujet est pathétique, et l'on se sent gagner d'une émotion douce en le regardant.' So affecting were the figures, continued Diderot, that they seemed to speak. The aged father was saying to his son-in-law, 'Jeannette est douce et sage; elle fera ton bonheur; songe à faire le sien' ... ou quelque autre chose sur l'importance des devoirs du mariage ... Ce qu'il dit est sûrement touchant et honnête.' While Diderot conceded that other artists had depicted scenes similar to that in L'Accordée, in his opinion they had not brought to bear the same artistic qualities as Greuze. This painter had 'plus d'élégance, plus de grâce, une nature plus agréable ... Ses paysans ne sont ni grossiers comme ceux de notre bon Flamand [Teniers], ni chimériques comme ceux de Boucher.'[8]

Diderot's discussion of L'Accordée tells us a great deal about eighteenth-century aesthetics. As a *philosophe* and a reformer Diderot did develop aesthetic theories which, in some respects, departed from seventeenth-century doctrines. In both his literary and artistic criticism he broadened the social framework in order to reach (and therefore edify) a larger audience. Clearly, Diderot's *drame* is far removed from Racine, just as Greuze could hardly be mistaken for Poussin. As different as they are in surface appearance, however, there is an important pattern of continuity between the seventeenth-century classical work and the eighteenth-century moralistic work. Both, after all, aimed to edify; both appealed to the higher feelings; both idealized and ennobled. Thus, Diderot, the very aesthetician who, in his *drame*, seemed to be arguing for a theatre of the everyday, was not, in fact, interested in real life.[9] Nor did he support realistic painting. What attracted him to Greuze was that artist's 'goût,' 'finesse,' and 'bonnes mœurs.' In depicting morally significant scenes Greuze covered himself with 'honneur.' Obviously he was no common artist; rather, he was a 'peintre savant' whose compositions were full of 'esprit' and 'delicatesse.' Just as Diderot was cultured, so too was the artist who won his favour; and just as seventeenth-century aesthetics were rooted in a high-minded, idealistic conception of art, so too were those of Diderot.

To Diderot, Chardin's family scenes were 'commune' and 'rude.' But in choosing such a subject as 'L'Accordée de village,' Greuze showed that

MUSÉE DU LOUVRE

1 Le Brun: Alexandre et Porus (detail)

2 Poussin: Apollon amoureux de Daphné

3 Giorgione: Fête champêtre

4   Rubens: Garden of Love

5   Watteau: Assemblée dans un parc

MUSÉE DU LOUVRE

6 Watteau: L'Embarquement pour Cythère

MUSÉE DU LOUVRE

7 Boucher: Berger et bergères

8 Fragonard: L'Escalade

9 Fragonard: La Poursuite

10 Fragonard: La Déclaration d'amour

11　Fragonard: L'Amant couronné

12 Boucher: Femme nue étendue: Louise O'Murphy

13 Boucher: Léda et le cygne

14 Fragonard: La Bacchante endormie

15 Fragonard: La Dormeuse

16 Fragonard: L'Armoire

17 Fragonard: Le Verrou

18 Fragonard: Le Baiser à la dérobée

19 Baudouin: Le Carquois épuisé

20 Lavreince: Le Roman dangereux

21 Lavreince: Le Lever

22　Lavreince: Le Lever

23 Lavreince: Le Repentir tardif

24 Baudouin: Le Fruit de l'amour secret

25 Baudouin: L'Epouse indiscrète

26 Lavreince: Le Billet doux

27 Lavreince: L'Heureux moment

28 Boilly: Le Vieillard jaloux

29 Schall: L'Attente

30 Mallet: Le Déjeuner

31 Mallet: Le Baiser

32 Mallet: Le Déjeuner du matin (detail)

33 Lavreince: Les Soins discrets (detail)

34 Chardin: Le Bénédicité

35 Greuze: L'Accordée de village

36 David: Combat de Minerve contre Mars

37   David: Bélisaire recevant l'aumône

38 David: Le Serment des Horaces

39 Greuze: La Voluptueuse

40 Greuze: La Cruche cassée

he was a man of *sensibilité* and 'bonnes mœurs.' The *sensibilité* and 'bonnes mœurs' which Diderot saw in Greuze helps explain his enthusiasm for that artist, whose didacticism was in fact grounded in sentimentalism. In Greuze's art it was through affecting scenes of family life that the innate moral sense of the viewer would be stirred. Just as the *sensibilité* of Marivaux rested upon a favourable view of human nature, so did the *sensibilité* of Greuze; just as sentimentalism implied moralistic tableaux in literature, so too did sentimentalism imply the same in painting. The function of *sensibilité*, then, was to idealize and edify. Thus, while Greuze depicted the 'people,' and even though he filled his paintings with realistic details, he was not a 'realistic' painter. In order to find a realistic family scene it is necessary to turn to such a work as Chardin's Le Bénédicité. Chardin's directness and freedom from ideological commitment made him the ideal painter of everyday life. By contrast, Greuze's sentimentalism, loftiness of purpose, self-conscious moralizing, 'goût,' and 'delicatesse' made him attractive to the cultured classes.[10]

Perhaps no painter in eighteenth-century France was such a financial success as Greuze. His first moralistic painting, Père de Famille expliquant la Bible, brought him a major reputation. Monsieur de la Live de Jully, a wealthy amateur, purchased this work in 1755, and in the following year the marquis de Marigny commissioned two works on behalf of his sister, Madame de Pompadour, to decorate her apartments at Versailles. Marigny himself purchased Greuze's second moralistic tableau, L'Accordée de village, for 39,000 *livres*.[11] This painting was acquired by the king in 1782. Other collectors who bought works by Greuze are Monsieur Damery, lieutenant of the French guards, the comte de Vence, Catherine II, and the duchesse de Gramont. Perhaps the best evidence of Greuze's popularity was the result of a reversal in the Academy. Having been *agréé* in 1755, Greuze neglected to submit his *morceau de reception*, which was to determine his status in the Academy. Finally, after a ruling that forbade him showing his paintings in the salons, he presented his reception piece in 1769, Septime Sévère et Caracalla. He chose this subject because he aspired to the most prestigious rank in the Academy, that of historical painter. Greuze's reception piece was rejected, probably in answer to his arrogance and frequent criticisms of the Academy. He himself was accepted, but as a specialist in a genre and not as a painter of history. This decision enraged Greuze, who was a man of immense vanity. In retaliation, he turned his shop into a kind of salon, in which he showed his own paintings. He timed the opening of his 'salon' to coincide with the official Salon of 1770. It was a huge success, and was visited in 1771 by

Gustavus III, Benjamin Franklin, and Joseph II. On May 31, 1777, Métra wrote in his diary that 'a crowd of curious people gather outside the celebrated Greuze's shop in order to see his new painting, "Le Fils ingrat" ... but this artist will only admit friends and princes of the blood.'[12] In August, 1777, Joseph II commissioned a picture and at the same time presented Greuze with the title of baron and 4000 ducats.

Greuze was also popular among print collectors, and reproductions of some of his smaller works were only moderately expensive. La Dormeuse sold for three *livres* (twice as much as Le Bénédicité) and L'Aveugle dupé brought four *livres*, but Le Silence (which, by the way, the *Mercure* described in glowing terms in a three-page notice) sold for sixteen *livres*. Altogether, Greuze earned as much as 300,000 *livres* from the sale of prints.[13]

The novelist whose popularity more or less matches that of Greuze was Jean-Jacques Rousseau. *La Nouvelle Héloïse*, along with *Candide*, was one of the two most popular novels of the eighteenth century. Forty editions were published between 1760 and 1778, and seventy between 1778 and 1800.[14] Like Greuze, Rousseau appealed (though not exclusively) to the 'cultured' classes. There is in Rousseau the same sentimentalism, philosophisizing, didacticism, affecting family tableaux, and loftiness of purpose as in Greuze. The cultured classes, then, lent their support to idealistic art and literature and in so doing they were perpetuating an important aesthetic pattern of the seventeenth century. The idealism and didacticism of the classical age was diverted in the eighteenth century into a new channel, that of sentimentalism.

The persistent vitality of certain seventeenth-century aesthetic criteria might help explain the reappearance of classicism in the second half of the eighteenth century, a period in which it flourished everywhere in Europe. It is often said that the excavations at Pompeii and Herculaneum contributed to a new interest in antiquity, and certainly the accurate representation of antiquity in painting seems to reflect a more thorough archaeological understanding of the classical past. But also, and especially in France, the return to classicism was a return to the seventeenth century. *Poussinisme* now replaced *rubénisme*. After half a century of reaction, French art returned to a past tradition. The loftiness of purpose associated with seventeenth-century aesthetics had continued to hold sway in the eighteenth century, but it had done so in genres that, stylistically, were anti-classical. After 1750, idealism returned to its original stylistic matrix.

In what might be described as a search for moral identity, the eighteenth century created two personas, one sentimental and the other classical. Thus, Rousseau, on one occasion, said that 'après avoir passé une vie obscure et simple, mais égale et douce, je serois mort paisiblement dans le sein des miens.'[15] But he also wrote that 'Sans cesse occupé de Rome et d'Athènes; vivant, pour ainsi dire, avec leurs grands hommes, né moi-même Citoyen d'une République, et fils d'un père dont l'amour de la patrie étoit la plus forte passion, je m'en enflamois à son example; je me croyois Grec ou Romain.'[16] The didactic tendencies of the eighteenth century could be realized through either sentimentalism or classicism. Both styles flourished after 1750, but especially in the 1770s and 1780s classicism gained in popularity. While there was a return to classicism in the second half of the eighteenth century artists who exploited its popularity often did so without being moralistic. It was not until Jacques-Louis David (1748–1825) worked out his distinctive style that classicism could fully realize the didactic aims which were searching for expression in French painting. Interestingly, David's stylistic innovations were intimately connected to the moral outlook that became an essential part of his art. As David worked out his style, he could see its didactic possibilities, and the closer he came to his mature style, the more he capitalized on those possibilities.

After David won the Grand Prix de Rome in 1774, he went to the Eternal City vowing that antiquity would not put him under its Spell. As a youth, he had studied briefly under Boucher (a distant relative) and then under Vien. Both of these artists introduced David to the *petite-manière*: even the classicist Vien had retained some of the refined elegance of the rococo. And there was much of the rococo in David's Combat de Minerve contre Mars (1771 Plate 36) with its flowing drapery, fluttering putto and birds, rich colour, and swirling cloud dissolving into diffuse masses. The foreground of this work is highly unclassical in its clutter.

Yet, even in this early work there is a suggestion of the classicism which ultimately became David's hallmark. The fallen Mars, in reeling back, shows a powerful set of arms and a muscular, forceful face which contain some of the elements of David's mature style. The trip to Rome brought out this tendency to paint in the grand manner. In Rome, David observed ancient sculpture, sarcophagi, and cameos, studied moulds from Trajan's column, made tracings from engravings of Greek vases, and read French translations of Winckelmann. He already knew Homer, Virgil, and Corneille, and perhaps at this time began reading Plutarch's *Lives*, which he came to know well and from which he could recite long passages. By 1777 his sketches were beginning to show a fluidity that indicated a growing feeling for classical form. David realized that his style was changing and admitted to Vien that the very thing he had vowed to prevent had taken place: antiquity had won him over.

It is interesting that Bélisaire recevant l'aumône (1781, Plate 37), which reveals the classical spell under which David had fallen, conveys a moral message. Justinian had come to fear his great general, and consequently had had him blinded. Belisarius, mutilated by the very prince he had served loyally, sits under his own triumphal arch, receiving charitable attention from a child and lady. The lady drops alms into a container held by the child, while behind the lady is one of Belisarius's soldiers, astonished at the plight of his once great leader. Stylistically, it was through a carefully worked out composition that David conveyed the tragedy of this event. Belisarius and the child form one unit, the woman and soldier another. The outstretched hands of Belisarius and the child are countered by the lady who bends toward them, giving alms. The lady's reply to their gestures is echoed by the soldier behind her, whose upraised arms and incredulous expression indicate his surprise at seeing Belisarius in such a state. In Bélisaire recevant l'aumône David has given his composition a classical equilibrium, and this equilibrium has helped contribute to a moralistic commentary. For David, the return to antiquity was bound up with morality.

The work which best demonstrates David's use of composition to emphasize an idea is Le Serment des Horaces (1787, Plate 38). Two preliminary sketches for this work, which was initially inspired by Corneille's Horace, have been preserved. Each version represents a further simplification and results in a more dramatic projection of an idea, which, in its finished form, proclaims the ideal of sacrifice to the fatherland.[17] In Rome's war with Alba Longa it was agreed that the issue would be determined by a combat between the Horatii and Curiatii families, the former being Roman, the latter Alban. Both families had three sons, by mothers who were twin sisters, and it was these sons who were to engage in mortal combat. In David's picture the three Horatii sons are swearing an oath to fight for their country, in spite of the blood connection between them and their opponents. This was David's way of giving artistic expression to the idea of patriotism; devotion to the fatherland overrides even family ties. To the side of the oath-swearing ceremony are the wives of the warriors, who lean on one another in mutual grief, and a nurse who shelters their children. By adding the women to his painting David has introduced the idea of family solidarity, which the principal event had denied. This is David's way of proclaiming the virtues of both patriotism and family unity. Furthermore, the differences between the stern, rigid, powerful men and the grieving women, whose limpid arms and drooping heads suggest weakness, provide an important contrast. One gets the impression that these prudently dressed wives with their tightly wrapped head-dresses, and the nurse who tends the children, belong in the home, while the men's role is to dedicate themselves to tougher problems, such as deciding the fate of the fatherland.

Through technical means David has given this composition an 'epigrammatic edge' (the phrase is Walter Friedlaender's) which allows him to narrate an important event with maximum precision, clarity and force. The viewer is struck by the powerful figures in the foreground: immediately, the eye is drawn to the warriors swearing their oaths before moving to the wives of these staunch heroes, who lament a ceremony which imperils the lives of their husbands. There are two themes, and two compact groupings of figures. In the background is an austere colonnade which both encloses the composition and serves as an appropriate setting for the serious event that is unfolding. Like the sentimental family paintings of Greuze, David has narrated a story whose obvious purpose is to edify the viewer. There were, in the second half of the eighteenth century, two styles of moralistic painting, sentimental and classical, and two types of subject, family and patriotic. All were idealistic, lofty, and serious.

Just as sentimental art appealed to the cultured classes, so did classical art. Elisabeth Vigée-Lebrun, Marie Antoinette's favorite painter, gave a dinner party in 1789, for which she went to considerable effort to establish an appropriately classical tone. Her guests, who were urged to dress in the antique fashion, entered to the strains of Gluck's *Dieu de Paphos et de Gnide*. Once they began to circulate they noticed Etruscan vases which the comte de Parois had loaned the hostess, and a golden lyre someone else had brought along. The poet Le Brun (called Le Brun Pindar) was crowned with a laurel wreath as he recited his translation of *Anacreon*. The hostess knew what she was doing: the evening was such a success that news of it raced through Parisian society.[18] In fact, high society played a major role in giving popularity to classicism. When Fragonard delivered the four magnificent rococo paintings now known as the Grasse Panels to Madame du Barry, who had commissioned them for the pavillion of Louveciennes, they were not installed. Madame du Barry had Vien execute four classical paintings instead. Classicism was the last of the major artistic styles of the eighteenth century, and like the others it was supported by the upper classes.

Classicism was also favoured by the Academy. In 1748 Lenormant de

Tournehem, head of the Academy, established a school in Rome, the *École royale des élèves protégés*, whose purpose was the promotion of historical painting. The location of this school, together with the subjects taught in it – mythology, ancient history, ancient costume, and ancient decoration – indicate the particular emphasis on historical painting at this time: it was the classical past to which the attention of the *élève protégé* was directed. In giving its support to classicism, the Academy was returning to the tradition of Le Brun, Louis xiv, and the seventeenth century.

That Tournehem should return to the style that the Academy had endorsed in the seventeenth century is not surprising. After a period of vitality under Louis xiv, the Academy underwent a period of decline in the first half of the eighteenth century. To return to the official style of the seventeenth century was to identify with a period in which it had flourished. Moreover, by 1748 the classical movement had already begun to emanate from the excavations at Pompeii and Herculaneum. The directors of The Academy who gave their support to the classical movement were moving in the same direction as various branches of the royal government, whose support they were undoubtedly receiving. In addition to favouring a particular style, the Academy placed its weight behind art which, through its didacticism, could contribute to the very reform movement that was permeating the governments of both Louis xv and Louis xvi.[19]

Louis xv, whose favorite painter was Boucher, did not fall in easily with the high-minded ambitions of the Academy. Cochin, secretary of the Academy, and a friend of the *philosophes*, was given charge in 1764 of decorating the chateau of Choisy, which until then had been ornamented with landscapes, hunting scenes, and light mythological paintings.[20] The Seven Years' War had just ended, and in Cochin's opinion this provided an appropriate occasion for selecting subjects which would point out the benefits of peace. Rather than celebrating military exploits, paintings would show rulers bringing prosperity and happiness to their people. Interestingly, in proposing a sequence depicting the beneficent deeds of Augustus, Trajan, and Marcus Aurelius, Cochin was hoping to convert his own monarch. He hoped that 'le Roy, en voyant célébrer leur vertus, reconnoisse quelques-unes de celles qui le rendent si cher à son peuple.'[21] It turned out that Louis did not respond favourably to the proposal, and got Boucher to execute the commission instead. But Boucher died (in 1771) before the project was completed and at this point there was an opportunity to complete a series of moralistic paintings for Choisy. J.B.M. Pierre, who had just succeeded Cochin, added classical paintings representing courage, vigilance, filial devotion, and humanity, to paintings that had already been executed depicting justice, mercy, benevolence, and generosity. All these works were finally installed.

Under the directorship of the comte d'Angiviller (1774–91) the Academy broadened its support for moralistic painting. During this period it encouraged historical art and discouraged art which was thought to be improper. In 1775, 'indecent and licentious' paintings were withdrawn from the Salon and in the Salon of 1777 a 'suite' of moralistic paintings treated such subjects as impartiality, industry, and constancy. Interestingly, the period in which the Academy was discouraging 'indecent and licentious' paintings and commissioning moralistic works coincides with the brief ministry of Turgot. In fact, d'Angiviller was a close friend of Turgot, and it was through Turgot's influence that he was appointed head of the Academy (As Director of Public Buildings). Although Turgot fell in 1776, the Academy continued to support moralistic art.

Given the moralistic propensities of the age, it was only natural that painting would serve the cause of reform. Further, the whole thrust of monarchical centralization had for centuries been to draw the French people together into a nation: by 1750 *patrie* came to mean all of France rather than the local area in which the individual Frenchman lived.[22] It was possible in the mid-eighteenth century to establish a more vital relationship between the state and the people, and the sentiment of patriotism was well suited to further that end. In the arts, patriotism was celebrated in scenes from classical history and in the depiction of important events in the history of France, to which the Academy gave its support.[23] Historical painting, whether the subject was taken from classical antiquity or French art, was capable of proclaiming the virtue of patriotism. In doing so, it entered into a common cause with the reform element in the government.

Both the sentimental and classical styles in eighteenth-century painting emerged from a social milieu that can be described as elitist. Even one as obviously committed to an egalitarian social order as Diderot accepted the aesthetic criteria of this society. While as a political thinker Diderot emphasized the concrete and the realistic, and set himself against the sentimental,[24] as an art critic he turned not to realism, but to sentimentalism. In this, he was only acting as a man of his times. Given the position in Diderot's thought of an associationist theory of psychology, and given his commitment to reform, it was logical that, in the realm of art, he would support a style that through its affectiveness was capable of edifying.

Diderot was not striking off on a new path when he championed the cause of morality in art. Seventeenth-century French classicism had been high-minded and idealistic, and idealism continued to hold sway, in the form of sentimentalism, in the eighteenth century. Both the classicism of the one century and the sentimentalism of the other emerged from an upper-class cultural milieu. Not even as radical a reformer as Diderot broke thoroughly from the aesthetic doctrines of this milieu; in fact, Diderot found the realistic, everyday art of Chardin 'rude,' 'basse,' and 'commune.' While Diderot's aesthetics were those of an ideologist and a reformer, they were also those of France's elitist artistic establishment.

Eighteenth-century moralistic painting, whether sentimental or classical, enjoyed the enthusiastic support of the upper classes. Furthermore, a government agency, the Royal Academy, threw its considerable influence behind diactic art, and at the same time discouraged painting in styles considered immoral. However, it happened that didacticism could serve the cause of revolution as well as that of reform. In any event, what was to become the official artistic style of the Revolution took shape before 1789, with the support of the cultural elite of France and the loyal servants of the king.[25]

11

Duality in literature
and painting

Not all eighteenth-century French literature and painting fits neatly
into the somewhat arbitrary erotic and moralistic categories which have
been discussed in previous chapters. Although an author's or artist's
intent or message, if any, is often sufficently clear for there to be little
difficulty in assigning a particular work to one of these categories, it is
interesting to note that some authors and artists produced both erotic and
moralistic works. The line between the erotic and the moralistic was not
hard and fast. Individual authors could be at times erotic, and at others
moralistic, while certain individual works are occasionally difficult to
classify. Still, the author's intention is usually clear, in spite of certain
contradictions in a given work. In *Angola*, for instance, the hero married a
virtuous young lady at the end of the story. Yet, the story is about
seduction, and love scenes are described wittily and often salaciously. La
Morlière actually riduculed marriage and even serious non-marital at-
tachments.

When La Morlière, like many writers of erotic stories, depicted aristocratic life as corrupt he was not really criticizing the aristocracy, but rather
amusing his readers through satire. Most other writers of erotic literature
intended to entertain their readers, rather than criticize a particular class.
But the same might not be true of Laclos, who, as we have seen, in addition
to depicting vicious aristocrats, explained the reasons for their depravity.
His characters had been brought up in a society which was unhealthy, and
seem therefore to have been products of that society. This suggests that
Laclos might be seen as a reformer, a moralistic critic who condemned
aristocratic life.[1]

This interpretation is supported by a recurring theme in *Les Liaisons dangereuses*: one of the principal causes of unhappy marriages was the custom of sending girls to convents for their education, and then marrying them off in *pactes de famille* to virtual strangers. A girl who was married in this way was often little more than an adolescent and could not easily adapt to a way of life for which she was completely unprepared. Having been isolated in a convent, she was thrust into the world in all her innocence, and forced to adjust to society and marriage under dangerous conditions. Cécile's naïveté, which was a product of her convent education, made possible her destruction by Valmont. The arranged marriage of the Marquise de Merteuil contributed to that depraved lady's cynicism. In criticizing these social abuses, Laclos appeared as a moralist and a reformer, as he did in two treatises he wrote on the education of women.

Was Laclos actually a reformer? If so, he conveyed his message in a book about seduction which, since its publication, some have thought indecent, if not scandalous. *Les Liaisons dangereuses* lends itself to various interpretations: a reader might, depending on his predilections, consider it either immoral or moral. The question remains: was Laclos a writer of licentious literature, or was he a moralist?

The same question must be asked of the Marquis de Sade who seems to have been a social critic as well as a pornographer. The vicious aristocrats in his novels lived off large incomes, which they enjoyed at the expense of the poor. In *La Nouvelle Justine* (1797), Sade indicated concern for the underprivileged when he said that by the 'peuple' he did not mean the bourgeoisie, but those unfortunates who 'ne peut vivre qu'à force de peines et de sueurs ... '[2] Moreover, a lower class character stated, 'Je veux l'égalité, je ne prêche que cela. Si j'ai corrigé les caprices du sort, c'est parce qu'écrasée, anéantie de l'inégalité de la fortune et des rangs, ne voyant que vanité, que tyrannie dans les uns, que bassesse, que misère dans les autres, je n'ai voulu ni briller avec le riche orgueilleux, ni végéter avec le pauvre humilié.'[3]

In *Aline et Valcour* (before 1788), Sade described the voyages of a young man which eventually led him to a Utopian South Sea Island. The king, Zamé, had been sent to Europe as a youth in order to discover the benefits of civilization. Except for the presence of some mechanical inventions, Europe disgusted him. In trying to understand the degradation and tyranny he saw there, he concluded that the principal causes of abuse were private property, class distinctions, religion, and family life. He therefore abolished or transformed these institutions on his own island. The state became the sole owner of property, all class distinctions were abolished, and religion was reduced to voluntary nature worship. There were no priests, and education was in the hands of the state. Children went to school until they were fifteen, and were instructed in patriotism and family morality. A youth was told that marriage was a mutual effort by husband and wife. When a boy reached the age of fifteen, he visited a girls' school, where he met with a girl for a week under the supervision of the masters and mistresses. At the end of the week they could marry by joint consent. In this state useful work was encouraged by the government. All luxury arts were forbidden, and the purpose of the arts was to inculcate morality. King Zamé frequently predicted revolution in France.

Duality is found also in the pornographic novels of Restif de la Bretonne.[4] *Le Paysan et la paysanne pervertis* (1784–1787) is a catalogue of virtually all the adventures, misadventures, and perversions of eighteenth-century literature. A brother and sister, both peasants, went to Paris, moved into upper-class society, and as a result became corrupt. Their virtue gave way first to self-indulgence, then to cynicism, and finally to hardened criminality. In passing through the stages of vice they encountered homosexuals, knife-wielding sadists, and out-and-out nihilists. The arch fiend in the story was a rich and powerful cleric, whose evil influence was instrumental in corrupting both hero and heroine. This cleric helped establish an incestuous relationship between the brother and sister and was himself in love with both. Indeed, it was because the sister belonged to the brother that he too was anxious to possess her. But at the same time, this devil wished to rid France of its abuses. He would divert incomes from monks to officers and other men who were useful in serving the country. All prelates in the kingdom would be taxed at the same rate, and religious orders would no longer be able to take in novices. Tenant farmers would be given ownership on the land they tilled, which would require the dismemberment of the large estates and bring about the ruin of countless nobles. In order to regenerate the people morally, special holidays and festivals, based upon those of the ancients, would be held in the villages. In short, reason and philosophy would reign everywhere. But so out of step was the present age, so decrepit had the human race become, that more than a physical or moral revolution was necessary. Perhaps the rejuvenation of society would require its complete overthrow. Like Sade, Restif de la Bretonne was at once a pornographer and a Utopian philosopher, and his novels contemplated the complete destruction of the established social and political order.

The same complexity in literature which superficially appears to be primarily erotic sometime confronts the reader of moralistic literature.

Were it not for the ultimate reform of the count in Duclos's *Confessions du Comte de* *** this work would appear to be just another string of intrigues and seductions. The moral point of a number of Marmontel's *Contes moraux* is blunted by a succession of salacious incidents, and Beaumarchais treated intrigue and seduction wittily and amusingly in *Le Mariage de Figaro*.

The writer of moralistic literature whose intentions are most complex, however, is Diderot. In *Jacques le Fataliste* he created two evil geniuses who bring to mind characters in the novels of Laclos and Sade.[5] The Marquise de Pommeraye was the mistress of the Marquis d'Aisnon, until he announced that, while they might as well remain friends, their relationship must end. The marquise, who was well able to dissimulate, appeared to accept her dismissal in good grace, but inwardly she seethed. Since the affront was more than she would tolerate, she planned her revenge. First, she gained control over a mother and her daughter, both of whom had been reduced by financial straits to prostitution. Then she set both up in a household, made them appear to be paragons of virtue, and introduced the marquis to them, hoping that he would become infatuated with the daughter, which he did. His infatuation continued to increase as the girl followed the marquise's orders by refusing his advances. Finally, the marquis proposed marriage, which the marquise had anticipated and planned on, and which was quickly accepted. The marquise then took her revenge by informing her former lover that he had married a prostitute.

Père Hudson was an abbot who imposed a strict rule on his monastery, but went to extreme measures to renounce such rigidity and conventional morality in his own life. He was the lover of every kind of woman, from virgin to prostitute. His oppressive policies provoked the enmity of his underlings, who knew about his way of life and planned to expose it. Père Hudson got wind of the plot, and through cunning and intelligence reversed it in such a way that his enemies appeared to be the guilty parties. In the Marquise de Pommeraye and Père Hudson, Diderot created two geniuses who refused to accept the normal standards of society, who felt constrained by it, and therefore broke away. But these characters were evil, like the heroes and heroines of Laclos, Sade, and Restif, and sexual manipulation figured importantly in their destructiveness.

There are a number of simply erotic scenes in *Jacques le fataliste*. Jacques lost his virginity when he was nineteen, after he and his boyhood friend, Bigre, fell in love with the same girl. At first, Bigre won the girl's favours, Jacques her ridicule. Bigre achieved his victory on a haystack, where he slept with his mistress every night. One morning, suspecting that his father had caught him, he told the girl to remain in hiding all day. Jacques, learning of her predicament, and with Bigre's father immediately beneath him, climbed into the loft under the pretext of taking a nap, found the girl, and took advantage of her situation.

By the time Jacques was twenty-two, his apprenticeship had long been completed: any clumsiness he might have had in his first experiences had been replaced by a considerable expertise. And yet, he liked to play the innocent. On one occasion two husbands broke into laughter when Jacques told them that he was still a virgin. Such a sight was so amusing that they told their wives about this absurd person, and all joined in the merriment. But then the two wives, without consulting one another, decided to seduce Jacques. The first, taking him into a field, supposedly to cut some brush, lay in a position that made her intentions unmistakeable. Jacques enjoyed her so expertly that she immediately realized his deception. 'Trompe-moi encore quelquefois de même, et je te le pardonne ... '6

The other wife persuaded Jacques' father to have him grind some grain for her at the mill, and then waited for him in a little patch of woods along the way. When she intercepted him, Jacques played the innocent again, claiming to know nothing about love. His would-be seductress made herself as languishing as possible, and then, pretending to faint, she lay on the ground, her breasts heaving, her lips trembling, her eyes closed, her mouth half-open. But Jacques did nothing, so she was forced to give up and appear to regain consciousness. Jacques suggested that she teach him whatever it was that he needed to know, and explain why everyone laughed at him. She refused, but nevertheless they held hands, and then kissed. By this time it was getting dark, and Jacques, playing his game to perfection, indicated that since she would not contribute to his education, they might as well go home. At this point, the woman seized Jacques' hand and put it on herself. 'Il n'y a rien! Il n'y a rien!'7 cried Jacques. Then they made love, many times, in a variety of ways.

This wife was so pleased with Jacques that she continued to lavish her favours on him. One day a foolish, stuttering priest caught them together, and launched into a tirade against the dissolute young man. To silence the priest, Jacques pitched him into a hayloft, and in his full view used his mistress on the back of a donkey. Just then the husband ran up and Jacques and his mistress rode off unnoticed. The husband saw the priest, got him on the end of a pitchfork and jeered at him as his wife and her lover disappeared.

These scenes in *Jacques le fataliste* suggest comparisons with erotic literature. In the *roman érotique* innocent men commonly 'neglected' ladies who had swooned, and clerics were often subjected to ridicule in seduction scenes. Furthermore, Diderot was well able to titillate. There is another story about a pretty girl called Denise, at whose house Jacques stayed after he had injured his leg. Since the leg was itchy, Denise scratched it for him; first with one, then two, three, and four fingers, and finally with her whole hand. First she went below the knee, then above it. Aroused by this activity, Jacques seized the girl's hand, and as Diderot commented in a double entendre 'la baisa.'[8] After exciting his reader Diderot enjoyed putting him down again.

In the *Supplement au Voyage de Bougainville* (1772; published 1796) Diderot accepted marriage only if it imposed no restraints. Conventional, monogamous, marriage was impractical for utilitarian reasons. One of the principal reasons for intercourse was the reproduction of children, on which the welfare of the entire state rested. Frequent reproduction could best be achieved by having individuals seek their pleasure, whenever and wherever they wished, either in or out of marriage. In this work, Diderot heaped scorn on a Jesuit priest, who hesitated to sleep with the daughter of a Tahitian chieftain. The chieftain argued that the daughter had never borne any children, and therefore no one would marry her. The Jesuit could do her no greater favour than to make her pregnant, and eventually he did try.

Like the Marquis de Sade, Diderot did not hesitate to describe sexual deviance. One of the leading characters in his novel *La Réligieuse* (1760; published 1796) was a lesbian abbess. In his *Rève de d'Alembert* (before 1796; published 1830) a Doctor Bordeau considered the scientific possibility of mating different species, and defended homosexuality. The supreme merit of love, in Diderot's opinion, was to 'réuni l'agréable à l'utile.[9]

Diderot's duality also came out in some utopian descriptions in the *Supplement* that bear a close resemblance to similar passages in Sade and Restif. All these novelists, after breaking away from Christian love and marriage, denounced the entire social and political order. Diderot mocked monogamy and contended that man's sexual rights had been subverted. This happened because the civil laws, the political philosophies of rulers, religious institutions, and disparities of rank and wealth required the tyranny of man over woman, and as a result man had departed from nature and given up his happiness. To recover it, he had only to return to the sovereign state of nature. Then, broadening his attack, Diderot said that the lawmakers of Europe had fashioned a rigid and awkward mould that crushed the people but served the interests of the established order. All civil, political, and religious institutions perpetuated time-worn abuses, but men were groaning under their tyranny and were anxious to escape from artificial customs and despotic government. Sometimes they left society and moved into the woods. The world was overcivilized; it had grown old. Only in Tahiti, where a 'natural' morality prevailed, were men happy.

Painters, like writers, moved back and forth between the erotic and moralistic genres, and sometimes combined elements of both in one work. We have seen that Fragonard executed a sizeable number of erotic drawings and paintings, particularly in the period 1765–72. A few years later, between 1777 and 1779, he specialized in moralistic family subjects. Even Boucher, Fragonard's master, painted an occasional domestic scene. These artists invested their family paintings with a sensibility wholly becoming to them. Fragonard, in particular, portrayed mothers whose solicitude for their children provided an appropriate setting for domestic happiness. And yet, he represented the female shape in these works much as he had in his erotic paintings. In Le Retour au logis and Le Maîtresse d'école of ca. 1778 he showed women of ample breast in the midst of their children. These women give Fragonard's domestic paintings a tone different from that of Chardin's. The same is true of a Boucher family painting, La Vie pastorale, undated, in which a mother as full-bosomed as any of Fragonard's appears engaged in her rustic houshold tasks, surrounded by children. Baudouin's Le Fruit de l'amour secret departs from the witty comments on love typical of the petits-maîtres by showing the grief caused by an illegitimate birth.

In a number of cases, painters who were best known for their moralistic works did not limit their artistic efforts to the praise of virtue. Greuze was both a moralist and an eroticist. La Voluptueuse, shown in the Salon of 1765 (Plate 39), shows a girl touching a letter and throwing a kiss to its author. Greuze emphasizes her amorous feelings by showing her thinly-covered bosom. He depicted the loss of virginity in a number of works which, because they convey a double meaning, are all the more salacious. Ostensibily they describe some small misfortune. A girl has dropped a basket of eggs (Les Oeufs cassés, shown in the 1757 Salon), broken a mirror (Le Miroir brisé, probably after 1767) or a pitcher (La Cruche cassée, before 1773, Plate 40). Consequently, in each of these works, the girl looks crestfallen over the accident, but the real sadness is caused by her loss of innocence. In Le Miroir brisé the girl who looks at herself in a cracked mirror sees a dishevelled image. Her hair is untidy and her dress is in a state of disarray, particularly around her neck and bosom. She had dressed up, gone out, and then returned to her bedroom. Scattered about are the cosmetics and jewelry that she had used for her make up. Upon returning, she seems to have picked up the mirror and dropped it. Her disconsolate expression suggests that she is also lamenting the recent loss of her virginity. The same meaning is apparent in La Cruche cassée, when the state of the girl's clothing suggests another meaning. In Les Oeufs cassés a mother sternly regards her daughter, pointing accusingly at the eggs she has dropped. But she also clutches a young man, apparently the daughter's lover, who is putting his hat on and is anxious to take his departure. The dejected girl seems to lament both her loss and her mother's discovery.

Writers and artists executed both moralistic and erotic works, because both were fashionable within the same audience. As we have seen, the moralistic and erotic conventions emerged simultaneously, and in the same, predominantly aristocratic, social and cultural milieu. Within this milieu there was to the very end of the Ancien Regime a demand for both moralistic and erotic subjects. Duality in painting and literature reflects this situation.

But it was not just in response to the market that artists and writers changed genres. In order to understand the cross currents of style, it is necessary to look at the content of art and literature. Each convention gave the writer or painter a particular orientation and provided him with certain motifs and themes. Basically, to turn to eroticism was to denounce Christian love and marriage. To work in the moralistic pattern was to reaffirm the significance of beneficence, compassion, marriage, and the family. The tone of an erotic work tended to be mocking and ironic, while the moralistic work was sincere, sentimental, and moving. This led to irreverence in the former and a plea for moral regeneration in the latter. Yet, antithetical as the two conventions were, they could, and did, converge at certain points.

Implicit in the call for moral regeneration in the moralistic convention was a programme for reform. Rousseau prescribed a way of life in *La Nouvelle Héloïse* that would replace another, corrupt, life style. In working out his scheme for reform, Rousseau covered politics and religion, in addition to the usual subjects of the sentimental novel. Already in *La Nouvelle Héloïse* Rousseau had covered some of the ground that he was later to travel in *Émile* and the *Contrat Social*.[10] Curiously, programmes for reform came also from the erotic convention. In a sense, the working out of erotic themes led inevitably to a call for moral regeneration. The society that was depicted in both the *roman érotique* and erotic painting was hedonistic and libertine. Lacking any serious purpose in life, aristocrats sought only to amuse themselves, moving through the elegant world of the opera, theatre, and masked ball. Other pastimes were the hunt, gambling, and trips to country estates. None of these diversions satisfied, and aristocrats, bored with life, turned to love. Love did bring pleasure, but sooner or later it palled. The next step was intrigue, and beyond intrigue lay the sick, perverted, criminal world of sadism. The truth is, condemnations of aristocratic life were far more scathing in the erotic than in the moralistic convention, and further, the call for reform came more strongly from the former. The society described in the erotic work was artificial, degenerate, and morally diseased. Thus, it was necessary to destroy the entire social and political order to make possible the creation of a new, moral, world. While the moralistic convention held consistently to a traditional orientation, the erotic convention broke from tradition and, as it worked out its own inner logic, rejected everything tied to the past. At this point, in some works, a programme was set forth which called for a total reorganization and regeneration of society.

12

Conclusion

At the time that this study was first conceived and written, George Lefebvre's interpretation of the Revolution seemed unassailable. In the interim, his 'orthodoxy' has come under attack. 'Revisionist' historians, their leader being Alfred Cobban, have criticized one of the most basic tenets of the 'orthodox' interpretation: that the Revolution was a conflict between two social classes, the aristocracy and bourgeoisie, and that this conflict was a result of ill-feeling that had been developing for several decades before Louis xvi summoned the Estates General. Cobban sees the Revolution not in these, but in other term. In his interpretation, the bourgeoisie and aristocracy are no longer locked in mortal conflict. On the contrary, their interests and ambitions sometimes overlap or coincide. In Cobban's opinion, Lefebvre allowed the Marxian analysis to cloud his thinking: assuming that the bourgeoisie had to come to power, he looked at the period before 1789 through tinted (if not tainted) glasses.

The dust has not yet settled from the debate between 'orthodox' and 'revisionist' historians. Perhaps, as Cobban suggests, a full understanding of the social background of the Revolution will come only upon the completion of extensive empirical research. In any event the debate is relevant to the argument set forth here, if only because it shows how the historian sometimes operates within a set of assumptions that, in part, are created by other members of his guild.

When first undertaken, this study assumed Lefebvre's interpretation, and it was only too easy to find the necessary supporting evidence. 'Bourgeois' literature did emerge, and at the very time that the eighteenth-century economy was booming. It seemed only logical that eulogies of the merchant, issuing from the rising economic importance of the bourgeoisie, signalled, as it were, a new class feeling of self-importance. Moreover, at the time that class lines hardened, a protest literature appeared which seemed to reflect contemporary social and political realities. But, even in the passages most heated with hostility there was a point of view still partly traditionalist. In condemning the elitism and injustice of his society, Bernardin de Saint-Pierre looked nostalgically to a time in French history when men low in birth but high in merit were properly rewarded by the state.

While the literature of protest did reflect contemporary attitudes, it did so in a way that was not at first apparent to this author. As much as looking ahead to a more fluid society dominated by the bourgeoisie, this literature looked back to a period in French history when the bourgeoisie had enjoyed opportunities for advancement within a stratified social order. Assuming that the bourgeoisie was 'rising,' the literature that began to appear in the 1750s seemed to be an index of contemporary social and economic change. But in fact, 'bourgeois' literature derived from the activity of intellectuals whose point of view agreed with that of reform-minded officials in the royal government. Furthermore, in both style and themes, it was greatly in the debt of novels and plays that emerged from an aristocratic social milieu. There was, then, no 'spontaneous bourgeois literature'; in this field the bourgeoisie did not proclaim their autonomy. Such a conclusion, interestingly, is analogous to one of the most clearheaded arguments by the historians of revisionism. By studying their wealth, George Taylor has decided that the bourgeoisie was non-captialist, because they preferred to invest in land, the aristocratic commodity. Following this argument to its logical conclusion, Taylor contended that 'in the spring of 1789 middle-class feelings toward the nobility were still benign. Far from wanting to abolish nobility, the Third Estate wanted to rehabilitate it.'[1]

But can the historian define the problem in quite this way, which is to imply that the bourgeoisie had made up its mind on the nobility one way or the other? Bourgeois attitudes toward the aristocracy were in fact deeply ambivalent, a complex and unstable compound of like and dislike, admiration and resentment, approval and disapproval. If we are to understand bourgeois attitudes on the eve of the Revolution, we must take this ambivalence into account, and we must try to recapture the ambience of life at this critical moment in French history by considering such elusive, intangible factors as 'climate of opinion' and 'ethos.' Sometimes people simply do not act as they should, or as the economic or political historian might assume that they should. In order to understand their motivation, it is necessary to know what ideas they had and how they got them. Certainly the bourgeoisie in the pre-Revolutionary period did not have only a benign idea of the aristocracy. But then neither did people from other classes, including the aristocracy itself. In fact, the idea of the libertine or perverse aristocrat had become a late eighteenth-century myth, and as such it contributed to the 'pre-Revolutionary ethos,' or, perhaps, even to the 'Revolutionary mentality,' once the Revolution occurred.

There is an element of paradox in the myth of the perverse aristocrat. Certainly the appearance of this myth was no historical accident. As Henri Carré has shown, the eighteenth-century French aristocracy did provide examples of lavish spending, disregard of marriage, arrogance, and violence.[2] But none of this was new; the diligent researcher could find ample evidence of all these 'abuses' in earlier centuries. While it is impossible to reconstruct completely the life of the eighteenth-century aristocracy, it is doubtful that immorality was very much more pronounced than before; in any event, until someone proves the contrary there is no reason for believing that it was.

But there were some important changes in aristocratic life, and particularly among the court nobility. For them the seventeenth century had been a time of constraint, which was first imposed internally, through a code requiring impeccable manners, strict observance of etiquette, and perpetual participation in ceremony, and then externally under Louis xiv, who realized fully the advantages in upholding the code. In creating a code the aristocracy fashioned an instrument that the king was to use to further his interests. From the beginning the code's purpose had been to assist the noble at court; when it became clear that the court took away more than it gave, it was inevitable that disillusionment would follow. The result was bitterness, a new feeling for irony, and a relaxation of the aristocratic code. The importance of this relaxation is not in that the aristocracy became corrupt and vicious, but rather that manners came to sanction greater freedom.

In literature, too, there was a reaction against the formalism of the seventeenth century. Just as the code had required moral conduct of the highest order, so too had the novel; indeed, the novel was one means of disseminating the code. Both the *roman* of the period 1600–60 and the *nouvelle* of 1660–1700 aimed to edify and instruct; both exclusively represented aristocratic life, and represented it favourably. This is not to say that aristocratic characters were always virtuous; but the presence of immoral characters necessitated a choice between right and wrong. The function of vice was to highlight virtue. Aristocratic heroes and heroines in the seventeenth-century novel, then, not only had to speak the right language and possess the right manners, but they had to be moral paragons as well. A new genre of literature appeared in the eighteenth century, the *roman érotique*, which both parodied and rejected the moral pattern of the seventeenth-century novel. The *roman érotique* was rooted in a hedonistic philosophy whose objective was to enlarge the scope of freedom. Given the traditional themes of the French novel, it was only natural that this freedom would be translated as sexual. In reacting against the traditional, Christian morality which dominated the seventeenth-century novel, the *roman érotique* became its dialectical opposite. As it worked out its inner logic the erotic novel passed through stages leading from gratification to satiety, to boredom, and eventually to perversity.

At the same time that the aristocracy was creating a literature of eroticism and libertinism, it was also developing a literature of sensibility. Parodoxically, the sentimental novel was also a reaction against the formalism of the seventeenth-century, and it too was rooted in, or at least influenced by, philosophical hedonism. But here the analogy ends, for the thrust of sentimentalism was moralistic. Man was innately good, and it was through the feelings that his goodness could be realized. The stirrings of the heart led to romantic love and compassion, both of which enlarged the scope for virtue. Unlike the libertine love of the *roman érotique*, its romantic counterpart in the sentimental novel deepened the moral sense. One variant of love cared only for self-gratification and was therefore strictly egotistical; the other, in bringing human beings closer together, made them considerate, and was therefore unselfish. Libertine or sentimental, the purpose of love was happiness, whether it was achieved through self-indulgence or by solicitude toward others.

Rousseau was not the first to champion romantic love, nor to see moral good in the sentiments. Aristocratic society had laid the foundations for the literature of sensibility as early as the 1690s, at the same time that a literature of eroticism was beginning to emerge from that society. Rousseau's moral program in *La Nouvelle Héloïse* was not a bourgeois reaction against aristocratic corruption; rather it represented an approach to moral problems that came from within aristocratic society itself. Rousseau not only presented an ideal pattern of rural, aristocratic life, but also argued for an organic society rooted in social differences but held together by fairness and responsibility. This had long been argued by aristocratic literature.

And yet, Rousseau was arguing against a certain pattern of aristocratic life, the very pattern that emerged from the *roman érotique*. The foolish, ironic, over-refined, mean, self-indulgent, libertine aristocrat that Rousseau denounced was not his own creation, but a stock type in the erotic novel. Further, Rousseau was not the first to denounce him. At the very time that the erotic novel accepted gratification as legitate, and in so doing began to move down the path of libertinism, the sentimental novel championed the cause of romantic love, threw its support behind the family, and through compassion and benevolence urged social responsibility and altruism. The call for moral regeneration did not originate with the *philosophes*; it sounded clearly from aristocratic literature of sentimentalism. In fact, many of the moral currents that passed into the Revolution came from the society of the French aristocracy. The royal government also lent its support to the cause of moral reform.

In conclusion, it is interesting to note that some of the leaders of the Revolution were well read in erotic literature, and indeed wrote some of it themselves. Of the eleven men described in J. M. Thompson's *Leaders of the French Revolution*, six wrote works which appear in Lemonyer's *Bibliographie des ouvrages relatifs à l'amour, aux femmes et au mariage*. J.B. Louvet de Cambray's *Amours et galanteries du chevalier de Faublas* (1786–9) was autobiographical, witty, libertine, sentimental, and, in Thompson's opinion, a revelation of the author's 'perpetual make-believe' world. Honoré Gabriel Riqueti, comte de Mirabeau, wrote a large amount of erotic literature, including the *Contes galantes* and *Contes gaulois*, *Le Degré des âges du plaisir, ou Jouissance volupteuses de deux personnes de sexes différentes* (all three of which were published posthumously), *Ma conversion, ou le Libertin de qualité* (1783), and a pornographic book, *Errotika Biblion* (1782). Perhaps the most interesting work by a revolutionary leader was the *Organt* (1789), by Antoine Louis de Saint Just, in which love affairs were described in considerable length, nuns were raped, kings, courtiers, generals, and priests denounced, and the right to pleasure was justified.

What manner of men were these, who wrote libertine literature yet also set themselves up as moralists, drifted across Europe before 1789, and were often romantic and sometimes given to utopian visions? Certainly the historian detects incongruities in these patterns. It is the author's contention that these incongruities were neither isolated nor accidental. The same themes and tensions that appeared in erotic literature written by revolutionary leaders also appeared in some of the literature studied in this book. Would these themes have appeared had there not been a reaction against the Christian idea of love and marriage in the eighteenth century? Would the moral climate otherwise have been so heated on the eve of the Revolution? Once the dikes of traditional morality broke, two responses took place. First, authors reacted against the severity of the seventeenth century, which led to a literature of libertinism and eventually of pornography. Secondly, an attempt was made to retain the loftiness of seventeenth-century morality, but to place that morality on new foundations, the result being sentimentalism and later, classicism. As these currents of moral thought developed and interacted they not only intensified their basic differences, but also, in some cases, became intertwined in a literature that can be called dualistic. This literature is at once romantic and anti-romantic, libertine and sentimental, moralistic and nihilistic. It combines hedonism, and sometimes perversity and pornography, with a condemnation of the social order, a call for moral regeneration, and a utopian vision of the future. In reacting against the traditional morality of the seventeenth century, the eighteenth century created a literature filled with incongruities and tensions which might well tell the historian something about the climate of opinion or ethos in the pre-Revolutionary period.

Notes

INTRODUCTION

1 Shafer, 'Bourgeois Nationalism,' 33
2 Volney, *La Loi naturelle*, 143
3 Stewart, *A Documentary Survey*, 574
4 Volney, *La Loi naturelle*, 144
5 *Social History*, 532
6 *Art and Social Life*, 146
7 Ibid., 140
8 See Cobban, *Social Interpretation*, and his reply to critics in 'The French Revolution.' Another important 'revisionist' article is Taylor, 'Non-capitalist wealth.'
   In the same number of the AHR see 'Class,' in which a debate over revisionism is
   carried on between J. Kaplow, G. Shapiro, and E. Eisenstein.

CHAPTER 1   The Christian idea of love and marriage

1 Crébillon *fils*, *La Nuit*, 17–19
2 Lewis, *The Allegory*, 59–60
3 Ibid., 60
4 Weiss, *Earliest Christianity*, 580–2
5 Troeltsch, *The Social Teaching*, 181–99
6 Labriolle, 'Le "mariage spirituel," ' 204–25
7 Dooley, *Marriage According to Saint Ambrose*, 43–56
8 Paredi, *Saint Ambrose*, 143

9 Taylor, *Sex in History*, 52–4
10 Ansolde, Abelard, and Berze are discussed in Epton, *Love and the French*, 12; Lombard, in Lewis, *The Allegory*, 15
11 Holmes, *A History*, 200–6, 317–20
12 Lewis, *The Allegory*, 32–43. See also Painter, *French Chivalry*, 100–1
13 Rougemont, *Passion*, 32–5
14 Levi, *French Moralists*, 49
15 Ratner, *Theory and Criticism*, 26
16 D'Urfé, *L'Astrée*, 147
17 Magendie, *Le Roman*, 380
18 Ibid., 380–3
19 Magendie, *La Politesse*, 226–37, 605–17
20 Dallas, *Le Roman*, 184–204
21 *La Princesse de Montpensier*, 59
22 *La Princesse de Clèves*, 237
23 Bénichou, *Morales*, 230–2

CHAPTER 2 The connection between the *nouvelle* and the *roman érotique*

1 *L'Honneste homme*, 185–7
2 *Le Gentilhomme*, 91–92
3 *La Fortune*, 164–6
4 *Suite*, 29
5 Ibid., 32
6 For a discussion of manuals that upheld the Christian side of *honnêteté*, see Lévêque, ' "L'Honnête homme," ' 620–32
7 For the decline of Soicism and the revival of Epicureanism, see Spink, *French Free Thought*, 133–68, and for the shifting moral climate among the court nobility, see Auerbach, 'La Cour et la Ville,' 133–79; Chill 'Tartuffe and Courtly Culture,' 133–79; and Bénichou, *Morales*, 159–70. For the spread of secularism among the upper classes, see Mornet, *Les Origines*, 51–68, 129–58, 267–318
8 Méré, *De la vraïe*, 101
9 La Rochefoucauld, *Œuvres*, 345
10 Magendie, *La Politesse*, 774–75
11 See *Letters*, 274, for his admiration of Epicurus and ibid., 137, 144, for Christian attitudes
12 Turnell, *The Novel*, 27–48
13 Ariès, *Centuries*, 388
14 For a brief discussion of paganism within the aristocracy see Mornet, *Les*

origines, 24–5. For the intellectual background, no one has gone beyond Hazard, *European Mind*

15 '"Précieux" Elements,' 99–107
16 'Uses of the Fairy Tale,' 116
17 Haac, 'Marivaux,' 255–67
18 *Mimesis*, 398–9
19 Varga 'La Désagregation,' 998–8
20 *Les Liaisons*, 'Introduction' by Harry Levin, x-xii
21 Magendie, *Le Roman*, 374–5
22 *Tant Mieux*, 128
23 *Angola*, 10–11
24 *Les Liaisons*, 79
25 *La Spleen*, 23
26 Ibid., 29–30
27 Ibid., 31

CHAPTER 3   Aristocratic manners

1 Michels, *First Lectures*, 11
2 *Suite*, 257–60
3 *La Politesse*, 63–87
4 *L'Honneste homme*, 7
5 Bitton, *The Crisis*, 80
6 Ibid.
7 Ariès, *Centuries*, 386–7. I find this passage interesting, as Grenaille did stress individual achievement, and considered nobility more 'honourable' if acquired by 'merit' rather than by birth. Yet, he thought that nobles were 'endowed by nature with an air of majesty.' It seems that he said this in spite of his different criteria for nobility.
8 *Mimesis*, 233–47
9 *Morales*, 15–79
10 In Aristotle see the *Politics*, III, 13, and in Cicero the discussion of Regulus in *De officia*, III, 10
11 *L'Honneste homme*, 44–5, 69–71
12 *Traité*, 194–5
13 *Le Gentilhomme*, 19
14 *Suite*, 249–65
15 *Renaissance Cavalier*, 58–62
16 *The Book of the Courtier*, 43
17 Ibid., 44

18 Mazzeo, *Rennaissance*, 145–6
19 *The Book of the Courtier*, 103
20 Lough, *Introduction to Seventeenth Century France*, 227
21 *De la vraïe*, 70
22 *Le Commerce*, 156
23 *De la vraïe*, 72
24 Ford, *Robe*, 10
25 *Mémoires*, vol. 16, 246
26 Ibid., vol. 14, 247
27 *L'Esprit*, 538
28 La Morlière, *Angola*, 302
29 Auerbach, 'La Cour,' 164–7
30 Green, *French Novelists*, 116
31 *Angola*, 54, 102
32 *Mémoires*, vol. 4, 8
33 Ibid., 8–9
34 Ibid., vol. 38, 216
35 Ibid., 213–14
36 Ibid., vol. 4, 84
37 Ibid., vol. 38, 208
38 Ibid., vol. 14, 247–8
39 Ibid., vol. 9, 262
40 *Caractères*, 215, 223–4, 235–8

CHAPTER 4   Aristocratic perversity in the *roman érotique*

 1 *Victorian England*, vi
 2 *Le Sopha*, 105
 3 *La Nuit*, 96
 4 *Histoire*, 169–71
 5 Sauroy, *Le Masque*, 198
 6 Ibid., 211
 7 'Comment étudier,' 204–16
 8 *Les Liaisons*, 372
 9 Ibid., 108–9
10 Ibid., 175–77
11 Ibid., 177
12 For a discussion of Valmont's wit see May, 'The Witticisms,' 181–7
13 Loy, 'Love-Vengeance,' 157–66
14 Thelander, *Laclos*, 121

15 *Les Liaisons*, 260–1
16 Ibid., 174
17 Loy, 'Love-Vengeance,' 157–66
18 Bloch, *120 Days*; and Ashbee, *Index*, *Centuria*, and *Catera*
19 'On the Universal Tendency,' 189–90
20 *Fragments*, 7
21 Ibid., 51
22 Ibid., 43
23 *Mémoires*, 25
24 *French Chivalry*, 101
25 *Centuries*, 353–6
26 For a discussion of Sombart see Mauzi, *L'Idée*, 269
27 *Other Victorians*, 195
28 *Memoirs*, 116

CHAPTER 5 Sentimentalism and moralistic literature

1 'Love-Vengeance,' 157–66
2 Barchillon, '"Précieux"' and 'Uses'; and Mylne, 'Sensibility,' 47
3 On the persistence of preciosity see Tilley, 'Preciosity', and Deloffre, *Marivaux*,
33–5
4 For an excellent discussion of the *Avis* see Deloffre, 'Premières idées,' 178–83
5 For an intelligent study of the relationship between Madame de Lambert and
Marivaux see Jamieson, *Marivaux*, 13–27, 43–9, 68–77, 110–11
6 *Avis a sa fille*, 80–1
7 Ibid., 81
8 Ibid., 61
9 Ibid., 51
10 Jamieson, *Marivaux*, 116–19
11 *Avis a son fils*, 41
12 Jamieson, *Marivaux*, 118
13 Ibid., 115
14 *Avis a son fils*, 45
15 Ibid., 13–14
16 *Traité*, 101
17 *Reflexions*, 161
18 Ibid., 162–3
19 Ibid., 155
20 Jamieson, *Marivaux*, 50
21 *La Vie de Marianne*, 43

22 Ibid., 184
23 Ibid., 211
24 Ibid., 346
25 Mylne, 'Sensibility,' 49
26 McKee, *The Theater*, 182–94, 222, 248–50
27 Gaiffe, *Le Drame*, 31–2
28 Lanson, *Histoire*, 660
29 *Œuvres esthétiques*, 192–7
30 *Œuvres complètes*, vol. 7, 222
31 Ibid., vol. 7, 211
32 Ibid., vol. 7, 297–8
33 Rouseeau, *La Nouvelle*, vol. 1, 81
34 For Rousseau's associationist psychology see Hall, 'The Concept,' 20–33
35 *Rousseau*, 137–72, 192–5, and *Minuet*, 409–21
36 *Œuvres complètes*, 444
37 Starobinski, 'The Illness,' 73
38 *Œuvres complètes*, 16
39 Ibid.
40 Ibid., 17
41 Ibid., 548
42 *La Nouvelle*, vol. 2, 38
43 This interpretation draws heavily from Grimsley's fine article, 'The Human Problem'
44 *La Nouvelle*, vol. 2, 33
45 Ibid.
46 Ibid., 35–6
47 Ibid., 115–16
48 Ibid., 172
49 Ibid., 183
50 Ibid., vol. 3, 91
51 Ibid., 88
52 Ibid., vol. 2, 36
53 Ibid., 17
54 Ibid., 171
55 In his edition of *La Nouvelle*, vol. 1, 335–57
56 Ibid., 367–70

CHAPTER 6 Marriage in moralistic literature

1 *Emile*, 383–4

2 Ibid., 244–5
3 Ibid., 389
4 *La Nouvelle*, vol. 2, 251
5 *Emile*, 490
6 *La Nouvelle*, vol. 4, 31–2
7 *Emile*, 589
8 Ibid., 596
9 *La Nouvelle*, vol. 2, 104–5
10 Ibid., 272
11 Ibid., vol. 4, 305
12 Ibid., 9
13 *Contes*, vol. 2, 118–19
14 Ibid., 129–30
15 Ibid., 132
16 Ibid., 111

CHAPTER 7   The social context of moralistic literature

1 *Sentimental Revolution*, 64
2 Jamieson, *Marivaux*, 23
3 Atkinson, *Sentimental Revolution*, 84
4 Madame de Miran, incidentally, was a fictionalized Madame de Lambert
5 *La Nouvelle*, vol. 4, 24
6 Hendel, *Rousseau: Moralist*, 84
7 *Emile*, Bk I, VII, 45–6
8 Ibid., X, 199–200
9 *La Nouvelle*, Part V, Letter II, l. 200
10 *Social Origins*, 491–6
11 Tilly, *The Vendée*, 23
12 Cited in Forster, *Nobility*, 152
13 Duby and Mandrou, *A History*, 354
14 Bloch, *French Rural*, 126–49
15 Further, Rousseau's views on marriage agree in many ways with those of the serious seventeenth-century novel. See Magendie, *Le Roman*, 371–7
16 Gaiffe, *Le Drame*, 93
17 Plekhanov, *Art and Social Life*, 140
18 Auerbach, *Mimesis*, 375–6
19 For a similar treatment of the bourgeoisie in the comic novel, see Strickland, 'Social and Literary Satire,' 182–92
20 Ratner, *Theory*, 94–101

21 Lough, *Paris Theatre Audiences*, 250
22 Adams and Baxter, *Dramatic Essays*, 372–73, 391
23 Ibid., 386
24 Wiley, *The Formal French*, 123
25 Gaiffe, *Le Drame*, 269
26 *Théâtre Complet*, vol. 1, 271–2
27 *Contes*, vol. 2, 121
28 Ibid., 152
29 Lough, *Paris Theatre Audiences*, 185–268
30 Ibid., 254
31 Grassby, 'Social Status,' 19–38
32 As Marcel Reinhard has shown ('Élite et noblesse,' 18), a number of merchants were in fact ennobled, but as they numbered only thirty-one between 1767 and 1787 one must conclude that the plan to create a commercial nobility failed.
33 Green, *Eighteenth Century*, 93–110
34 Levy-Brühl, 'La Noblesse'
35 Adams and Baxter, *Dramatic Essays*, 374
36 Ibid., 365
37 For Diderot's bohemianism, see Wilson, *Diderot*, 20–46
38 France, 'The Literature,' 78–99. See also Perkins, 'Diderot's Concept', and Barbu, 'The New Intelligentsia.' Barbu inclines to my point of view: that the intellectual identified with no social class.
39 Such as Groethuysen, *The Bourgeois*; Mauzi, *L'Idée*, 269–89; and Barber, *The Bourgeoisie*, 34–54
40 Watt, *Rise*, 69–92
41 Bloch, *Feudal Society*, 325
42 Stone, *Crisis*, 163–82
43 Ranum, *Paris*, 162–9
44 Mousnier, *La Venalité*
45 For an example of how 'bourgeois' literature has been misunderstood, see Lafarge, 'The Emergence.' Lafarge sees such 'realistic' novels as Challes' *Les Illustres Françoises* (1713) as 'reflecting the rise of the bourgeoisie which in the eighteenth century reached an apex which was to be consecrated by the Revolution.' Lafarge argues that Challes' heroes reflect 'the self-assurance of those who have come to terms with their social status,' and that, being 'socially independent,' they 'need no affectations in dealing either with their peers or inferiors.' This conclusion follows a quote from the *Illustres Françoises* describing a bourgeois, Monsieur Pelletier, whose outlook was obviously aristocratic, and whose self-assurance derived from this fact. It was precisely the success with which he appeared aristocratic that led the 'man of quality' to join him in his carriage.

46 Mornet, in *Le Sentiment*, 108–17, sees the return to the simple life theme against the background of agrarianism. He comments on the interest with which agriculture was studied and adds that Rousseau's position has been misunderstood. Rather than making rural life fashionable, he moved with an already well-developed fashion. For a study of the return to the simple life theme in literature before 1750, see Atkinson, *Le Sentiment*

CHAPTER 8   Social Discontent in French Literature

1 *Romans*, 567
2 Ibid., 737
3 *Théâtre*, 248
4 Ibid., 449
5 Deloffre, in his introduction to *Le Petit Maître corrige*, 41–67
6 Greene, *Marivaux*, 70–1, 97
7 *La Nouvelle*, vol. 2, 313
8 Ibid., 364
9 Ibid., 375
10 Ibid., 371. See n.1 for comments on marriage by other writers
11 *La Nouvelle*, vol. 2, 333
12 Ibid., 363
13 Ibid., 371
14 Ibid.
15 Haac, 'Marivaux,' 262
16 *Théâtre de Beaumarchais*, 258
17 Ibid., 311
18 Ibid., 260
19 Ibid., 311
20 Ibid., 260
21 *Theater*, 67–9, 82
22 Lemaitre, *Beaumarchais*, 48–54
23 Barber, *The Bourgeoisie*, 99–146
24 The realignment of the aristocracy is described in Ford, *Robe and Sword*
25 Bernardin de Saint-Pierre, *Paul et Virginie*, 19
26 Ibid., 80–1
27 Ibid., 181–2
28 Ibid., 164–8

CHAPTER 9   Erotic love in eighteenth-century painting

1 Hartle ('Le Brun's Histoire,' 90–103) discusses Louis XIV's interest in Alexan-

der as a subject for both painting and theatre. In this work Le Brun painted Alexander to resemble Louis

2 Hauser, *Social History*, 516
3 Panofsky, 'Poussin,' 300
4 Curtius, *European Literature*, 187–90
5 Huizinga, *Waning*, 134–8
6 Prints of *fêtes galantes* that became fairly common after 1685 are another source of Watteau's work. See Adhémar and Huyghe, *Watteau*, 105–17
7 Goncourt, *French Painters*, 12
8 Munro, 'Moral Occupations,' 1045–54
9 Adhémar and Huyghe, *Watteau*, 5–6
10 Jamieson, *Marivaux*, 15
11 *The Nude*, 150
12 Ibid., 149

CHAPTER 10   Didacticism in eighteenth-century painting

1 In discussing bourgeois values and the way of life of the bourgeoisie Barber (*The Bourgeoisie*, 34–54, 75–98) points out their ambivalence toward stratification. The bourgeois who accepted middle-class values would tend to remain in his social station. Mauzi (*L'Idée*, 279–89) discusses idealizations of the bourgeoisie. His sources, like Barber's, tend to be ideological and philosophical, and therefore have a different orientation from Chardin's paintings. In addition, Barber's and Mauzi's sources are either upper middle class or bourgeois who became nobles, such as Madame Thiroux d'Arconville, the daughter of a farmer general and the wife of a president of a *chambre des enquêtes* (Mauzi, 273, n. 2). For a discussion of Chardin's modest way of life see Goncourt (*French Painters*, 109–14, 137–40, 145–48)
2 See the letter, signed by Louis xv, appointing Boucher chief court painter, in Goncourt (*French Painters*, 81–2). See also pp. 78–81 for a discussion of Boucher's popularity at court, and pp. 62–4 for his libertinism. In a letter on p. 100 Boucher signed himself 'Le Chevalier Boucher.' See also Cailleux ('François Boucher', 247–52)
3 See Goncourt (*French Painters*, 138–9) for a discussion of the low prices of Chardin's paintings. The Goncourts claim that 'at no stage, even during his last years, was [he] able to earn his living by his art.'
4 'Bourgeois, Rentiers,' 25–46
5 'Further Evidence,' 257
6 In addition to 'Further Evidence' see Green's 'Realism.' For critical attitudes that helped nurture realism see May (*Le Dilemme*, 47–74, 106–38). On pp.

163–78 May discusses the role played by the English novel in the rise of realism in French literature, an influence to which Green attaches little importance. By emphasizing the continuity between realism in the French novel of the eighteenth century with that of the seventeenth century ('The Critic') Green develops what I consider the most convincing interpretation of realism. He sees it as a product of French social attitudes, and he traces its development in literary genres other than idealistic. Further, Green sees the same dichotomy between realism and idealism in painting ('The Critic,' 294)

7 *Salons*, vol. 1, 125

8 Ibid., 143

9 I am pleased to say that I arrived at this conclusion before finding a similar interpretation in Green (*Minuet*, 147–8). For a different interpretation of Diderot's realism, see Leith, *The Idea of Art*, 38

10 For Greuze's self-conscious moralizing, and his attempt to use painting as a medium of reform, see his description of La Belle-Mère and La Veuve et son Curé in Goncourt (*French Painters*, 219–21). Greuze wrote descriptions of these works for the *Journal de Paris*, and addressed that of the latter painting to the parish priests of France.

11 For the enthusiasm elicited by this painting see Diderot (*Salons*, vol. 1, 99). Seznec and Adhémar call the 39,000 livres paid for L'Accordée an enormous price

12 Brookner, 'Jean-Baptiste Greuze,' 192

13 Rivers, *Greuze*, 231

14 *La Nouvelle*, vol. 1, 178–209, 232

15 *Confessions*, 43–4

16 Ibid., 9

17 Friedlaender, *David*, 15

18 Brookner, 'Aspects,' 67–73

19 For a brief but intelligent discussion of the reform movement see Cobban, *A History*, 97–109

20 Locquin, *La Peinture*, 19–20, and Leith, *The Idea of Art*, 74–6

21 Leith, *The Idea of Art*, 75

22 Palmer, The National Idea, 95–111; Shafer, Bourgeois Nationalism, 34; and Hyslop, *French Nationalism*, 152–60

23 Leith read a most informative paper on this subject at the New York Association of European Historians annual conference in the fall of 1968. The paper, entitled 'Nationalism and the Fine Arts,' describes the rising popularity of paintings based on themes taken from French history. In a statistical study Leith has show that in works shown in the Salons, national subjects increased steadily from 1750 to 1789. In the fifties national subjects constituted 2.03 per

cent of the exhibited works, in the sixties 2.91 per cent, in the seventies 4.35 per cent, and in the eighties 6.46 per cent. Classical subjects were far more popular, by at least two to three times.

24 Wilson, 'The Development,' 1873–87

25 For studies of art during the Revolution see Leith, *The Idea*; Dowd, *Pageant-Master*; Dowd's articles cited in Leith, Ibid., 168–9; and Idzerda, *Art and the French State*. See also Parker, *The Cult*

CHAPTER 11   Duality in literature and painting

1 Two recent articles, Greshoff, 'The Moral Structure,' and Perkins, 'Irony and Candour,' have argued that Laclos was a moralist. Perkins studies the 'atmosphere' and 'esthetic milieu' of Laclos by looking at two novels written in the 1770s, Jacob Vernes' *Confidence philosophique* and Philippe Gerard's *Liaisons dangereuses: le comte de Valmont* that resemble Laclos' novel, *Les liaisons dangereuses*, and might well have influenced it. Both of these novels were moralistic tracts against atheism, which leads Perkins to deduce a similar objective in Laclos.

2 *Œuvres*, vol. 7, 361–2

3 Ibid., 378

4 Porter discusses the connection between Restif and Rousseau ('Restif, Rousseau,' 262–73)

5 See Crocker, 'Jacques le Fataliste'

6 *Œuvres completes*, vol. 6, 212

7 Ibid., 216

8 Ibid., 285

9 Ibid., vol. 2, 183

10 See Ellis, *Julie*

CHAPTER 12   Conclusion

1 Taylor, 'Non-Capitalist,' 492

2 Carré, *La Noblesse*, 154–207

Bibliography

BIBLIOGRAPHIES

ASHBEE, HENRY SPENCER. *Index Librorum Prohibitorum*, 1877
– *Centuria Librorum Absconditorum*, 1879
– *Catena Librorum Tacendrorum*, 1885
CABEEN, D.C. *A Critical Bibliography of French Literature*, ed. George Havens and Donald F. Bond. Syracuse, 1951. Vol. 4, and *Supplement*, 1968
JONES, S. PAUL. *A List of French Prose Fiction from 1700 to 1750*. New York, 1939
LANSON, GUSTAVE. *Manuel bibliographie de la littérature française moderne, xvi*, *xvii*, *xviii* et *xix* siècles*. Paris, 1921
LEMONYER, J. *Bibliographie des ouvrages rélatifs à l'amour, aux femmes et aux mariage*. 4 vols. Lille, 1894–1900

PRIMARY SOURCES

BEAUMARCHAIS, PIERRE AUGUSTIN DE *Théâtre complet* ed. G. D'Heylli and F. DeMarescot 4 vols. Paris, 1967: *Eugenie*, 1967; *Les deux amis*, 1770
– *Theatre de Beaumarchais*, ed. Maurice Rat. Paris, 1961: *Le Barbier de Seville*, 1775; *Le Mariage de Figaro* 1784
BERNADIN DE SAINT-PIERRE, JACQUES HENRI. *Paul et Virginie*. Paris, 1889
BESENVAL, PIERRE VICTOR, BARON DE. *Contes de M le Baron de Besenval*, ed. Octave Uzanne (Paris, 1881): *La Spleen*, 1777
BIBIENA, JEAN GALLI DA. *The Fairy Doll*, trans. H.B.V. London, 1925

BOUFFLERS, STANISLAS-JEAN DE. *Contes du Chevalier de Boufflers*, ed. Octave Uzanne. Paris, 1878

BRUYÈRE, JEAN DE LA. *Œuvres complètes*, ed. Julien Benda. Paris, 1951: *Les Caractères*, 1688

CAILLIÈRES, JACQUES DE. *La Fortune des gens de qualité*. Paris, 1663

CAPELLANUS, ANDREAS. *The Art of Courtly Love*, trans. John Jay Perry. New York, 1941

CASTIGLIONE, BALDASSARE. *The Book of the Courtier*, trans. Charles S. Singleton. New York, 1959

CHALESME, DE. *L'Homme de qualité, ou les moyens de vivre en homme de bien, et en homme du monde*. Paris, 1671

CORNEILLE, PIERRE. *Œuvres complètes*, ed. André Stegmann. New York, 1963: *Le Cid*, 1636

COURTIN, ANTOINE DE. *Nouveau traité de la civilité qui se pratique en France parmi les honnestes gens*. Paris, 1682

– *Suite de la civilité française, ou traité du point-d'honneur, et des règles pour converser et se conduire sagement avec les Inciviles et des Fâcheux*. Paris, 1675

CRÉBILLON, CLAUDE PROSPER JOLYPOT DE (called Crébillion *fils*). *Œuvres Complètes*. 5 vols. Paris, 1929–30: *Le Sylphe*, 1730; *Lettres de la marquise de M*** au comte de R****, 1732; *L'Écumoire*, 1734; *Les Egarements du cœur et de l'esprit*, 1736–38; *Le Sopha*, 1742; *La Nuit et le moment*, 1755; *Le Hasard du coin du feu*, 1763

DIDEROT, DENIS. *Diderot's Thoughts on Art and Style*, ed. Beatrix L. Tallemache. London, 1893

– *Œuvres Complètes*, ed. Jules Assézat and Maurice Tourneaux. 20 vols. Paris, 1875–7: *Le fils naturel*, 1757; *Père de famille*, 1758; *La réligieuse* 1760; *Rêve de d'Alembert*, 1769; *Supplement au Voyage de Bougainville*, 1772; *Jacques le fataliste*, 1773

– *Œuvres esthétiques*, ed. Paul Vernière. Paris, n.d.

– *Rameau's Nephew and Other Works*, trans. Jacques Barzun and Ralph H. Bowen. Garden City, 1956

– *Salons*, ed. Jean Adhémar and Jean Seznec. 4 vols. Oxford, 1957–67

DUCLOS, CHARLES PINOT. *Les Confessions du Comte de****, trans. *A Course of Gallantries*. London, 1775

– *Memoires secrets sur les regnes de Louis XIV et de Louis XV*, trans. *Secret Memoirs of the Regency* by E. Jules Meros. London, 1912

FARET, NICOLAS. *L'Honnête homme, ou l'art de plaire à la cour*. Paris, 1637

FROMAGET, NICOLAS. *Contes de Fromaget*, ed. Octave Uzanne. Paris, 1878

HOGUETTE, P. FORTIN DE LA. *Testament, ou conseils fidèles*. Paris, 1661

LACLOS, CHODERLOS DE. *Les Liaisons dangereuses*, ed. Yves le Hir. Paris, 1961

LA FAYETTE, MADAME DE. *Romans*, ed. Raoul Audibert. Paris, n.d.

LAMBERT, MADAME DE. *Œuvres morales de la Mise de Lambert*. Paris, 1883: *Avis d'une mère à son fils*, 1726; *Réflexions sur les femmes*, 1727; *Avis d'une mère à sa fille*, 1728; *Traité de l'amitié*, 1732

LA MORLIÈRE, JACQUES-ROCHETTE DE. *Contes du Chevalier de la Morlière*, de. Octave Uzanne. Paris, 1879: *Angola*, 1747

LANDOIS, PAUL. *Silvie The First French Tragédie Bourgeoise*, ed. Henry Carrington Lancaster. Baltimore, 1954

LAUZUN, ARMAND LOUIS DE GONTAUT, DUC DE. *Mémoires du Duc de Lauzun*. Paris, 1858

LIGNE, CHARLES JOSEPH, PRINCE DE. *Fragments de l'histoire de ma vie*, ed. Felicien Leuridant. 2 vols. Paris, 1927

MARIVAUX, PIERRE CARLET DE. *Romans, suivis de Recits, Contes et Nouvelles estraits des Essais et des Journaux de Marivaux*, ed. Marcel Arland. Paris, 1949: *La vie de Marianne*, 1731–41; *Le paysan parvenu*, 1735–6

– *Théâtre complet*, ed. Marcel Arland. Paris, 1949: *La double inconstance*, 1723; *La mère confidente*, 1735; *La femme fidèle*, 1755

– *Le Petit-Maître corrigé*, ed. Frédéric Deloffre. Geneva, 1955

MARMONTEL, JEAN FRANCOIS. *Contes Moraux*. 3 vols. London, 1780

– *Memoirs of Marmontel*, trans. Brigit Patmore. London, 1930

MERCIER, LOUIS-SÉBASTIEN. *Le Tableau de Paris*, trans. *The Picture of Paris* by Wilfrid and Emilie Jackson. New York, 1929

– *Le Tableau de Paris*, trans. *The Waiting City: Paris, 1782–88* by Helen Simpson. London, 1933

MÉRÉ, ANTOINE GOMBAUD, CHEVALIER DE. *Œuvres*, ed. Charles-H. Boudhors. 3 vols. Paris, 1930: *De la vraïe*, 1700; *Le commerce*, 1700

MONCRIF, AUGUSTIN PARADIS DE. *Contes de A. Paradis de Moncrif*, ed. Octave Uzanne. Paris, 1879: *Les égarements de Zeloide*, 1715

MONTESQUIEU, CHARLES LOUIS etc. *Lettres Persanes*, ed. Élie Carcassonne. 2 vols. Paris, 1949

– *Œuvres complètes*, ed. Daniel Oster. New York, 1964: *L'esprit des lois*, 1748

PASQUIER, NICOLAS. *Le Gentilhomme*. Paris, 1911

RACINE, JEAN. *Œuvres complètes*, ed. Raymond Picard. 2 vols. Paris, 1950–60: *Phèdre* (1677)

REFUGE, DE. *Traicte de la cour, ou instructions des courtisans*. Paris, 1627

RESTIF DE LA BRETONNE. *Le Paysan et La Paysanne Pervertis*. trans. *The Corrupted Ones* by Alan Hull Walton. London, 1967

ROCHEFOUCAULD, FRANCOIS DE. La *Œuvres complètes*, ed. A. Chassang. 2 vols. Paris, 1883–4: 'Entretien avec Méré,' 1682

ÉTIEMBLE, RENÉ, ed., *Romanciers du XVIIIᵉ siècle*. 2 vols. Paris, 1960–5: Denon, Vivant. *Point de Lendemain!* 1777

ROUSSEAU, JEAN-JACQUES. *Œuvres complètes*, ed. Bernardin Gagnebin and

Marcel Raymond. 2 vols. Paris, 1959–64. *Confessions*, 1770
- *The Confessions of Jean-Jacques Rousseau*, trans. J.M. Cohen. London, 1953
- *Emile, ou de l'Éducation*. Paris, 1911
- *Œuvres complètes de J.J. Rousseau*. 4 vols. Paris, 1846: *Contrat Social*, 1762; *Lettre à d'Alembert*, 1758
- *La Nouvelle Héloïse*, ed. Daniel Mornet. 4 vols. Paris, 1925
- *La Nouvelle Héloïse*, trans. *Julie, or the New Eloise. Letters of Two Lovers, Inhabitants of a Small Town at the Foot of the Alps* by Judith H. McDowell. Philadelphia, 1968
SADE, DONATIEN ALPHONSE etc., Marquis de. *Œuvres complètes*, ed. Gilbert Lely. 16 vols. Paris, 1966–7: *Cent journées de Sodome*, 1785; *Aline et Valcour* before 1788; *La Nouvelle Justine*, 1797
SAINT-ÉVREMOND, CHARLES MARGUETEL, SEIGNEUR DE. *Œuvres en Prose*, ed. René Ternois
- *The Letters of Saint Evremond*, ed. John Hayward. London, 1930
SAINT-SIMON, LOUIS DE ROUVROY, DUC DE. *Memoires*. 40 vols. Paris, 1853
SAUROY, JOSEPH, DUREY DE. *Le Masque, ou Anecdotes particulières du Chevalier de ****, 1782: *Histoire d'une fille celebre*
TILLY, ALEXANDRE, COMTE DE, *Memoirs of the Comte Alexandre de Tilly*, intro. Havelock Ellis. New York, 1932
URFÉ, HONORÉ D'. *L'Astrée analyse et extraits*, ed. Maurice Magendie. Paris, 1928
VOISENON, CLAUDE HENRI FUZÉE DE. *Contes de l'abbé Voisenon*, ed. Octave Uzanne. Paris, 1878: *Histoire de la felicité*, 1751
- *Tant mieux pour elle!* trans. *All the Better for Her! and other Stories* by H.B.V. London, 1927
VOLNEY, CONSTANTIN FRANÇOIS. *La loi naturelle, ou catéchisme du citoyen français*, ed. Gasto-Martin. Paris, 1934

SECONDARY SOURCES

ACOMB, FRANCES. *Anglophobia in France, 1763–1789*. Durham, 1950
ADHÉMAR, HÉLÈNE and RENÉ HUYGHE. *Watteau; sa vie, son œuvre, l'universe de Watteau*. Paris. 1950
ANANOFF, ALEXANDRE, *L'Œuvre dessiné de Jean-Honoré Fragonard*. 2 vols. Paris, 1963
ARIÈS, PHILIPPE. *Centuries of Childhood*, trans. Robert Baldick. New York, 1962
ATKINSON, GEOFFROY. *Le Sentiment de la Nature et le retour à la vie simple,*

1690–1740. Geneva and Paris, 1960

– *The Sentimental Revolution*. Seattle, 1966

AUERBACH, La Cour et la Ville.' In *Scenes from the Drama of European Literature*, New York, 1959

– *Mimesis. The Representation of Reality in Western Literature*, trans. Willard Trask. Princeton, 1953

BARBER, ELINOR, *The Bourgeoisie in Eighteenth-Century France*. Princeton, 1955

BARBU, ZEB. 'The New Intelligentsia.' In *French Literature and its Background. The Eighteenth Century*, ed. John Cruickshank. Oxford, London, New York, 1968

BARCHILLON, JACQUES. ' "Précieux" Elements in the Fairy Tale of the Seventeenth Century,' *L'Esprit Createur* 3, (fall, 1963) 99–107

– 'Uses of the Fairy Tale in the Eighteenth Century.' *Voltaire Studies* 24, (1963) 111–38

BARINE, AVÈDE. *Bernardine de Saint-Pierre*, trans. J.E. Gordon. London, 1903

BARNWELL, H.J. *Les Idées morales et critiques de Saint-Évremond*. Paris, 1957

BATIFFOL, LOUIS. *The Great Literary Salons*. London, 1930

BAUS, KARL. *From the Apostolic Community to Constantine*. New York, 1965

BEACH, VINCENT W. 'The Count of Artois and the Coming of the French Revolution.' *Journal of Modern History* 80 (Dec. 1958), 313–24

BECKER, CARL. *The Heavenly City of the Eighteenth-Century Philosophers*. New Haven, 1932

BEHRENS, BETTY. 'Nobles, Privileges and Taxes in France at the End of the Ancien Regime.' *Economic History Review* vol. 15 3 (1963), 451–75.

BÉNICHOU, PAUL. *Morales du grand siècle*. Paris, 1948

BISHOP, MORRIS. *The Life and Adventures of La Rochefoucauld*. Ithaca, 1951

BITTON, DAVIS. *The French Nobility in Crisis 1950–1640*. Stanford, 1969

BLOCH, IWAN. [Eugene Duehren] *120 Days of Sodom and the Sex Life of the French Age of Debauchery*. New York, 1934

BLOCH, MARC. *Feudal Society*, trans. L.A. Manyon. Chicago, 1961

– *French Rural History: An Essay on its Basic Characteristics*, trans. Janet Sondheimer. London, 1966

BLUNT, ANTHONY. *Art and Architecture in France: 1500–1700*. London, 1953

BRAY, RENÉ. *La Formation de la doctrine classique en France*. Paris, 1927

BRERETON, GEOFFREY. *A Short History of French Literature*. London, 1954

BROOKNER, ANITA. 'Aspects of Neo-Classicism in French Painting.' *Apollo* LXVIII (Sept. 1958), 67–73

– 'Jean-Baptiste Greuze.' 2 parts. *Burlington* XCVIII (May, June, 1956), 157–62, 192–9

BRUNETIÈRE, FERDINAND. *Conférences de l'Odéon: les époques du théâtre Français*. Paris, 1896

BURY, J.B. *The Idea of Progress: An Inquiry into its Origins and Growth*. London, 1920

CAILLEUX, JEAN. 'Francois Boucher, The King's First Painter.' *Burlington* XCVI (May 1964), 247–52

CARRÉ, HENRI. *La Noblesse de France et l'opinion publique au XVIIIe siècle*. Paris, 1920

– *Le règne de Louis XV*. Paris, 1911

CASSIRER, ERNST. *The Philosophy of the Enlightenment*. Boston, 1955

– *The Question of Jean-Jacques Rousseau*, ed. Peter Gay. Bloomington, 1963

CASTELOT, ANDRÉ. *Philippe-Égalité*. Paris, 1950

– *Queen of France*, trans. Denise Folliot. New York, 1957

CHAMARD, HENRI. 'Three French Moralists of the Seventeenth-Century.' *The Rice Institute Pamphlet* (Jan. 1931), 1–43

CHÉREL, ALBERT. *De Télémaque à Candide*. Paris, 1958

CHERPACK, CLIFTON. *An Essay on Crebillon Fils*. Durham, 1962

CHILL, EMANUEL. 'Tartuffe, and Courtly Culture.' *French Historical Studies* 3 (1959), 133–79

CLARK, KENNETH. *The Nude: A Study in Ideal Form*. New York, 1956

COBBAN, ALFRED. *A History of Modern France: Old Regime and Revolution, 1715–1799*. Harmondsworth, 1957

– *In Search of Humanity*. London, 1960

– *The Social Interpretation of the French Revolution*. Cambridge, England, 1964

COVENEY, PETER. *The Image of Childhood: The Individual and Society. A Study of the Theme in English Literature*. Baltimore, 1967

CROCKER, LESTER G. 'Jacques le Fataliste: An "expérience morale".' In *Diderot Studies* III, ed. Otis Fellows and Gita May. Geneva, 1961

CURTIUS, ERNST. *European Literature and the Latin Middle Ages*, trans. Willard Trask from the original 1948 edition. New York, 1953

DACIER, ÉMILE. *La Gravure de Genre et de Mœurs*. Brussels, 1925

– *L'Art au XVIIIème siècle en France: époques régence Louis XV, 1715–1740*. Paris, 1955

DALLAS, DOROTHY. *Le Roman francais de 1660 à 1680*. Paris, 1932

DEBU-BRIDEL, J. 'La Préciosité héroïque de la Vie.' *Revue de France* 18. 1938, 195–216

D'HAUTRIVE, G. Grandsaignes. *Le Pessimisme de la Rochefoucald*. Paris, 1914

DELOFFRE, FRÉDÉRIC. *Marivaux et le marivaudage: une préciosité nouvelle*. Paris, 1955

- 'Premières idées de Marivaux sur l'art du roman.' *L'Esprit Créateur* 1 (1961), 178–83
DE TOCQUEVILLE, ALEXIS. *The Old Regime and the Revolution.* New York, 1955
DIECKMANN, HERBERT. 'Diderot's Conception of Genius' *Journal of the History of Ideas* II (1941), 151–82
- 'The Presentation of Reality in Diderot's Tales.' In *Diderot Studies* III, 101–82.
DOOLEY, WILLIAM JOSEPH. *Marriage According to Saint Ambrose.* Washington, D.C., 1948
DOWD, DAVID LLOYD. *Pageant-Master of the Republic.* Hastings, 1948
ADAMS, HENRY HITCH and BAXTER HATHAWAY, eds. *Dramatic Essays of the Neo-Classic Age.* New York, 1950
DUBY, GEORGES, and MANDROU, ROBERT, *A History of French Civilization,* trans. James Blakely Atkinson. New York, 1966
DUCROS, LOUIS. *French Society in the Eighteenth Century,* trans. W. de Geijer. London, 1926
DUPLESSIS, GERARD. *Les Mariages en France.* Paris, 1954
DURKIN, THOMAS J. 'Three Notes to Diderot's Aesthetic.' *Journal of Aesthetics* (March, 1957), 331–9
EISENSTEIN, ELIZABETH. 'Who Intervened in 1788? A Commentary on the Coming of the French Revolution.' *American Historical Review* LXXI (1965)
- 'A Reply.' *American Historical Review,* 514–22 LXXII (1967)
ELLIS, M.B. *Julie, or La Nouvelle Héloïse: A Synthesis of Rousseau's Thought (1749–59).* Toronto, 1949
EPTON, NINA. *Love and the French.* New York, 1959
FAY, BERNARD. *The Revolution Spirit in France and America.* London, 1928
FELLOWS, OTIS E. 'The Theme of Genius in Diderot's Neveu de Rameau' In *Diderot Studies* II, ed. Otis E. Fellows and Norman L. Torrey. Syracuse, 1952
FELS, FLORENT. *L'Art et l'Amour.* 2 vols. Paris, 1952
FIDAO-JUSTINIANI, J.E. *L'esprit classique et la préciosité au XVII'' siècle.* Paris, 1914
FORD, FRANKLIN. *Robe and Sword: The Regrouping of the French Aristocracy after Louis XIV.* Cambridge, Mass., 1953
FORSTER, ROBERT. *The Nobility of Toulouse in the Eighteenth Century* (Baltimore, 1960)
FOSTER, J.J. *French Art from Watteau to Prud'hon.* 3 vols. (London, 1905)
HINE, A.M., ed. *Fragonard, Moreau Le Jeune and French Engravers, Etch-*

ers, and Illustrators of the Later XVIII *Century*. New York, 1911

FRANCE, PETER. 'The Literature of Persuasion.' In *French Literature and its Background. The Eighteenth Century*, ed., John Cruickshank. (Oxford and New York, 1968, 62–79

FREUD, SIGMUND. 'On the Universal Tendency to Debasement in the Sphere of Love' in *The Standard Edition of the Complete Psychological Works of Sigmund Freud*, ed., James Strachey. 24 vols. London, 1953–63, vol. 11

– *Jokes and their Relationship to the Unconscious*, ed. James Strachey. New York, 1963

The Frick Collection: Paintings. New York, 1963

FRIEDLANDER, WALTER. *David to Delacroix*. Cambridge, Mass., 1952

FUNCK-BRENTANO, FRANZ. *The Old Regime in France*. New York, 1929

GAIFFE, F. *Le Drame en France au* XVIIIe *siècle*. Paris, 1910

GAUTHIER, M. *Watteau*. New York, 1964

GAY, PETER. *The Enlightenment: An Interpretation. The Rise of Pagan Humanism*. New York, 1965

– *The Enlightenment: The Science of Freedom*. Vol. 2. New York, 1969

– *The Party of Humanity: Essays in the French Enlightenment*. New York, 1964

GLOTZ, MARGUÉRITE and MADELEINE MAIRE. *Salons du* XVIIIe *siècle*. Paris, 1945

GONCOURT, EDMOND DE and JULES DE GONCOURT. *L'Art du dix-huitième siècle*. 2 vols. Paris, 1880

– *La femme au dix-huitième siècle*. 2 vols. Paris, n.d.

– *French* XVIII *Century Painters*, trans. Robin Ironside. London, 1948

GOOCH, G.P. *Louis* XV: *The Monarchy in Decline*. London, 1956

GORER, GEOFFREY. *The Life and Times of the Marquis de Sade*. New York, 1963

GRASSBY, R.S. 'Social Status and Commercial Enterprise under Louis XIV.' *Economic History Review* 13 (1961), 19–38

GREEN, FREDERICK CHARLES. 'The Critic of the Seventeenth Century and his Attitude toward the French Novel.' *Modern Philology* 24 (1926–7), 285–95

– *Eighteenth Century France*. London, 1929

– *French Novelists, Manners, and Ideas: From the Renaissance to the Revolution*. London, 1928

– 'Realism in the French Novel in the First Half of the xviiith Century.' *Modern Language Notes* XXXVIII (1923) 321–29

– 'Further Evidence of Realism in the French Novel of the Eighteenth Century.' *Modern Language Notes* 40 (May, 1925), 257–70

– 'The Eighteenth-Century French Critic and the Contemporary Novel.' *Modern Language Review* 23 (1928), 174–87

– *Jean-Jacques Rousseau. A Study of His Life and Writings.* Cambridge England, 1955
– *Minuet. A Critical Survey of French and English Literary Ideas in the Eighteenth Century.* London, 1935
GREENE, E.J.H. *Marivaux.* Toronto, 1965
GRESHOFF, C.J. 'The Moral Structure of *Les Liaisons Dangereuses.*' *French Review* 37 (Feb. 1964), 383–99.
GRIMSLEY, RONALD. 'The Human Problem in *La Nouvelle Heloise.*' *Modern Language Review* 53 (1958), 171–84
GROETHUYSEN, BERNARD. *The Bourgeois. Catholicism vs. Capitalism in Eighteenth-Century France,* trans. Mary Ilford. New York, 1956
GUY, BASIL. 'The Prince de Ligne, Laclos, and the *Liaisons dangereuses*: Two Notes.' *Romanic Review* 55 (1964), 260–67
GUÉRARD, ALBERT. *France in the Classical Age The Life and Death of an Ideal.* New York, 1965
HAAC, OSCAR A. 'Marivaux and the Honnête Homme.' *Romanic Review* 50 (Dec. 1959), 255–67
HALL, G. GASTON. 'The Concept of Virtue in *La Nouvelle Héloïse.*" *Yale French Studies* 28 (1962), 20–33
HATZFELD, HELMUT R. *Literature Through Art.* New York, 1956
HAUSER, ARNOLD. *The Social History of Art,* trans. Stanley Goodman. 4 vols. New York, 1957
HAUTECŒUR, LOUIS. *Les peintures de la vie familiale.* Paris, 1945
HAVENS, GEORGE. *The Age of Ideas. From Reaction to Revolution in Eighteenth Century France.* New York, 1955
HAYES, CARLTON J.H. *The Historical Evolution of Modern Nationalism.* New York, 1931
HAZARD, PAUL. *The European Mind* (1680–1815). trans. from the original 1935 French edition titled *La Crise de la conscience européenne* by J. Lewis May. New Haven, 1952
– *European Thought in the Eighteenth Century: From Montesquieu to Lessing,* trans. J. Lewis May from the original 1946 edition. New Haven, 1954
HECKSCHER, ELI F. *Mercantilism.* 2 vols. London, 1955
HENDEL, CHARLES W. *Jean-Jacques Rousseau: Moralist.* 2 vols. in 1. New York, 1962
HEROLD, J. CHRISTOPHER. *Love in Five Temperaments.* New York, 1961
HEXTER, J.H. 'The Education of the Aristocracy in the Renaissance.' *Journal of Modern History* 22 (March, 1950), 1–20
HOLMES, URBAN TIGNER. *A History of Old French Literature. From the Origins to 1300.* New York, 1937

HOPE, QUENTIN M. *Saint-Evremond: The Honnête Homme as Critic.* Bloomington, 1962

HOURTICQ, LOUIS. *La Peinture française:* XVIII *siècle* Paris, 1939

HUDON, E. SCULLEY. 'Love and Myth in Les Liaisons dangereuses' *Yale French Studies* XI (1953), 25–38

HUIZINGA, JOHAN. *The Waning of the Middle Ages,* trans. from the original 1919 Dutch edition. New York, 1956

HUNT, NORTON. *The Natural History of Love.* New York, 1959

HYSLOP, BEATRICE FRY. *French Nationalism in 1789 According to the General Cahiers.* New York, 1934

IDZERDA, STANLEY. 'Art and the French State during the French Revolution 1789–1795.' Unpublished dissertation. Western Reserve, 1952

JAMIESON, RUTH KIRBY. *Marivaux. A Study in Sensibility.* New York, 1937

JOUVENEL, BERTRAND DE. 'Rousseau, the Pessimistic Philosopher.' *Yale French Studies* 28 (1962), 83–92

KAPLOW, JEFFRY. 'The Social Interpretation of the French Revolution' [Review of Cobban]. *American Historical Review* LXX (July, 1965)

– 'Class in the French Revolution; A Discussion on "Who intervened in 1788".' *American Historical Review* LXXII (1967) 497–502

KERN, EDITH. '"L'Honnête Homme" Postscript to a Battle of the Scholars.' *Romanic Review* 54 (April, 1963), 110–15

KOHN, HANS. *The Idea of Nationalism* (New York, 1934)

KRISTELLER, PAUL OSKAR. 'The Platonic Academy of Florence.' *Renaissance News* XIV (1961), 147–59

Labriolle, Pierre de. 'Le "mariage spirituel" dans l'antiquité chrétienne.' *Revue Historique* 137 (1921), 204–25

LABROUSSE, C.E. *La crise de l'économie française à la fin de l'Ancien Régime et au debut de la Revolution.* 2 vols. in 1. Paris, 1943

LAFARGE, CATHERINE. 'The Emergence of the Bourgeoisie,' *Yale French Studies* Vol. 32 (1964), 40–9

LANCASTER, HENRY CARRINGTON. *French Tragedy in the Time of Louis* XV *and Voltaire. 1715–1774.* 2 vols. (Baltimore, 1950)

LANSON, GUSTAV. *Histoire de la littérature française.* 17th ed. Paris, 1922

– 'La Transformation des Idées morales et la naissance des morales rationelles de 1680–1715.' *Revue des Mois* (1910), 5–28

– *Nivelle de la Chausee et la comédie larmoyante.* Paris, 1887

LAWRENCE, FRANCIS L. 'La Princesse de Clèves Reconsidered.' *French Review* 29 (Oct. 1965), 15–21

LAWRENCE, H.W. and B.L. DIGHTON. *French Line Drawings of the Late* XVIII *Century.* London, 1910

LEFEBVRE, GEORGES. *The Coming of the French Revolution.* New York, 1957
– *Études sur la Revolution française.* Paris, 1954
LEITH, JAMES A. *The Idea of Art as Propaganda in France, 1750–1799: A Study in the History of Ideas.* Toronto, 1965
LEMAITRE, GEORGES. *Beaumarchais.* New York, 1949
LEVÊQUE, ANDRÉ. "'L'Honnête homme" et "L'Homme de bien" au XVIIIe siècle.' *Publications of the Modern Language Association of America* 72 (Sept. 1957), 620–32
LEVI, ANTHONY. *French Moralists. The Theory of the Passions, 1548 to 1649.* Oxford, 1964
LEVIN, HARRY. 'Introduction.' *Les Liaisons dangereuses.* New York, 1961
LEVRON, JACQUES. *Daily Life at Versailles in the Seventeenth and Eighteenth Centuries,* trans. Claire Elaine Engel. London, 1968
LEVEY, MICHAEL. *Rococo to Revolution. Major Trends in Eighteenth-Century Painting.* New York, 1966
LEVY-BRÜHL, HENRI. 'La Noblesse de France et le commerce à la fin de l'Ancien Régime.' *Revue d'Histoire Moderne* 3, (1933), 209–35
LEWIS, C.H. *The Scandalous Regent.* New York, 1961
– *The Splendid Century: Life in the France of Louis* XIV. New York, 1957
LEWIS, C.S. *The Allegory of Love: A Study in Medieval Tradition.* Oxford, 1936
LINDSAY, JACK. *The Death of the Hero.* London, 1960
LOUGH, JOHN. *An Introduction to Eighteenth Century France.* London, 1960
– *An Introduction to Seventeenth Century France.* London, 1954
– *Paris Theatre Audiences in the Seventeenth and Eighteenth Centuries.* London, 1957
LOCQUIN, JEAN. *La Peinture d'Histoire en France de 1747 à 1785.* Paris, 1912
LOVEJOY, ARTHUR. *Essays in the History of Ideas.* New York, 1960
LOY, J. ROBERT. 'Love-Vengeance in the Late Eighteenth-Century Novel.' *L'Esprit Créateur* 3, (1963) 157–66
MCCLOY, SHELBY. *The Humanitarian Movement in Eighteenth Century France.* Lexington, 1957
MCFALL, HALDANE. *Boucher: The Man, His Times, His Art, and His Significance, 1703–70.* London, 1908
MCKEE, KENNETH N. *The Theatre of Marivaux.* New York, 1958
MCMANNERS, J. 'France.' In *The European Nobility in the Eighteenth Century : Studies of the Major European States in the pre-Reform Era,* ed. A. Goodwin. London, 1953
MCNEILL, GORDON H. 'The Cult of Rousseau and the French Revolution.' *Journal of the History of Ideas* VI (1945), 197–212
MAGENDIE, MAURICE. *La Politesse mondaine et les théories de l'honnêteté en*

France, au XVII*ᵉ siècle, de 1600 à 1660.* 2 vols. Paris, 1925

– *Le Roman français de 1660 à 1680.* Paris, 1932

MANDROU, ROBERT. *La France aux* XVII*ᵉ et* XVIII*ᵉ siècles,* Paris, 1967

MANUEL, FRANK. *The New World of Henri Saint-Simon, 1760–1825.* Cambridge, Mass., 1956

MARCUS, STEVEN. *The Other Victorians. A Study of Sexuality and Pornography in Mid-Nineteenth-Century England.* New York, 1966

MARTIN, KINGSLEY. *The Rise of French Liberal Thought: A Study of Political Ideas from Bayle to Condorcet.* New York, 1956

MATHIEZ, ALBERT. *The French Revolution,* trans. Catherine Alison Phillips. New York, 1928

MAUCLAIR, CAMILLE. *Jean-Baptiste Greuze.* Paris, 1907

MAUZI, ROBERT. *L'Idée du bonheur dans la littérature et la pensée française au* XVIII*ᵉ siècle.* Paris, 1960

MAY, GEORGES. *Le Dilemme du roman au* XVIII*ᵉ siècle: Étude sur les rapports du roman et de la critique, 1775–1761.* Paris, 1963

– 'The Witticisms of Monsieur de Valmont.' *L'Esprit Créateur* 3 (1963) 181–7

MAZZEO, JOSEPH ANTHONY. *Renaissance and Revolution. Backgrounds to Seventeenth Century English Literature.* New York, 1967

MICHELS, ROBERTO. *First Lectures in Political Sociology,* trans. Alfred de Grazia. New York, 1965

MITFORD, NANCY. *Madame de Pompadour.* New York, 1954

MOORE, G. BARRINGTON, JR. *Social Origins of Dictatorship and Democracy. Lord and Peasant in the Making of the Modern World.* Boston, 1966

MORNET, DANIEL. 'Comment étudier les écrivains ou les ouvrages de troisième ou quatrième ordre (Le Mercure galante de 1672 a 1700).' *Romanic Review* 28 (Oct. 1937), 204–16

– 'Les enseignements des bibliothèques privées.' *Revue d'histoire littéraire de la France* XVIII (1910), 449–96

– *Histoire de la littérature française classique, 1660–1700, ses caractères véritables, ses aspects inconnus.* 3rd ed. Paris, 1947

– *Les origines intellectuelles de la révolution française, 1715–1787.* 5th ed. Paris, 1954

– *Le Pensée française au* XVIII*ᵉ siècle.* Paris, 1962

– *Le Sentiment de la Nature en France: de J.J. Rousseau à Bernardin de Saint-Pierre.* Paris, 1907

– *A Short History of French Literature.* New York, 1935

MOSSIKER, FRANCES. *The Queen's Necklace.* New York, 1961

MOUSNIER, ROLAND. *La Vénalité des offices sous Henri IV et Louis XIII*. Rouen, 1945

– *Les XVIe et XVIIe siècles: La grand Mutation intellectuelle de l'Humanité, l'Avènement de la Science moderne et l'expansion de l'Europe*. 3rd ed. Paris, 1961

MUNRO, JAMES S. 'Moral and Social Occupations in early eighteenth-century French Comedy.' *Voltaire Studies* 57 (1967), 1031–54

MYLNE, VIVIENNE. *The Eighteenth-Century French Novel*. London, 1965

– 'Sensibility and the Novel.' In *French Literature and its Background. The Eighteenth Century*, ed. John Cruickshank (Oxford and New York, 1968), 45–61

NICOLSON, HAROLD. *Good Behavior, being a Study of Certain Types of Civility*. London, 1956

PAINTER, SIDNEY. *French Chivalry: Chivalric Ideas and Practices*. Ithaca, 1957

PADOVER, SAUL K. *The Life and Death of Louis XVI*. New York, 1939

PALACHE, JOHN GARBER. *Four Novelists of the Old Regime*. New York, 1926

PALMER, R.R. *The Age of Democratic Revolution: A Political History of Europe and America, 1760–1800*. 2 vols. Princeton, 1959, 1964

– 'The National Idea in France before the Revolution.' *Journal of the History of Ideas* I (1940), 95–111

PANOFSKY, ERWIN. 'Poussin and the Elegiac Tradition.' *Meaning and the Visual Arts* (Garden City, 1956), 295–320

– *Studies in Iconology. Humanistic Themes in the Art of the Renaissance*. Oxford, 1939

PAREDI, ANGELO. *Saint Ambrose. His Life and Time*. Notre Dame, 1964

PARKER, HAROLD T. *The Cult of Antiquity and the French Revolutionaries*. Chicago, 1937

PARODI, DOMINIQUE. 'L'honnête homme et l'idéal moral du XVIIe et du XVIIIe siècle. *Revue Pedagogique* LXXVII (1921), 79–99; 178–93

PELLES, GERALDINE. *Art, Artists and Society: Origins of a Modern Dilemma, Painting in France and England, 1750–1850*. Englewood Cliffs, 1963

PERKINS, JEAN. 'Diderot's Concept of Virtue.' *Voltaire Studies* 23 (1963) 77–91

– 'Irony and Candour in Certain Libertine Novels.' Ibid. 60 (1968), 245–59

PEVSNER, NICOLAS. *Academies of Art: Past and Present*. Cambridge, England, 1940

PEYRE, HENRI. 'The Influence of Eighteenth Century Ideas on the French Revolution.' *Journal of the History of Ideas* X (1949), 63–87

PICARD, ROGER. *Les Salons littéraires et la société françaises, 1610–1789.* New York, 1943

PILON, EDMOND. *La Vie famille au XVIIIe siècle.* Paris, 1933

PINTARD, R. *Le Libertinage érudit dans la première moitié du dix-septième siècle.* Paris, 1943

PLEKHANOV, G.V. *Art and Social Life.* London, 1953

PORTER, CHARLES. *Restif's Novels: or, An Autobiography in Search of an Author.* New Haven, 1967

– 'Restif, Rousseau, and *Monsieur Nicolas*,' *Romanic Review* 54, (1963), 262–73

RANUM, OREST. *Paris in the Age of Absolutism. An Essay.* New York, 1968

RATNER, MOSES. *Theory and Criticism in the Novel from L'Astrée to 1750.* New York, 1938

RÉAU, LOUIS. *L'Art au XVIIIème siècle en France: style Louis XVI, 1760–1789.* Paris, 1955

– *Histoire de la Peinture française au XVIIIe siècle.* 2 vols. Paris, 1925, 1926

RIVERS, JOHN. *Greuze and His Models.* London, 1912

ROBIQUET, JEAN. *La Femme dans la peinture française: XVe–XXe siècle.* Paris, 1938

ROSENBERG, PIERRE. *Chardin.* Geneva, 1963

ROTHKRUG, LIONEL. *Opposition to Louis XIV. The Political and Social Origins of the French Enlightenment.* Princeton, 1965

ROUGEMONT, DENIS. *Passion and Society*, trans. Montgomery Belgion. London, 1956

ROWLANDSON, BENJAMIN R. JR. *The Classical Tradition in Western Art.* Cambridge, Mass., 1963

SAGNAC, P. *La Fin de l'ancien régime et la révolution americaine, 1763–1789.* 2 vols. Paris, 1941

SAISSELINES, RÉMY G. 'The Rococo as a Dream of Happiness.' *Journal of Aesthetics* (1960), 145–52

SALOMON, ALBERT. *In Praise of Enlightenment: Essays in the History of Ideas.* New York, 1963

SEZNEC, JEAN. *The Survival of the Gods: The Mythological Tradition and its Place in Renaissance Humanism and Arts.* trans. Barbara F. Sessions from the original 1940 edition. New York, 1953

SHACKELTON, ROBERT. *Montesquieu: A Critical Biography.* Oxford, 1961

SHAFER, BOYD C. 'Bourgeois Nationalism in the Pamphlets on the Eve of the French Revolution.' *Journal of Modern History* X (1938), 31–50

SHAPIRO, GILBERT. 'The Many Lives of Georges Lefebvre.' *American Historical Review* LXXII (1967), 502–14

SHAW, EDWARD P. *François-Augustin Paradis de Moncrif, 1687–1770*. New York, 1958

SPINK, J.S. *French Free-Thought from Gassendi to Voltaire*. London, 1960

STAROBINSKI, JEAN. 'The Illness of Rousseau.' *Yale French Studies* 28 (1962) 64–74

– *The Invention of Liberty 1700–1789*. trans. Bernard C. Swift. Geneva, 1964

STEWART, JOHN HALL. *A Documentary Survey of the French Revolution*. New York, 1951

STONE, LAWRENCE. *The Crisis of the Aristocracy, 1558–1641*. Abridged ed. Oxford and New York, 1967

STRICKLAND, WILLIAM EMILE. 'Social and Literary Satire in Furetière's Roman Bourgeois.' *French Review* 27 (1954), 182–92

SYDENHAM, M.J. *The Girondins*. London, 1961

TAYLOR, GEORGE V. 'Non-Capitalist Wealth and the Origins of the French Revolution.' *American Historical Review* 72 (Jan. 1967), 469–96

TAYLOR, G. RATTRAY. *Sex in History*. New York, n.d.

THELANDER, DOROTHY R. *Laclos and the Epistolary Novel*. Geneva, 1963

THOMAS, KEITH. 'Work and Leisure in Pre-Industrial Society.' *Past and Present* no. 29 (1964), 50–62

THOMPSON, J.M. *Leaders of the French Revolution*. Oxford, 1965

– *Robespierre*. 2 vols. New York, 1936

THUILLIER, JACQUES and ALBERT CHATELET. *French Painting: From Fouquet to Poussin*. Geneva, 1963

– *French Painting from Le Nain to Fragonard*. Geneva, 1964

TILLEY, ARTHUR. 'Préciosité after *Les Précieuses ridicules*.' *Modern Language Review* 11 (1916), 33–47, 176–85, 302–15

– *The Decline of the Age of Louis XIV or, French Literature 1687–1715*. Cambridge, 1929

TILLY, CHARLES. *The Vendée. A Sociological Analysis of the Counterrevolution of 1793*. Cambridge, 1964

TREASURE, GEOFFREY. *Seventeenth Century France*. New York, 1967

TROELTSCH, ERNST. *The Social Teaching of the Christian Churches*, trans. Olive Wyon. New York, 1931

TURNELL, MARTIN. *The Novel in France*. New York, 1951

VALENTINER, W.R. *Jacques-Louis David and the French Revolution*. New York, 1929

VARGA, A. KIBÉDI. 'La Désagregation de l'idéal classique dans le roman français de la première moitié du XVIIIe siècle.' *Voltaire Studies* 26 (1963), 965–98

VOVELLE, M. and ROCHE, D. 'Bourgeoisie, Rentiers, and Property Owners: Elements for defining a Social Category at the End of the Eighteenth Century.' *New Perspectives on the French Revolution: Readings in Historical Sociology*. New York, 1965

WADE, IRA O. *Voltaire and Madame du Châtelet: An Essay on the Intellectual Activity at Cirey*. Princeton, 1951

WATT, IAN. *The Rise of the Novel: Critical Studies of Defoe, Richardson, and Fielding*. Berkeley, 1967

WEISS, JOHANNES. *Earliest Christianity. A History of the Period* A.D. *30–150*, trans. Frederick C. Grant. 2 vols. New York, 1959

WEITZMAN, ARTHUR J. 'The Oriental Tale in the Eighteenth Century: a Reconstruction' *Voltaire Studies* LVIII (1967), 1839–55

WELCH, OLIVER J.G. *Mirabeau: A Study of a Democratic Monarchist*. London, 1951

WHITE, JOHN S. *Renaissance Cavalier*. New York, 1959

WILDENSTEIN, GEORGES. *The Paintings of Fragonard: Complete Edition*. London, 1960

WILENSKI, R.H. *French Painting*. Boston, 1949

WILEY, W.L. *The Formal French*. Cambridge, Mass., 1967

WILSON, ARTHUR M. *Diderot: The Testing Years, 1713–1757*. New York, 1957

– 'The Development and scope of Diderot's political thought.' *Voltaire Studies* XXVII (1963), 1873–87

YOUNG, G.M. *Victorian England Portrait of an Age*. London, 1963

Index